SOLIDARITY POLITICS FOR MILLENNIALS

The Politics of Intersectionality

Series Editors:

Ange-Marie Hancock, *University of Southern California*
Nira Yuval-Davis, *University of East London*

Solidarity Politics for Millennials
Ange-Marie Hancock

Solidarity Politics for Millennials

A Guide to Ending the Oppression Olympics

Ange-Marie Hancock

First published in hardcover in 2011 by PALGRAVE MACMILLAN® in the United States—a division of St. Martin's Press LLC, 175 Fifth Avenue, New York, NY 10010.

Where this book is distributed in the UK, Europe and the rest of the world, this is by Palgrave Macmillan, a division of Macmillan Publishers Limited, registered in England, company number 785998, of Houndmills, Basingstoke, Hampshire RG21 6XS.

Palgrave Macmillan is the global academic imprint of the above companies and has companies and representatives throughout the world.

Palgrave® and Macmillan® are registered trademarks in the United States, the United Kingdom, Europe and other countries.

ISBN: 978–1–137–38600–7

Library of Congress Cataloging-in-Publication Data

Hancock, Ange-Marie.
    Solidarity politics for millennials : a guide to ending the oppression olympics / Ange-Marie Hancock.
        p. cm.—(Politics of intersectionality)
    Includes bibliographical references.
    ISBN 978–0–230–10800–4 (alk. paper)
      1. Generation Y—United States—Attitudes. 2. Generation Y—Political activity—United States. I. Title. II. Series.

HQ799.7.H345 2011
320.973084'2—dc22   2011007630

A catalogue record of the book is available from the British Library.

Design by Newgen Knowledge Works (P) Ltd., Chennai, India.

First PALGRAVE MACMILLAN paperback edition: December 2013

10 9 8 7 6 5 4 3 2 1

For Charles R. and Theresa M. Hancock

Contents

Figures and Tables

Figures

Tables

SERIES INTRODUCTION: THE POLITICS OF INTERSECTIONALITY

The Politics of Intersectionality series builds on the longstanding insights of intersectionality theory from a vast variety of disciplinary perspectives. As a globally utilized analytical framework for understanding issues of social justice, Leslie McCall, Mary Hawkesworth, and others argue that intersectionality is arguably the most important theoretical contribution of women's and gender studies to date.[1] Indeed the imprint of intersectional analysis can be easily found on innovations in equality legislation, human rights, and development discourses.

The history of what is now called "intersectional thinking" is long. In fact, prior to its mainstreaming, intersectionality analysis was carried for many years mainly by black and other racialized women who, from their situated gaze, perceived as absurd, not just misleading, any attempt by feminists and others to homogenize women's situation, particularly in conceptualizing such situations as analogous to that of racialized others. As Brah and Phoenix point out,[2] many black feminists fulfilled significant roles in the development of intersectional analysis, such as the Combahee River Collective, the black lesbian feminist organization from Boston, who pointed out the need of developing an integrated analysis and practice based upon the fact that major systems of oppression interlock rather than operate separately. However, the term "intersectionality" itself emerged nominally from the field of critical legal studies, where critical race feminist Kimberle Williams Crenshaw wrote two pathbreaking articles, "Demarginalizing the Intersection of Race and Sex: A Critique of Antidiscrimination Doctrine, Feminist Theory and Antiracist Politics"[3] and "Mapping the Margins: Intersectionality, Identity Politics, and Violence against Women of Color."[4] At nearly the same time, social theorist Patricia Hill Collins was preparing her landmark work, *Black Feminist Thought: Knowledge, Consciousness and the Politics of Empowerment*,[5] which characterized intersections of race, class, and gender as mutually reinforcing sites of power relations.

Both Crenshaw and Collins gave the name "intersectionality" to a far larger and more ethnically diverse trajectory of work, now global in nature, that speaks truth to power sited differentially rather than centralized in a single locus. What could also be called intersectional analysis was in fact developing at roughly the same time among European and postcolonial feminists, including, for example, Anthias & Yuval-Davis,[6] Brah,[7] Essed,[8] Ifekwunigwe,[9] Lutz,[10] Meekosha,[11] and Min-ha.[12] Indeed, it seems that, in a manner parallel to that which Sandra Harding characterizes the evolution of standpoint theory,[13] intersectionality was an idea whose time had come precisely because of the plethora of authors working independently across the globe making vastly similar sets of claims. Around the world, those interested in a more comprehensive and transformative approach to social justice—whether sociologists, legal scholars, feminist theorists, policy makers, or human rights advocates—have used the language and tenets of intersectionality to more effectively articulate injustice and advocate for positive social change.

The books in this series represent an interrogation of intersectionality at various levels of analysis. They unabashedly foreground the politics of intersectionality in a way that is designed to both honor the legacy of earlier scholarship and activism as well as push the boundaries of intersectionality's value to the academy and most importantly to the world. We interpret the series title, The Politics of Intersectionality, in two general ways:

First, we emphasize the **politics** of intersectionality, broadly conceived; that is to say, we include debates among scholars regarding the proper conceptualization and application of the term "intersectionality" as part and parcel of the series' intellectual project. Is intersectionality a paradigm?[14] Is intersectionality a normative political (specifically feminist) project?[15] Is it a method or epistemological approach? Is it (merely) a concept with limited applicability beyond multiply marginalized populations?[16] Our own idiosyncratic answers to these questions are far less important than the open dialogue we seek by including them within the scholarly discourse generated by the series.

What this means pragmatically is that rather than dictatorially denote an extant definition of intersectionality and impose it on every author's manuscript, as series editors our task has been to meaningfully push each author to grapple with their own conceptualization of intersectionality and facilitate their interaction with an ever-growing body of global scholarship, policy, and advocacy work as they render such a conceptualization transparent to readers, reflexive as befits the best feminist work, and committed to rigorous standards of quality no matter the subject, the method, or the conclusions. As editors we have taken such an active role precisely because grappling with the politics of intersectionality demands our adherence to the normative standards of transparency, reflexivity, and speaking to multiple sites of power for which intersectionality is not only known but lauded as the gold standard. It is our honor to build this area of scholarship across false boundaries of theory and praxis; artificially distinct academic disciplines; and the semipermeable line between scholarship and activism.

No less importantly, we emphasize politics to mean, well, politics, whether everyday senses of justice—so-called formal politics of social movements, campaigns, elections, policy, and government institutions—or personal politics of identity, community, and activism across a broad swath of the world. While this general conceptualization of politics lends itself to the social sciences, we define social sciences in a broad way that again seeks to unite theoretical concerns (whether normative or positive) with interpretive and empirical approaches across an array of topics far too numerous to list in their entirety.

The second way we interpret the series title—simultaneously, as one might expect of intersectionality scholars—is with an emphasis on the word **intersectionality**. That is, the books in this series do not depend solely on 20-year-old articulations of intersectionality, nor do they adhere to one particular theoretical or methodological approach to study intersectionality; they are steeped in a rich literature of both substantive and analytical depth that in the twenty-first century reaches around the world. This is not your professor's "women of color" or "race-class-gender" series of the late twentieth century. Indeed an emphasis on up-to-date engagement with the best and brightest global thinking on intersectionality has been the single most exacting standard we have imposed on the editing process. As series editors, we seek to develop manuscripts that aspire to a level of sophistication about intersectionality as a body of research that is in fact worthy of the intellectual, political, and personal risks taken by so many of its earliest interlocutors in voicing and naming this work.

Currently, intersectionality scholarship lacks a meaningful clearinghouse of work that speaks across (again false) boundaries of a particular identity community under study (e.g., Black lesbians, women of color environmental activists), academic disciplines, or the geographical location from which the author writes (e.g., Europe, North America, Southeast Asia). For this reason, we expect that the bibliographies of the manuscripts will be almost as helpful as the manuscripts themselves, particularly for senior professors who train graduate students and graduate students seeking to immerse themselves broadly and deeply in contemporary approaches to intersectionality. We are less sanguine, however, about the plethora of modifiers that have emerged to somehow modulate intersectionality—whether it be intersectional stigma,[17] intersectional political consciousness,[18] intersectional praxis,[19] post-intersectionality,[20] paradigm intersectionality,[21] or even Crenshaw's original modes of structural and political intersectionality.[22] Our emphasis has been on building the subfield rather than consciously expanding the lexicon of modes and specialities for intersectionality.

INTRODUCTION TO THE PAPERBACK EDITION

When W.E.B. Du Bois published *The Souls of Black Folk* in 1903, he spoke of a kind of double consciousness "Negro Americans" faced. For him, the two "unreconciled strivings" were the reviled political identity—"Negro"—and the simultaneously lauded "American" identity. Moreover the revulsions regarding Negroes and other minority groups were a constitutive element of American identity. These contradictions affected each Negro American, but they also affected Blacks as a group, the Civil Rights Movement's agenda and strategy in the 20th century, and America as a whole. 110 years later *Solidarity Politics for Millennials* argues for a related double consciousness: privilege and disadvantage co-exist, not just in our world, but within a single person, a single group, and a single social movement.

I initially wrote this book as an accessible introduction to the 21st century challenges people of all generations face as they seek to recognize and confront their own privilege even as they assiduously pursue social justice. It presents intersectionality theory and deep political solidarity as complementary tools for 21st century activism without engaging in many of academic debates about their origins or futures because frankly most activists aren't focused on theoretical treatises. They are grappling with what it means to practice intersectionality in a fast-moving political environment and confront their own hidden biases.

One of the challenges of writing a 21st century book using real-world politics and popular culture is that both are ever-changing targets. This book discusses the Californians who woke up the morning after election day 2008 experienced the whiplash of elation and disappointment in the election of Barack Obama and the passage of Proposition 8. They were not alone. In December 2010, on the same day that the Senate voted to repeal Don't Ask, Don't Tell (DADT), they defeated the DREAM Act. The second session of the 112th U.S. Congress and the 2012–2013 term of the Supreme Court likewise reflected the confusing combination of empowerment, privilege and discrimination that persists in the United States.

This introduction to the paperback edition explores more recent changes—some positive, some negative—that continue to challenge those of us who are activists and those of us who aspire to become or support social justice activists. Two hard-fought 20th century victories regarding women's health care have been challenged over the past four years. Decades of progress on breast cancer research and prevention and access to contraception were both threatened. Senator Patty Murray (D-WA) said it best: "Reading the news this morning was like stepping into a time machine and going back 50 years."[23]

In 2009 the U.S. Preventive Services Task Force (USPSTF) raised the recommended age at which biennial mammograms should commence to 50 from the prior standard of care, which was 40 years old.[24] The task force used evidence from population studies that failed to acknowledge both the increasing demographic changes among the U.S. population and the incidence of more aggressive forms of breast cancer in younger women, many of whom are African American.[25] All breast cancers, in other words, were assumed to be "alike," when it came to recommendations for mammograms. Although seven of the sixteen members of the Task Force were female, no members were oncologists. Clearly unfamiliar with intersectionality, the USPSTF remained unmoved by the responses of most cancer research organizations[26] or the likelihood that insurance companies would stop covering such preventive mammograms for women under 50. Despite strong evidence of higher risk and later stage diagnosis among less privileged women,[27] the general recommendation went into affect with little more than a yawning howl of protest.

Much of the progress in the past 30 years regarding access to early diagnosis tests like mammograms and government policies to support treatment protocol research is credited to the Susan G. Komen For a Cure Foundation. Founded in 1982, Komen enjoyed near-universal acclaim as the premier breast cancer research and advocacy organization in the world. Most importantly, that acclaim seemed to transcend politics, for everyone wanted to find a cure, no matter their political beliefs. But in 2011 Komen's outstanding reputation was severely damaged when the foundation went against its own previous endorsements of expanded access to mammograms and changed its grant regulations in a way that would affect just one grantee in particular: Planned Parenthood.

Planned Parenthood had been a grantee in good standing, providing over 6,000 mammograms and 170,000 clinical breast exams to low income women using Komen funding for five years prior to this policy change. They convincingly framed the policy change as an attack on their provision of safe medical terminations of unwanted pregnancies, which were funded independently and constituted only 3% of Planned Parenthood's activities. The ensuing media controversy hurt Komen far more than it did Planned Parenthood. Komen was pressured to rescind the policy and to continue to fund Planned Parenthood's mammogram program, further inciting backlash from the anti-abortion side of the debate.

The transcendence of politics and class, religious, and ideological diversity that Komen seemed to achieve for 30 years proved to be a chimera. Komen's brand equity was destroyed in response to their handling of the controversy. That damage has lingered. 18 months after the debacle Komen continued to cancel previously successful mass events like Race for the Cure around the country due to low participation—50% of their 3-day walks for 2014 have been canceled.[28] Ultimately, Komen's long-term ability to financially support early diagnosis and research has declined precipitously.

For women *with* health insurance, the passage of the Affordable Care Act (aka "Obamacare") expanded access to mammograms. Insurers were required to cover preventive exams like mammograms and pap smears (which offer early diagnoses of cervical cancer) and contraception without co-payment or additional charge by 2012. News of these changes was later overshadowed by a controversial hearing of the House Committee on Oversight and Government Reform, chaired by Darrell Issa (R-CA).

Unfortunately, women's access to health care, whether through private funding like the Komen Foundation or government policy like "Obamacare" was again up for debate, 39 years after *Roe v. Wade* and 47 years after *Griswold v. Connecticut*. In February 2012 Issa convened a hearing on employer requirements to provide contraceptive coverage with a list of witnesses that read like the setup to a bad joke. On the topic of employer requirements for religious organizations, the panel consisted of a priest, three ministers and a rabbi...none of whom was female. Representative Rosa DeLauro (D-CT) was yielded time by her male colleague to speak during the hearing but Issa interrupted her within the first 30 seconds of her statement. While Representative Elijah Cummings (D-MD), the ranking Democrat, attempted to intervene, Issa continued to use parliamentary tactics, cutting DeLauro off after another minute and a half because her time had expired. DeLauro sarcastically marked the moment by replying, "Talk about abridging freedom of speech."

Privilege left unchecked and disadvantage left unattended continued the debate about women's autonomy over their own bodies through the November elections. Senate candidates in Missouri and Indiana articulated anti-abortion positions that suggested women's bodies could prevent pregnancy in the event of "legitimate rape" (Missouri) or such rape-created pregnancies were like any other pregnancy, a "gift from God" (Indiana). Voters across the country responded by electing and re-electing women to the House and Senate, sending a record 20 women to the Senate for the 113th session of Congress.

While much has been made of this "1 in 5 Senators will be female" statistic, these elected representatives bring intersectional diversity to their chamber. Through both their ascriptive identities of race and sexual orientation, along with their chosen identities of veteran and naturalized citizen, the new female members of Congress have many policies where their voices could presumably be valuable in the 113th Congress: comprehensive immigration reform, sexual assault in the military, and the Employment Non-Discrimination Act (ENDA). Mazie Hirono (D-HI) is both the first Asian American female senator and the first Buddhist senator. Tammy Baldwin (D-WI) is America's first openly lesbian senator, and she is joined in the House by Rep. Kirsten Sinema (D-AZ), who is openly bisexual. Hirono and freshman representative Tammy Duckworth (D-IL) share the categorical intersection of Asian American, female, naturalized citizens of the United States.[29] Two new female representatives, Duckworth and Tulsi Gabbard (D-HI) are both veterans of the Iraq War. Finally, Deb Fisher (R-NE) is the sole newly elected Republican female.

Will these women agree with each other on everything? Probably not. We can expect each one to participate in governance and ideally provide additional opportunities for underserved and underrepresented groups to have seats at the policy-making table. While we might expect naturalized citizens Hirono and Duckworth to care about immigration reform, will Sinema and Baldwin care just as much that the Leahy Amendment, which protected binational same-sex couples' rights, was dropped from the final bill approved by the

Senate in July of 2013? They may in fact care, but as Rep. DeLauro discovered at the House Oversight Committee hearing, having a seat at the table isn't always enough.

If seats at the Congressional policy table are important, so too are those more permanently inhabited by the justices of the Supreme Court. In its 2012–2013 term the Supreme Court handed down a series of decisions as contradictory for social justice advocates as that 2010 Senate vote on DADT and the DREAM Act. In the space of 48 hours the Court declared the federal Defense of Marriage Act (DOMA) unconstitutional; effectively ended the proponents of Proposition 8 in California's efforts to permanently remove the right to marry from gays and lesbians; and gutted section four of the Voting Rights Act of 1965. While the LGBT community and their allies celebrated, advocates of strong protections against state policies intended to depress the votes of people of color, immigrants, young people, and the elderly were all still reeling from the Court's voting rights decision favoring Shelby, Alabama (and all similarly situated jurisdictions) 24 hours earlier.

All three outcomes were 5–4 decisions, indicating sharp divisions among justices. Writing for the majority in *Windsor v. United States*, the DOMA case, Justice Anthony Kennedy stated outright: "DOMA is unconstitutional as a deprivation of the equal liberty of persons that is protected by the Fifth Amendment."[30] The message was clear: married LGBT people could not be denied the 1000 rights granted to heterosexual married people that section 3 of DOMA mandated be withheld. Writing for the majority in *Shelby County v. Holder*, Chief Justice John Roberts was just as clear about how difficult it would be to prove racially disparate outcomes: "Regardless of how one looks at [today's] record, no one can fairly say that it shows anything approaching the 'pervasive,' 'flagrant,' 'widespread,' and 'rampant' discrimination that clearly distinguished the covered jurisdictions from the rest of the Nation in 1965."[31]

For social justice activists who are committed to both voting rights and marriage equality, it can be daunting to respond. Celebration is clearly in order for marriage equality advocates, yet 38 states still do not grant same-sex couples the right to marry. While many in the United States have declared us to be living in a post-racial society and the Supreme Court clearly agrees, how do we contend with the rash of restrictive voter identification laws that Texas and other states introduced in their legislatures within days of the court's decision? Can we say that the work of either the LGBT or the Civil Rights Movement is complete under these circumstances of victory and defeat? Can we say that the healthcare victories of the second wave women's movement or the DREAMers' 2012 deferred action victory are permanently safe from harm?

Clearly we can't. One of the main audiences for this book are people of different generations who believe their tolerance and their more liberal views on social justice issues of our time are sufficient to permanently move the needle in their favored direction. They will get a wake-up call: the practice of deep political solidarity is not an episodic, one-time Herculean effort to win. It is instead very much like learning a new language, where we are ushered into a culture of practices and a discourse about power that will easily become incomprehensible without frequent efforts to speak and act out solidarity. Put another way: how many of us took languages in high school that we can no longer speak, whether it has been two years or twenty (or more) since we graduated? Deep political solidarity functions requires similar vigilance.

Will *Shelby County v. Holder* be the Civil Rights Movement's Prop 8 moment—a wake up call to discuss racial justice once again? Will they cultivate enough solidarity around the fundamental value of one man, one vote in this nation? Or will we enter a nadir of limited voting rights for the emerging demographic populations we discuss in this book? Is change or hope still possible?

Some states did not wait for the Supreme Court to decide Shelby County. Anxieties about future demographic changes produced state-level efforts to change requirements and access to voting during the 2012 presidential election. In Florida, Ohio, and Pennsylvania activists fought efforts to require additional identification and restrict early voting, two policy changes that would disparately impact low income people of color, highly transient college students, and single women, who all use such policies to participate in our democracy's most celebrated tradition, elections.

Behind the scenes in these and other states were activists using a new strategy, integrated voter engagement, which sought to blend the best aspects of long-term grassroots organizing with the best elements of electoral campaigns.[32] The result was a victory for those like Dessaline Victor, a 102 year-old Haitian American woman who stood in line for hours waiting to vote in Florida. Re-electing President Obama under daunting electoral circumstances was the easy part. It's now up to us as a community committed to social justice to determine what comes next. Whatever it will be, it will require ongoing attentiveness to equality and justice for all, which is of course the meaning of participatory democracy.

NOTES

1. McCall, Leslie. "The Complexity of Intersectionality." *Signs: A Journal of Women and Culture in Society* (2005): 1771; Hawkesworth, Mary. *Feminist Inquiry: From Political Conviction to Methodological Innovation.* 2006.
2. Brah, Avtar and Ann Phoenix. "Ain't I a Woman? Revisiting Intersectionality," *Journal of International Women's Studies* 5.3 (2004): 80.
3. *University of Chicago Legal Forum* 139 (1989).
4. 43 *Stanford Law Review* (1991).
5. New York: Routledge, 1990.
6. Anthias, F. and N. Yuval-Davis."Contextualising Feminism: Gender, Ethnic & Class Divisions." *Feminist Review* 15 (November 1983): 62–75; Anthias, F. and N. Yuval-Davis. *Racialized Boundaries: Race, Nation, Gender, Colour and Class and The Anti-Racist Struggle.* London: Routledge, 1992.
7. Brah, Avtar. *Cartographies of Diaspora.* London: Routledge, 1996.
8. Essed, Philomena. *Understanding Everyday Racism: An Interdisciplinary Theory.* Newbury Park, CA: Sage, 1991.
9. Ifekwunigwe, J. *Scattered Belongings.* London: Sage, 1999.
10. Lutz, H. Migrant women of "Islamic background." *Amsterdam Middle East Research Associates* (1991).
11. Meekosha, H. and L. Dowse. "Enabling Citizenship: Gender, Disability and Citizenship in Australia." *Feminist Review* 57 (1997): 49–72.
12. Minh-ha, Trinh T. *Woman, Native, Other: Writing Postcolonialism and Feminism.* Bloomington: Indiana University Press, 1989.
13. Harding, Sandra. "Comment on Hekman's 'Truth and Method: Feminism Standpoint Theory Revisited': Whose Standpoint Needs Regimes of Truth and Reality?" *Signs: Journal of Women in Culture and Society* 22.2 [1997]: 382–91; p. 389.
14. Hancock, A-M. "When Multiplication Doesn't Equal Quick Addition: Examining Intersectionality as a Research Paradigm." *Perspectives on Politics* 5.1 (2007): 63–79.
15. Yuval-Davis. "Intersectionality and Feminist Politics." *European Journal of Women's Studies* 13.3 (2006): 193–209.
16. Jordan-Zachery. "Am I a Black Woman or a Woman Who Is Black? A Few Thoughts on the Meaning of Intersectionality." *Politics and Gender* 3.3 (2007): 254–263.
17. Strolovitch, Dara. *Affirmative Advocacy: Race, Class and Gender in Interest Group Politics.* Chicago: University of Chicago Press, 2007.
18. Greenwood, Ronni Michelle. "Intersectional Political Consciousness: Appreciation for Intragroup Differences and Solidarity across Diverse Groups." *Psychology of Women Quarterly* 32.1 (2008): 36–47.
19. Townsend-Bell, Erica. "What Is Relevance? Defining Intersectional Praxis in Uruguay." *Political Research Quarterly* 64.1 (2011): 187–199.

20. Kwan, Peter. "Intersections of Race, Ethnicity, Class, Gender and Sexual Orientation: Jeffrey Dahmer and the Cosynthesis of Categories." 48 *Hastings Law Journal* (1997).

21. Hancock, A-M. *Solidarity Politics for Millennials: A Guide to Ending the Oppression Olympics*. New York: Palgrave-Macmillan, 2011.

22. Crenshaw, K. W. "Demarginalizing the Intersection of Race and Sex: A Critique of Antidiscrimination Doctrine, Feminist Theory and Antiracist Politics." *University of Chicago Legal Forum* 139 (1989).

23. Quoted in Miller, Sunlen (2012). "Birth Control Hearing Was Like Stepping into a Time Machine." ABC News.go.com Last accessed July 8, 2013.

24. Nelson, Heidi D., Kari Tyne, Arpana Naik, Christina Bougatsos, Benjamin K. Chan, and Linda Humphrey, (2009). "Screening for Breast Cancer: An Update for the U.S. Preventive Services Task Force" *Annals of Internal Medicine* 151, 727–737.

25. The USPSTF decision was based primarily upon a meta-analysis of seven randomized clinical studies conducted over the past 25 years. These studies were selected primarily based on their rigorous randomization and clinical protocols (Nelson et al. 2009). What's interesting about these studies is that the populations under study in all seven projects made it nearly impossible to conclude multiple factors might be a significant part of the causal story because all had little if any relationship to the 21st century social reality of the United States. First, four of the seven studies were of Swedish women, a population that is 85% ethnically Swedish. A Canadian study drew from a population estimated to be 66% European (British, French, Irish or other European) and only 6% Asian, Arab or African *combined*. The sixth study from the United Kingdom shares a similar set of racial ethnic groups represented as Canada. The final study, from the United States, was published the earliest (1986) and in fact depends on data collected from as long ago as 1968[3]. What is notable here about all of these studies is that the populations in each of the nations (including a 1960s United States) are vastly different from the United States of 2011. Most glaringly in relationship to the recent 2010 Census, *none* of the studies had any information regarding Latinas, who have been part of the largest ethnic group in the United States for more than 10 years.

26. The recommendation was opposed by the American Cancer Society, the American College of Obstetricians and Gynecologists, the American College of Radiology, the American Society of Breast Surgeons and the Susan G. Komen For the Cure Foundation, among many other groups.

27. Weber, Lynn and Elizabeth Fore (2007). Race, Ethnicity and Health: An Intersectional Approach. In: Joe Feagin and Hernan Vera, eds., *Handbook of the Sociology of Racial and Ethnic Relations*. New York, NY: Springer, 191–218.

Weber, Lynn and Deborah Parra-Medina (2003). "Intersectionality and Women's Health: Charting a Path to Eliminating Health

Disparities." *Gender Perspectives on Health and Medicine: Key Themes / Advances in Gender Research* 7: 181–230.

Wells, Kristen J and Richard G. Roetzheim (2007). "Health Disparities in Receipt of Screening Mammography in Latinas: A Critical Review of Recent Literature." *Cancer Control* 14:4, 369–379.

28. On June 5, 2013 NBC News reported that Komen had cancelled walks in seven cities: Boston, Chicago, Cleveland, Phoenix, San Francisco, Tampa, and Washington DC. Komen's official statement revealed that these chapters had not met fundraising goals and that participation was down by 37%. Garza, Lisa Maria (2013). "Susan G. Komen for the Cure Cancels 7 [sic] Charity Walks in U.S. Cities" Reuters Newswire; last accessed July 8, 2013.

29. Hirono was born in Japan, while Duckworth was born in Thailand.

30. *United States v. Windsor*, p.2

31. *Shelby County v. Holder*, p.4

32. Pastor, Manuel, Gihan Perera, and Madeline Wander (2013). "Moments, Movements and Momentum: Engaging Voters, Scaling Power, Making Change." Los Angeles: USC Program for Environmental and Regional Equity.

1

Introduction: Why Geraldine Ferraro Needs to Meet Jay-Z

It all began in April 2008 with a trip to a live studio taping of the American women's talk show *The View*.

My brother-in-law gave us the tickets he'd received four months *after* he'd visited us in New York City. I invited my mother, who talks about cohosts Joy Behar, Whoopi Goldberg, Elizabeth Hasselbeck, Sherri Shepard, and Barbara Walters as if she's a fellow member of their bridge club, to visit me and attend the taping. She flew in from Ohio with my father in tow, who joined three other husbands of his age in holding up the walls and serving as de facto escorts for the overwhelmingly female audience.

While waiting in the studio lobby Mom and I got into our latest debate regarding the Democratic primary, which focused on whether I would cast my general election vote for Hillary Clinton if she was designated the nominee long after it was mathematically impossible for her to win the delegates on her own. Masterfully playing the guilt card, Mom reminded me that my dearly departed grandfather would turn over in his grave if I didn't show up at the polls in November no matter who the candidate was.

Two elderly Jewish women in front of us turned and smiled, perhaps in recognition of a kindred guilt-monger. We began to chat about why the two lifelong New Yorkers were Hillary supporters; one acknowledged that her daughter and son-in-law would likely vote for Barack Obama in Delaware. They said their piece about how much they respected Hillary, and my Mom, a fervent Obama supporter, said hers about her admiration of Obama. Neither side convinced the other to change, and given the pleasant atmosphere, I cracked that as a political science professor I really wouldn't be able to refuse to vote and look my students in the face on Wednesday November 5. The gentleman ahead of us, another of the reluctant husbands in attendance, chuckled, and we welcomed him and his wife into the conversation.

That's when everything began to turn sour.

The wife, who was from Scranton, Pennsylvania, represented Hillary's core demographic—the "older, white female voter""that so many pundits discussed on television. She came into the conversation as I was telling my story of support—that I was a true and undecided fan of both candidates, but turned toward Obama when Clinton's campaign began to make racially inappropriate comments ahead of the South Carolina primary.

"What comments?" the woman from Scranton inquired.

When I explained the situation involving the former president, the woman from Scranton dismissed it: "That's her husband's actions." She went further: she "just didn't know" about Obama, his policies, or anything about him, but knew she wouldn't vote for him.

It took only one question from my steel magnolia, retired reading specialist mother:

> "Have you read either of his books?"
> "No," the woman replied.
> "Oh, well then ..."
> Mom was finished, turning her attention back toward the two Jewish ladies with whom we'd begun the conversation.
> "Well you don't have to read his books to know about him!" the woman from Scranton tried to interject.

I would have warned her not to try to stay in the conversation, because now my mother suspected that other kinds of ignorance were at work that didn't have anything to do with reading books.

Mom enunciated precisely: "I can't lie, I just happen to love tall...intelligent...buh-lack men. And I married one." She then pointed at my unsuspecting dad, who stood against the wall out of earshot, waiting innocently to be admitted to *The View*.

By now the tension was getting thick. As the youngest member of this conversation, I tried to get it back on track with a joke: "Well I married a short, skinny, white guy and I'm voting for Obama too ..." The husband of the woman from Scranton again chuckled, as did the elderly ladies. His wife, however, didn't join in the laughter.

The damage was done, and the conversation crumbled. Ninety minutes later, when we were finally admitted to *The View* studio, ticket holder #1, the woman from Scranton, looked genuinely afraid that our family, ticket holders #3, 4, and 5, would leapfrog over her place in line to get one of the 150 or so seats available to everyone. Instead of a friendly debate grounded in the reality that Democrats of good conscience could disagree, the subtexts of race and class fractured the conversation among women instead of bringing them together. And the distrust lingered.

We traditionally think of leapfrog as a children's game. In the world of gender, race, class, and sexual orientation politics, however, it's become an Olympic sport. The paranoid fear of leapfrogging over those who patiently stood in line, waiting their turn, seems to be part of most discussions of gender, race, and class. It often exists just as it did in that line for *The View*: unaddressed or discussed in ways that reinforce resentful silence rather than open dialogue. Instead of rehashing the same problems we all know, *Solidarity Politics for Millennials* offers intersectionality—the most cutting-edge approach to the politics of gender, race, sexual orientation, and class—as a solution to this long-standing political problem.

The Oppression Olympics: A Threat to Our Democracy

At *The View*, my family physically stepped aside to let the couple from Scranton enter first. If we instead had attempted to enter first, what would have happened? Of course, we now know that Barack Obama conducted his campaign for the presidency with no deference to the idea that Hillary Clinton held nomination ticket #1. Following the long primary season both campaigns criticized each other; Clinton's people demanded greater deference, and Obama's people pointed to the scoreboard to remind them who won. The need for recognition and attention created serious tensions throughout the summer, which diverted party attention from the quest to win the presidency in November.

This kind of internecine warfare is evidence of the Oppression Olympics at work. Elizabeth Martinez first coined the term *Oppression Olympics* in a 1993 *Z Magazine* article, and lamented its existence:

> For a Latina to talk about recognizing the multi-colored varieties of racism is not, and should not be, yet another round in the Oppression Olympics. We don't need more competition among different social groups for that "Most Oppressed" gold. We don't need more comparisons of suffering between women and Blacks, the disabled and the gay, Latino teenagers and white seniors, or whatever.[1]

"Oppression Olympics" is an evocative term to describe intergroup competition and victimhood. The language resonates precisely because it continues to describe the state of intergroup relations in U.S. politics, preventing recognition of common ground and frames of political solidarity. Using *The View* taping, a primary campaign controversy covered by *The Today Show*, and analyses of Hurricane Katrina I'll examine five dimensions of the Oppression Olympics, later proposing the theory of intersectionality as a solution. Figure 1.1 displays the contemporary Oppression Olympics. Each dimension in the Oppression Olympics thwarts rather than facilitates democratic deliberation and political solidarity within and between politically relevant categories of difference. Throughout the book I'll argue that the introduction of intersectionality into our public discourse will give us better tools to handle today's more nuanced challenges of gender, race, class, sexual orientation, and age in the United States, ultimately helping us overcome the Oppression Olympics. In so doing intersectionality defies some "conventional wisdom" about the automatic nature of political change based on generational progress.

Figure 1.1 Oppression Olympics.

Oppression Olympics Day-One Event:
Leapfrog Paranoia

The question of "Who's first in line?" for the presidency arose directly in the national media, with different answers across the generations. In May 2008, former vice-presidential candidate and member of Congress Geraldine Ferraro and talk show host Rachel Maddow appeared on *The Today Show* in an interview with anchor Meredith Vieira about the role of gender in the 2008 Democratic primary campaign. Ferraro raised the subject of Senator Obama's symbolic gesture at a rally in North Carolina as an example of his sexism and dismissive attitude toward Senator Clinton. Maddow, the far younger feminist, read the gesture as a mimic of hip-hop star Jay-Z, which was neither sexist nor dismissive of Clinton. The exchange among the three women is telling:

> *Ms. Ferraro*: You asked for specifics, and let me just give you specifics. Women are looking at how this has gone on. [Senator Barack Obama] just—he—when he—after one of the—she mentioned after Philadelphia that she had—before Philadelphia, that she had gone out and she had learned to shoot a gun. He kind of ridiculed her, "Who does she think"—like a stand-up comedian walking up and down with a mike in his hand, "Who does she think she is, Annie Oakley?" And then, when something else was said about the campaign, this thing [Ferraro brushes imaginary dirt off her shoulders], flicking it off, diminishing her. I mean, sorry, that's not done.
>
> *Vieira*: Rachel . . .
>
> *Ms. Ferraro*: Women don't like that.
>
> *Vieira: Is he in trouble with women voters, people who feel this is—this was our time and it was taken from us? Are they going to blame Barack Obama?*
>
> *Ms. Maddow*: I think some will. I mean, when you cite those examples, I didn't see either of those examples as sexist. I saw this as him referencing a hip-hop video where Jay-Z does that.
>
> *Ms. Ferraro*: Oh, that's generational. She's had a problem with women—I mean, I did not—I don't see this hip-hop stuff. Maybe that's cool and maybe that's why a lot of people are voting for him. But I didn't see that.
>
> *Ms. Maddow*: Or maybe that's the—that's the—I think that's important that our perception is different, that both of us as women . . .
>
> *Ms. Ferraro*: It's very different.
>
> *Ms. Maddow*: . . . looking at the Democratic candidates seeing that treatment differently depending on our own lens.[2]

To provide some context, here is a video transcript of Obama's action, which took place at a campaign rally in Raleigh, North Carolina, on April 17, 2008:

> Yeah, that's why [Hillary Clinton]'s only airing negative attacks on TV in Pennsylvania like most places. Look, I understand that because that's the textbook Washington game. That's how our politics has been taught to be played [*sic*]. That's the lesson that she learned when the Republicans were doing that same thing to her back in the 1990s. So I understand it and when you're running for the Presidency, then you've got to expect it, and you know you've just got to kinda kinda [Obama brushes imaginary dirt off shoulders] kinda let it [Brushes off shoulder again]. You know. That's what you gotta do. That's what you gotta do.[3]

Maddow traced Obama's gesture to pop culture: the chorus of hip-hop artist Jay-Z's "Dirt Off Your Shoulder" features the refrain, "You gotta get, that, dirt off your shoulder."[4] But regardless of what Obama actually said and did, the questions asked by Meredith Vieira— "Is he in trouble with women voters, people who feel this is—this was our time and it was taken from us? Are they going to blame Barack Obama?"—echo the concerns I highlighted in the introduction. Vieira is articulating the precise kind of **Leapfrog Paranoia** in a political context that the woman from Scranton seemed concerned about as we all entered the studio taping of *The View*. Leapfrog Paranoia is just one lingering trend of intergroup relations that contributes to what Elizabeth Martinez called the Oppression Olympics.

Vieira's questions about "our time" and "something being taken from us" are based on a political lens that pits race against gender in a zero-sum context. This political lens has a long history. Second-wave feminist historians have long interpreted the tension between prominent abolitionist and women's rights supporter Frederick Douglass and prominent women's rights activist Elizabeth Cady Stanton in the nineteenth century as evidence that the United States was *more* sexist than racist when Douglass accepted the right to vote offered to black men in the nineteenth century. Some suffragettes, succumbing to Leapfrog Paranoia in light of the proposed Fifteenth Amendment, resorted to racialized appeals in an attempt to obtain the vote. They were aghast that racism was remedied *first*, through the proposed Fifteenth Amendment instead of either resolving sexism *first* or remedying both simultaneously.[5] With passage of the Fifteenth Amendment Congress's institutional power was able to destroy a coalition that had previously enjoyed tremendous political solidarity based on its shared work to abolish slavery. Many suffragettes then working to enfranchise women came of political age through their (suffragettes') antislavery work. Similarly many women in the second wave of the women's movement also came to their opinions about gender based on their prior political experience in the civil rights and antiwar movements nearly a century later.[6]

In 2008 Ferraro clearly emulated the outrage of those nineteenth-century feminists, drawing the same conclusion: that racism is unfairly considered "more serious" and thus gets primary attention over sexism:

> Meredith, there is a real difference in this country. It is—it is not OK to be racist, it is just not. It is almost acceptable to be sexist. When [Clinton] appeared at a rally up in New Hampshire, somebody held up a sign that said, you know, "Iron my shirt." Now, suppose somebody had gone up to a Barack Obama rally [and] said "Shine my shoes." The press would have been on top of that shine my shoes and on top of that person, saying, "What are you, a racist?" Nothing done. When Hillary—[we] barely saw a story on this thing.[7]

In a *New York Times* editorial following Obama's Iowa caucus victory, Gloria Steinem also made a similar point:

> So why is the sex barrier not taken as seriously as the racial one? The reasons are as pervasive as the air we breathe: because sexism is still confused with nature as racism once was; because anything that affects males is seen as more serious than anything that affects "only" the female half of the human race; because children are still raised mostly by women (to put it mildly) so men especially tend to feel they are regressing to childhood when dealing with a powerful woman; because racism stereotyped black men as more "masculine" for so long that some white men find their presence to be masculinity-affirming (as long as there aren't too many of them); and because there is still no "right" way to be a woman in public power without being considered a you-know-what.[8]

Although neither woman legitimizes racism, their mode of speech clearly communicates their ideas about the relationship between gender and race to say that we have not made nearly the progress on gender that we have on race, either socially or politically. Both Ferraro and Steinem, as women of a particular generation as well as race and gender, privilege gender as the primary threat to our democracy. That Steinem and Ferraro arrive so easily at this conclusion reflects their particular type of feminism—one that is distinct from a type that appeals to younger feminists who see the world as one of constant progress. These younger feminists see no danger posited by acts like brushing dirt off the shoulder or "Iron my shirt" because in a context of constant progress, women can never go back to the pre-Steinem and Ferraro days of limited opportunities. According to these third-wave feminists, "Feminism is like fluoride. We scarcely notice that we have it—it's simply in the water."[9]

While Steinem says later in the article that she's not "advocating a competition for who has it toughest,"[10] when she offers no alternative framework for interpreting her editorial many Americans will in fact take her point to be that women have it toughest. In general, Leapfrog Paranoia and zero-sum approaches are chronically accessible filters for understanding gender and race politics, thanks to the work of the mass media.[11] Leapfrog Paranoia reinforces the idea that U.S. politics is always and forever a zero-sum game. Such cognitive filters contribute to the ongoing "Oppression Olympics" between groups.

OPPRESSION OLYMPICS DAY-TWO EVENT: WILLFUL BLINDNESS

We could argue empirically with a host of statistics on either side of the debate: Who has it toughest? Racial minorities? Women? The lesbian/gay/bisexual/transgender (LGBT) community? But we'd spin our wheels, as we have for over a century, because we are using the wrong lens and asking the wrong questions. To be fair, just as we've criticized Steinem et al for their gloss-over of racism, Martinez only attended to gender in passing when she coined the term "Oppression Olympics," a subtle way to give race primary status. My point is that neither move is legitimate—these inegalitarian traditions are equally yet not identically threatening to our democracy. I'll come back to this point throughout the book.

Ferraro and Steinem's resistance to seeing racism and sexism as equal but not identical threats is not swayable using dueling statistics; it is grounded in a centuries-old filter, which was inculcated during their trailblazing second-wave women's activism of the 1960s and 1970s. During this era "consciousness-raising strategies" were wildly successful in mobilizing white, middle-class women into the workforce and the political arena. Although Maddow herself recognizes much of this era's success, many younger women are often surprised to learn that the athletic scholarships they receive, the sports they got to play as kids, the advent of maternity leave, and enhanced enforcement against domestic violence are all available courtesy of the second-wave women's movement.[12] More importantly, they are generally resistant to the idea that these long-standing policies could ever suffer any backlash and are unaware that several women's groups use the rhetoric of choice to do precisely that: repeal laws that were the bedrock of the second-wave women's movement.[13]

As an inculcation process feminist consciousness-raising was a wildly successful but double-edged sword for three reasons. First, as we can see from the Ferraro and Steinem examples, it didn't replace the nineteenth-century race-versus-gender lens with a more accurate vision of the relationship between race and gender. Consciousness-raising strategies brought attention to the disadvantaged aspect of middle-class, white women's lives while mostly leaving the privileged aspects as "invisible norms."[14]

Second, the success of the grassroots approach also produced mixed but politically significant responses among men and women. Second-wave successes produced backlash movements of men and women that were antithetical to the goals of second-wave feminism. Among its features, the antifeminist response includes interest groups of women that pursue tort reform to protect businesses that are sued for jeopardizing women's health.[15]

In a similar vein, while consciousness-raising worked phenomenally for white, middle-class women, many other women who were poor, women of color, lesbians, or any and all of the above were demobilized by such activities. Women of color in particular resisted the notion that gender functioned analogously to race. They did not believe that a movement that focused only on gender applied to them. Often the evidence for such beliefs emerged from the mouths of feminists themselves, when they used loaded terms that raised red flags for women of color or lesbians. On *The Today Show*, for example, Ferraro focuses here on Obama's offense in a way that can be interpreted as racialized. Referring again to the shoulder gesture, she notes her husband's disapproval of Obama's action, but in different terms:

> *Ms. Ferraro*: Like I also tell you, my husband will sometimes look at this thing and if he says something, he'll go—and—because it offended him as well. He thought it was very arrogant.[16]

The offense, expressed by Ferraro and (according to her) her husband as well, was characterized as "arrogance." The idea that it was Obama who was the arrogant interloper in the primary is suffused with racial implications, even as Clinton supporters like Ferraro and Gloria Steinem had the primary goal of turning our attention to gender. Just as Ferraro interpreted Obama's brush-off as putting

Hillary in her place, so, too, do some African Americans see a red flag when an educated, upper-class black person like Obama is called "arrogant" or "uppity" because they behave contrary to stereotypical expectations. *New York Times* columnist Brent Staples explained the vernacular racial subtext of a general election controversy featuring Republican Congressman Lynn Westmoreland's characterization of the Obama family as uppity: "The discomfort with certain forms of black assertiveness is just too deeply rooted in the national psyche— and the national language—to just disappear. It has become a persistent theme in the public discourse since Barack Obama became a plausible candidate for the presidency."[17] Just as former president Bill Clinton's comments in South Carolina about Obama turned off African American voters (including myself), women who felt disconnected from the women's movement found other paths to political participation when the movement's language and action overlooked the role of equally significant categories such as race and sexual orientation. In this way consciousness-raising as a strategy failed to produce the solidarity among all women that feminists sought.

Finally, consciousness-raising as a strategy contains internal tensions that can threaten the ability of its practitioners to build transformative egalitarian coalitions among women and between women and men. As Mary Hawkesworth notes: "The ideal of heightened consciousness incorporated a stringent conception of human perfection: those who have completed the process are expected to have cultivated *uncompromising* commitments to women in particular and social justice in general...That this project is advanced in the language of liberation does not preclude the possibility that it bears *coercive* implications for concrete individuals involved in the transition to the good society."[18] It is this sense of uncompromising judgment that sparks tension across the generations, again compromising solidarity. Queer theorist and activist Amber Hollibaugh makes this point in her description of the generational disconnect she observes:

> I often find myself in conversation with two oppositional groups at the same university or activist event: on the one hand the early intellectuals and activists of sex, gender and feminist studies who are disaffected and angry at the theories and movements they helped create but no longer recognize; on the other, the new generation of intellectuals and activists, who often feel disparaged and incriminated by those earlier people, as though their fresh, sometimes awkward inquiries and directions were betraying the world views that birthed them.[19]

My point here is not to question Ferraro, Steinem, or any other person's understandable outrage regarding both the obvious and subtle sexism during the 2008 presidential election cycle. I, too, saw sexism directed toward Senator Clinton. Instead I want to focus on the two words I highlighted in the first passage: *uncompromising* and *coercive*. Others have noted that an uncompromising stance may serve a legitimate movement purpose: "Framing issues in ways that lack cultural resonance allows groups to maintain a vision of the possible that otherwise would not exist."[20] However, this disengagement either with like-minded, otherwise well-intentioned women who happen to be younger feminists like Maddow, who are perceived to lack standing because "hip-hop stuff" is "generational," or with differently minded women who are presumed to be falsely conscious or mouthpieces of men because they are politically conservative,[21] poses great risks for a vibrant feminism's future. Author Ronee Schreiber emphasizes the growing power of conservative women, who currently play the game on feminists' home turf[22] but reframe issues in a way that speaks to the increasing number of moderate and independent women. Indeed, the nomination of Alaska governor Sarah Palin as a candidate for vice-president partly represents the recognition of growing political power among socially and/or economically conservative women in the Republican Party.

Whether it's nineteenth-century or second-wave feminists who overlooked the race and class privileged that shaped their policy agenda,[23] or black women who refuse to recognize their heterosexual privilege when black lesbian women like Sakia Gunn are murdered,[24] when we deliberately choose not to see our own power and privilege, we are engaging in ***Willful Blindness***. Willful Blindness emerges from a persistent vision of oneself or one's groups as *solely* victims. In our absolute focus on our own victimhood, we willfully and pathologically blind ourselves to our own agency. Whereas Leapfrog Paranoia is a game of which former victim goes first in obtaining access to political resources, Willful Blindness has become a sport of who's the *purest* victim. Both political phenomena threaten our democracy, independently and collaboratively, by locking in the zero-sum, winner-take-all framework that exists for elections throughout the rest of the political system. How, for example, can marginalized groups develop the necessary political trust and build egalitarian coalitions when the only true victim they are willing to see is their own, single, marginalized group? In such a context, how can we fault people for their obsession with going first or their refusal to see the political reality of other groups? Later chapters will examine some of the most recent outcomes of this blindness.

In reality, as I noted before, Steinem, Ferraro, Vieira , and Maddow are not just women. They are all white. Steinem, Ferraro, and Vieira are all straight and older, while Maddow is openly gay and younger. Maddow argued, "I think that's important that our perception is different, that both of us as women...looking at the Democratic candidates seeing that treatment different depending on our own lens."[25] Rather than dismiss Maddow's characterization of the brush-off as related to popular culture, it deserves further inspection. Online responses to Obama's gesture among older comment posters noted that the gesture is older than either Jay-Z's "Dirt Off Your Shoulder" (released in 2003) or Obama himself. One eighty-three-year-old woman accurately responded through her daughter's post that Fred Astaire had a song and dance with a similar gesture. That 1936 movie, *Swing Time*, featured Fred Astaire and his longtime partner Ginger Rogers singing and dancing to a song entitled "Pick Yourself Up," featuring the following chorus:

> Pick yourself up
> Dust yourself off
> Start all over again[26]

Online responses to the gesture more frequently echoed Maddow's interpretation, not Ferraro's.[27] Although Internet use is more common among young people, many specifically noted their advanced age or lack of familiarity with hip-hop even as they confirmed their agreement with Maddow's analysis. Maddow's willingness to see multiple legitimate interpretations of the same gesture is helpful to women of good conscience who want to think through the implications of an Obama presidency for gender equality, including that cracked but not yet shattered glass ceiling of the U.S. presidency.

Was Obama justified in using the gesture? Can we call it sexist even if all women don't agree with it? More importantly, is this the conversation and debate that we really want to be having—whether in May 2008 or now? Is it sufficient or even necessary? Many scholars have critiqued this kind of conversation as unproductive because it successfully allows groups to be divided and conquered, when political coalitions are more urgently needed in a majoritarian democracy like the United States.

Moreover, these discussions cannot only attend to only gender *or* only race. While Ferraro and Steinem rightly turn our attention to sexism (but wrongly place gender ahead of race in importance), Martinez rightly brings subtlety to racism, making our knowledge far broader than just black vs. white, even as she is willfully blind to gender in that article. Binary thinking along the black-white dichotomy involves an act of Willful Blindness to Latinos/as, Asian Americans, and Native peoples in politically significant ways. Specifically, Martinez brings to light numerous populations who otherwise remain invisible—Latinos/as especially.[28] Martinez's race critique identifies a variant of Willful Blindness that complements rather than supplants Ferraro and Steinem's charge against socially sanctioned sexism.

To overcome both Leapfrog Paranoia and Willful Blindness, then, we must not only attend to race and gender as conceptually distinct phenomena that produce the groups that vie for the Oppression Olympics gold, we must also look at them simultaneously as multiple categories of difference. Using this strategy (and including additional categories like class, sexual orientation, religion, or national status) breaks the tendency to use the zero-sum, category-versus-category lens used by nineteenth-century suffragettes and twenty-first-century Democrats. While the previous discussion explains how the first two Oppresion Olympics events, Leapfrog Paranoia and Willful Blindness prevent solidarity among groups returning to, Martinez suggests two additional dimensions of the Oppression Olympics.

OPPRESSION OLYMPICS DAY-THREE EVENT: MOVEMENT BACKLASH

In another article, "Beyond Black/White," Martinez offers us two additional "events" in the Oppression Olympics. The Oppression Olympics–oriented *Movement Backlash* focuses on the idea that the gains of social movements for civil rights or women's rights are creating a new class of formerly privileged victims who are now unfairly disadvantaged. This includes the claim of reverse discrimination in affirmative action cases like those filed by Allan Bakke[29] and Jennifer Gratz.[30] Martinez first describes the Movement Backlash against the gains of the twentieth-century civil rights movement agenda.[31] In addition to Martinez's identification of the problem, scholars have conducted a plethora of studies concerning legal backlash in the areas of racial integration, educational equity, and workplace discrimination. For example, Derrick Bell's *Silent Covenants* reappraises the legacy of *Brown v. Board of Education*.[32] In a very different way, David Theo Goldberg discusses antiregulatory legal backlash as a key factor contributing to the Hurricane Katrina debacle.[33] Unfortunately for our purposes, all three authors analyze race and mention other categories (like class or gender) in passing only; like Steinem and

Ferraro they are conducting a single-category analysis, which has limitations that will be articulated in subsequent chapters.

Movement Backlash enters previously privileged groups into the competition for "most oppressed" by redefining victimhood to include the collateral damage caused by social justice remedies. Within the policy domain of same-sex marriage, evidence of Movement Backlash emerges from the numerous statewide propositions and constitutional amendments proposed and passed by forty states that cast the religious institution of heterosexual marriage as the victims of an overly aggressive court system and a mobilized gay rights movement.[34] Though heterosexual marriage is the hegemonic institution throughout history, as proponents of anti-same-sex marriage Proposition 8 in California freely admit,[35] the logic of Movement Backlash makes it feasible for them to frame the institution of marriage as a "victim" of activist judges and marriage equality activists.

Susan Faludi's well-known book, *Backlash,* provided the public with myriad instances of gender backlash.[36] More recently, Movement Backlash also involves the anti–Title IX activism of the Independent Women's Forum, which argues, "Current Title IX enforcement has institutionalized discrimination against men and demeaned athletic and academic accomplishments of women."[37] Conservative organizations like Concerned Women for America and the Independent Women's Forum emerged in response to the success of the second-wave women's movement, and they have admitted leveraging that prior success for their own advantage.[38] Like the race-focused analyses of Martinez and others, however, Faludi's path-breaking book about gender only mentions other politically relevant categories in passing. As we will see in chapters 2 and 4, fighting Movement Backlash is much harder to do when the attendant steps to avoid the zero-sum analyses that perpetuate Leapfrog Paranoia and Willful Blindness aren't also simultaneously addressed.

OPPRESSION OLYMPICS DAY-FOUR EVENT: DEFIANT IGNORANCE

In an analysis of Arizona Senator John and wife Cindy McCain's marital body language, *Huffington Post* authors Kathlyn and Gay Hendricks make passing mention of a bumper sticker featuring the question, "What are you pretending not to know?"[39] The fourth dimension of the Oppression Olympics is **Defiant Ignorance**. Defiant Ignorance denies the existence of any and all victimhood or stratified systems of political power. Often linked to stories of American exceptionalism and Horatio Alger visions of success, Defiant Ignorance is a defense mechanism designed to resist responsibility for and advantage from inegalitarian traditions in the United States. For privileged groups, the responses and logic might proceed as follows: "Denying the validity of the information that is being presented, or psychologically or physically withdrawing from it. The logic is, 'If I don't read about [it], talk about [it], watch those documentaries or special news programs, or spend time with those people...I won't have to feel uncomfortable."[40] While psychologist and Spelman College president Beverly Tatum is describing here the response of racially privileged whites, such logic has been discussed with regard to gender and race in connection to each other as well.[41]

There are two different ways Defiant Ignorance operates. Martinez's original construction unfortunately focused again just on race[42] when in the 1990s she noted the continuation of "stunning ignorance" about Latinos, echoing an assertion made in 1972 by Robert Blauner.[43] As the wealth of scholarship and attention to Latino issues continues to grow,[44] those who would remain ignorant serve as a bitter reminder of how far there is yet to go in terms of full political inclusion. *Washington Post* columnist Marie Cocco provides a similar example as she describes the impact of Defiant Ignorance when the Democrats failed to recognize the sexism of the 2008 primary campaign:

> I will not miss the deafening, depressing silence of Democratic National Committee Chairman Howard Dean or other leading Democrats, who to my knowledge (with the exception of Sen. Barbara Mikulski of Maryland) haven't publicly uttered a word of outrage at the unrelenting, sex-based hate that has been hurled at the former first lady and two-term senator from New York. Among those holding their tongues are hundreds of Democrats for whom Clinton has campaigned and raised millions of dollars. Don Imus endured more public ire from the political class when he insulted the Rutgers University women's basketball team.[45]

In the end Cocco unfortunately uses the same race-versus-gender filter that Ferraro and Steinem do, cuing the Oppression Olympics lens.[46] There must be a better way to delineate the problem sexism continues to pose for American society without using this persistently problematic zero-sum filter.

The second way that Defiant Ignorance is problematic for society is the public positioning of knowledgeable experts. As Martinez and Blauner point out, omissions can make certain groups invisible to the public eye. As well, Defiant Ignorance can involve the deliberate appropriations of cultural products for the benefit of the privileged. Academics gain recognition, for example, for insights originally discovered by scholars from marginalized groups.[47] Popular mid-twentieth century cover artists like Pat Boone, Ricky Nelson, and the McGuire sisters gained some of their fame singing songs originated by black artists. Defiant Ignorance allows for such appropriation without attribution or recompense. The appropriation of another's work, whether in academe, in the workplace, or in popular culture, expresses a certain kind of imperial impunity—a belief that attribution is not important because the originator is not important. This belief dehumanizes originators who are members of marginalized groups specifically because their sociopolitical location comes with the baggage of being "less than" to begin with. We will examine one ugly outcome of this approach in chapter 4's discussion of California's recent ban on same-sex marriage, Proposition 8.

One very problematic aspect of Defiant Ignorance is its cultural currency beyond race-, gender-, or sexuality-based privilege. When Defiant Ignorance becomes a modus operandi for politics and government writ large, then the "class warfare card," to paraphrase conservative *New York Times* columnist David Brooks, devolves into "a disdain for the educated class as a whole . . . with a corrosive effect"[48] for our democracy as well as our intergroup relationships.

OPPRESSION OLYMPICS DAY-FIVE EVENT: COMPASSION DEFICIT DISORDER

In addition to the 2008 primary, other recent events have revealed evidence of the Oppression Olympics in the twenty-first century. In a manner akin to Movement Backlash within political institutions, *New York Times* columnist Judith Warner describes **Compassion Deficit Disorder** as a product of multiple realities: "one is the degree to which the meaning of the historical battle of America's long-discriminated against populations has been corrupted, and the other is the degree to which everyone seems to feel that the deck is stacked against them."[49] The wide-scale resolution to deny victim status to any and all groups—often going beyond such denial to actual victim blame—is one outcome of a politics of disgust,[50] which is notable for its dehumanizing effects. From a political point of view, people for whom no compassion can be generated are seen as less than human and therefore are politically and practically expendable. The failed governmental response to Gulf Coast residents immediately following

Hurricane Katrina illuminated the degree to which Compassion Deficit Disorder has infiltrated our nation's consciousness. David Theo Goldberg argues that political attitudes favoring "starving the state" of funding has forced the widespread decay of government capabilities in a pernicious way based on the idea that those who might need those services are less than human, and therefore undeserving of compassion or government assistance. Once such capabilities are hamstrung by deliberate mismanagement and drastic funding cuts, it becomes far easier in the wake of a devastating hurricane to let the targets of Compassion Deficit Disorder die.[51]

Compassion Deficit Disorder also misplaces compassion. After rapper Kanye West stunned the nation by calling attention to President George W. Bush's own Compassion Deficit Disorder when he stated, "George Bush doesn't care about black people," scholars and activists explored the role of race in the outcomes following Hurricane Katrina. At about the same time, former North Carolina Senator John Edwards kicked off his 2008 presidential campaign with a focus on poverty and class-based issues to address the aftermath of Katrina. Political institutions were suspicious of either race- or class-based explanations, and sought to address possible fraud in Katrina relief as a primary concern based on compassion for taxpayers over compassion for storm victims.

Compassion Deficit Disorder, then, becomes the foundation for the Oppression Olympics in political contexts like that of the post-Katrina Gulf Coast. Race scholar Lawrence Bobo traces the Katrina tragedy to the classification of storm evacuees as part of an "open racial secret": the unacknowledged yet widely present laissez-faire racism of the post-civil rights United States. The oxymoron of prior public invisibility of the populations most devastated by the storm—whether the segregated black working poor or the undocumented Latino population—called their worthiness for government-based remedies into question. Because such individuals don't deserve our compassion, we exercise our Willful Blindness and our Defiant Ignorance of their suffering unrepentantly. David Crowe expresses such Compassion Deficit Disorder succinctly: "Katrina was an act of God upon a sin-loving and rebellious nation, a warning to all who foolishly and arrogantly believe there is no God, and that if He did exist, 'would not have done such a thing.'"[52] In this sense, Compassion Deficit Disorder serves as a post hoc rationalization for ongoing Willful Blindness and Defiant Ignorance prior to the storm.

There is one major political implication of groups denied protection based on the Compassion Deficit Disorder of other groups. Such people are branded hopelessly and irreparably dysfunctional. Such branding reduces the number of justifiable political options to either complete oversight of their entire lives (e.g., imprisonment or institutionalization), often through a government contractor, or, in an era of devolution, public invisibility that translates into complete eradication from the earth during a natural disaster.

THE TWENTY-FIRST CENTURY OPPRESSION OLYMPICS

The vast majority of authors I've cited so far in this introduction follow twentieth-century convention—they focus on one category in depth and sometimes mention another one or two in passing. But Willful Blindness to the simultaneous roles of race, class, and sexual orientation in organizing human lives and political culture alienates like-minded women and men from each other in their commitment to gender equality.[53] As well, race scholars like Martinez ignore a tremendous amount of relevant political complexity among and between groups when the roles of gender, class, and sexual orientation are minimized. Although it's clear that the games of the Oppression Olympics are still played in the twenty-first century, we can't simply look for race-based Willful Blindness or gendered Leapfrog Paranoia alone. In order to effectively diagnose and correct the presence of the Oppression Olympics, we need to update our approach to account for changes in the twenty-first century.

Too often we pay lip service to some categories while paying attention to our pet category. This move comes at a cost of accurate explanations and, politically, at the cost of valuable coalition-building opportunities. For example, instead of Goldberg's or West's focus on race *versus* Edwards's focus on class, research has shown that in terms of Hurricane Katrina, neither explains the outcomes on its own. Instead, scholars have found that class and race are complementary rather than competing factors to explain outcomes such as rates of evacuation[54] and post-storm return.[55] It seems so logical, yet it's still not part of our mainstream culture to focus in depth on multiple categories simultaneously in this intersecting way. In fact the political complexity of the twenty-first century doesn't lend itself to reductionist, single-category approaches. Instead, intersectionality theory argues for full and simultaneous attention to multiple categories like race, gender, sexual orientation, and class in order to adjudicate among competing priorities and perspectives.

Intersectionality theory's most central and still controversial claim effectively combats the reductionist tendencies of the Oppression

Olympics. The competition for the title "most oppressed" stagnates when everyone is revealed to have some form of privilege and political agency within a larger structure of stratification. But how would this recognition of *categorical multiplicity* change our political analysis?

One interesting outcome of this deep attentiveness to multiple categories is that it becomes increasingly difficult to pinpoint any pure victims—a clear obstacle to the perpetuation of Willful Blindness. In the context of the 2008 primary, this would mean that we should look at Hillary Clinton not simply as a woman, but as a *rich, white* woman. The late-stage public hand-wringing regarding sexism (after far too many months of suffering in silence) caricatured Senator Clinton as a second-wave feminist victim, with little space in which to frame herself as an agent of her own destiny.[56] This caricature goes directly against the kind of individual that Americans tend to elect as president, and in fact contradicts Clinton's own vast capabilities and qualifications for the presidency.

Next, consider Clinton's statement to *USA Today* in May 2008: "I have a much broader base to build a winning coalition on," she said...As evidence, Clinton cited an Associated Press article 'that found how Senator Obama's support among working, hard-working [sic] Americans, white Americans, is weakening again, and how whites in both states who had not completed college were supporting me. There's a pattern emerging here,' she said." To recognize one's privilege, as Clinton did inadvertently here, is an uncomfortable, troubling form of agency, but it is still agency nevertheless, and part of what is revealed by a practice of deep simultaneous attention to multiple categories.

The recognition of such privilege should cause a moment of reflection at a minimum, disrupting the automatic slide into the Oppression Olympics. It is, as I discuss in chapter 3, a moment of identity conflict. What if, instead of resorting to self-construction as a pure victim, Clinton chose to address the sexism head on in a way that cast her as neither the stereotypical victim nor as gender-free? What if she used the recognition of agency as a way to start a conversation rather than avoid the topic or wallow in it? Could there have been a speech, campaign event, or ad that recognized the glass ceiling as both a barrier and an opportunity for girl power? There is an affirmative, chronically accessible "9 to 5" feminism in ways that embrace gender affirmatively rather than victim-like. It's the humorous ways three women outsmart their boss in the movie and now musical "9 to 5," yes, but it's also the affirming woman power of Mothers Against Drunk Driving (MADD), the Million Mom March, the GoGirlGo program of the Women's Sports Foundation, and the Women's Voices for Change website. Of course, hindsight is 20/20 and I don't mean to minimize the virulence of the campaign-trail sexism. But disrupting the Oppression Olympics involves disrupting some defeatist habits in ourselves as well as transforming the world around us.

Similarly, we can't look at Barack Obama as simply an African American, but as a *rich* African American *male*. One particular example stands out in a way that reveals Obama's male privilege and agency in a very clear way. In April 2008 Obama very publicly played an early morning game of pick-up basketball with members of the University of North Carolina Tar Heels Men's Basketball team, including 2008 Player of the Year Tyler Hansbrough.[57] Women supporters of Hillary Clinton saw Obama's usage of sports metaphors in battleground states and such public basketball games as a way to solidify Obama's image as a male politician among males who would otherwise vote for Hillary if she weren't a woman. Yet we cannot divorce the image of Obama, vying at the time to be the country's first African American president, from the public identity of black male athletes who, whether celebrated or castigated, are in all sectors a black male public identity that is familiar to mainstream America. A black male president who plays basketball with the most accomplished athletes in the sport is that much more familiar than a black president with an untraditional name or lineage. Nevertheless, in the twenty-first century we have to recognize that this image is structurally available to Obama due to his gender, and the leveraging of such an image constitutes an exercise of agency.

Last but certainly not least, analyzing race, class, and gender simultaneously reveals a more complete picture of former Republican vice-presidential nominee Sarah Palin. Early on there was much debate in the blogosphere about whether Palin was selected as an olive branch to the vocal Clinton contingent who vowed never to vote for Obama. If so, then why select Palin over numerous better-qualified women, including Governors M. Jodi Rell (CT) and Linda Lingle (HI), and Senators Kay Bailey Hutchinson (TX), Olympia Snowe (ME), or Elizabeth Dole (NC)? In part because Palin embraces a class-driven kind of white womanhood that is intended do more than speak volumes about gender politics. It is also intended to distinguish her quite clearly from the racialized Democratic presidential candidate Barack Obama.

For example, Palin recently told country singer Gretchen Wilson that she has publicly identified as the subject of Wilson's most popular song, "Redneck Woman," which opens with the potentially feminist statement, "Well, I ain't never been the Barbie doll type." Confronting the impossible standards dolls like Barbie and media images of female celebrities create for masses of women has long been a cause supported by feminist theorists and activists alike, who argue that the distorted senses of body image and disordered eating afflicting many women and girls are partly attributable to long-standing popular-culture phenomena like Barbie. But Wilson's song isn't just a statement about gender. It features as well the following class-driven chorus:

> Cause I'm a redneck woman
> And I ain't no high class broad[58]

Certainly, the combination of class and gender, as seen here, were part of Sarah Palin's self-presentation to the United States when she emerged as a virtual political unknown in August 2008. Several aspects of her personal life were marketed as emblematic of the "Jane Six-Pack" image reflected not just in the Wilson song but in popular culture, masking part of the important gender change she represented for the Republican party and, if she had been elected, for the nation writ large. As with Obama and Clinton, who had combinations of advantaged and disadvantaged traditions to draw upon, Palin's class politics and race were familiar to Americans, though her gender was relatively new. Her public image in this regard, including its class-driven image of whiteness, stood in stark contrast to the persistent rumors swirling around the identity of Barack Obama.

Late in the campaign Palin's own speeches were designed to focus attention on the "Joe the Plumbers" of the world in a distinctly racialized way that drew on whispering campaigns characterizing Senator Barack Obama as a Muslim or noncitizen, a particularly powerful contrast in light of the 9/11 analysis conducted in chapter 5. Responding to the rampant antibank bailout sentiment in the United States, Palin characterized business owners and wannabe business owners like Samuel "Joe the Plumber" Wurzbacher as the true victims of a possible Obama administration, thus engaging in Movement Backlash.

As is clear from the examples of Clinton, Obama, and Palin, attending to multiple categories produces information that can interrupt the reflexive turn to the Oppression Olympics. Recognizing all three officials as raced, classed, and gendered reveals similarities and differences that are invisible when using a single category filter. We can also use these nuanced accounts to examine the connections *between* the five elements of the Oppression Olympics. In the public presentation of Sarah Palin, we can connect the class and gender redefinition of victimhood present in Movement Backlash and the racialized Willful Blindness. Tapping into what John Dovidio has termed "aversive racism," undecided white voters are encouraged to engage in a little Willful Blindness to cast their vote for the "authentic American" Palin as "real" instead of the "questionably American" Obama. Moreover, Willful Blindness and Movement Backlash allow them to do so without feeling like they are overtly racist, preserving their personal sense of self as unprejudiced individuals. Like the woman from Scranton, they can say they just "don't know" about Obama or his policies and remain Defiantly Ignorant of the racial cues and implications of such statements. Second, with regard to Hurricane Katrina, empirical evidence about the race and class factors links Defiant Ignorance (systematic "not knowing" about racial inequality) and Compassion Deficit Disorder ("not caring about it") among white respondents who were asked their opinions about the evacuees.[59] The demonstrable connections among these five dimensions suggest the larger existence of the Oppression Olympics.

To summarize, Martinez's original construction of the Oppression Olympics remains useful in the twenty-first century political context, but in a more complicated way. While Martinez identifies the competition itself, part of how it functions is to create confusion rather than clarity about the complex politics that swirl in discussions of resource allocation, identity, and political behavior. When Steinem and Ferraro correctly point out the sexism evident in the 2008 election, they do so through a lens that obfuscates the role of race and class because it is grounded in a framework that automatically pits race and gender against each other. Obama is not solely African American, and neither Clinton nor Palin is solely female. The Oppression Olympics framework remains lodged in our psyches because it encourages reductionist interpretations for political expediency's sake in an era where the discussions we have about race, gender, class, and sexual orientation are much more nuanced than they were in the twentieth century.

PLAN OF THE BOOK

The presentation of the Oppression Olympics here is a call to start a conversation rather than settle for the dueling statistics debate of "who has it toughest." It is a call to engage across differences rather than resign from the political arena. From both a pragmatic political perspective and a normative perspective, intersectionality theory can resolve the multiple challenges posed by Leapfrog Paranoia, Willful Blindness, Movement Backlash, Defiant Ignorance, and Compassion Deficit Disorder in a way that addresses both the challenges of multiple categories of difference like race, gender, class, and sexual orientation as well as the connections between the five-pronged threat to our democracy, the Oppression Olympics.

Oppression Olympics is an evocative term that means what it says in many ways. To the average reader, the term intersectionality is not nearly as clear. In the chapters that follow we'll explore the theory of intersectionality and its potential for resolving the dominance of the Oppression Olympics filter. I argue that we can define and use intersectionality theory as a justice-oriented tool to think about how to interrogate multiple categories like race, class, gender, and sexual orientation in a way that doesn't illegitimately maximize one category's influence in politics over the other. In particular, intersectionality provides a lingua franca for multiple generations to discuss the contemporary political context in a way that both acknowledges the past and clears a path for the future. It does so through its ability to produce opportunities for building what I term "deep political solidarity."

The complexity of twenty-first-century globalized politics forces otherwise well-intentioned, committed people into greater paralysis as they think through the classic democratic question, "What are we to do?" Two examples illustrate the complexity:

- We know that buying local, in-season produce not only helps our farmer neighbors but preserves the environment by cutting the transportation distance (and thereby the carbon footprint) dramatically. Yet such actions, if enacted en masse, have the power to harm developing economies in other nations that depend on the export of produce. Clearly, preserving the environment can be a democratically agreed-upon good, but so can aiding less developed nations in their pursuit of economic self-sufficiency. What is an otherwise well-intentioned individual to do?
- A second example further illustrates the complexity. We can certainly agree that the devastation produced by Hurricane Katrina obligates us to do something to remedy the suffering of those affected. If a professional association elects to contribute to the economic recovery by holding its annual conference of 7,000 people in New Orleans, how do we reconcile this good intention with the fact that Louisiana (and Orleans Parish) overwhelmingly passed

a statewide defense-of-marriage act that denies rights to LGBT people? In that case, what is an otherwise well-intentioned individual to do?

The remaining chapters of this book aim to explore these kinds of political solidarity dilemmas from the perspectives of individuals, groups, and public policy.

Chapter 2 uses the Don Imus – Rutgers University women's basketball team controversy and the science fiction film *The Matrix* as springboards to explain intersectionality theory and its utility for politics. *The Matrix*, in particular, provides resources for understanding the complexity of our twenty-first-century political world. Far more than a prescription to engage multiple categories at once, intersectionality is a justice-oriented analytical framework that forces us to attend to changes over time and institutions, in addition to diversity within groups previously assumed to be monolithic. The chapter concludes by introducing three substantive justice-oriented contributions from intersectionality: new ways for the privileged to stand in solidarity, opportunities for counterintuitive egalitarian political coalitions, and new tools to handle the challenge of causal complexity. All three of these contributions are critical for politics in the twenty-first century.

Chapter 3 extends the first contribution of intersectionality, standing in solidarity, by examining the individual resources and practices necessary for deep political solidarity. The chapter begins with the character of Helo from the popular science fiction television series *Battlestar Galactica* to develop a prototypical form of citizenship that is essential to the new, twenty-first-century politics of solidarity. Helo serves as an example of how the intersectionally privileged can stand in solidarity, while political theorist and former Zionist Hannah Arendt and African American scholar-activist W. E. B. Du Bois illustrate the crucial steps of selfcraft from the perspective of the multiply disadvantaged. Individuals who develop intersectional consciousness end up in the final stage of the selfcraft process with a life project that consists of traveling among multiple margins and centers, rather than remaining stuck in a single monolithic location.

Chapters 4 and 5 build on the theory outlined in the first two chapters by examining how intersectionality can facilitate deep political solidarity at the group and policy level, respectively, by looking at the youngest voters in the 2008 election. Millennials are expected to carry the social justice hopes of entire communities based on the artifacts of their recent birth into a more diverse generation. But are

Millennials, in fact, more liberal? We'll examine the facts regarding these assumptions and the challenges to solidarity that they can create. Chapter 4 draws upon the real-life political dilemmas created during the campaign against Proposition 8, a constitutional ballot initiative that banned marriage for same-sex couples in California. This combination of political theory and pragmatic politics encourages us to open a space in which to practice critical marginality from a distance. To break the ossified, bifurcated us-versus-them identities observed on either side, chapter 4 returns to the complicated relationship between victimhood and agency, challenging our view of pure victims in ways that promote healing rather than hatred.

Chapter 5 examines one of the most challenging public policy arenas facing nation-states in the twenty-first century: immigration. Taking seriously the vehemence of debates surrounding immigration policy, it uses paradigm intersectionality to identify potential obstacles for deep political solidarity beyond the realm of pure identity politics. The focus here is on a second contribution of intersectionality theory, the formulation of counterintuitive coalitions, but from a policy-related rather than an identity-movement point of view.

Chapter 6 concludes with a call to action regarding the integration of complexity and the expansion of intergenerational conversation. It serves as a "new politics instruction manual" that requires something of every person involved in the political process. It thus falls within the domain of participatory democracy from a pragmatic rather than a utopian perspective.

While the book is steeped in contemporary politics, extended profiles of real-world activists and organizations are not a feature of this book for two reasons. First, to choose a subset of real-world people or groups would necessarily allow readers to "bond" with like-identified people, taking those examples closer to heart, perhaps, than others. Second, this book is less an instruction manual that details how others have done each step than an action-oriented book that allows each reader to get out there and do it for themselves. For that reason, the chapters end in a manner far different from most political science books—by encouraging action and reflection across the generation gap.

CONCLUSION: A NEW WAY TO MAKE THE TRANSITION

Demographers have identified a "cultural generation gap" that exists between the two largest generations: Baby boomers and Millennials.[60]

This book aims to exploit the positive potential of the current generation gap in American politics by concluding each chapter with practical strategies across the generational divide. Studies have shown distinct similarities between Millennials (those born between 1981 and 2000) and the Greatest Generation (those born between 1910 and 1920 who fought in World War II) in their opinions about government's ability to solve problems.[61] In light of the Greatest Generation's shrinking numbers, it is up to the Millennials to take up the cause. While Millennials are far more tolerant in their attitudes about race, gender, class, and sexual orientation than their older counterparts because they have been raised in a far different society,[62] Millennials often fail to recognize that gains taken for granted today were hard-fought victories that can and do disappear regularly if no one is watching, deeply affecting citizens' lives. The cross-generational conversations are thus designed to inject some levity while allowing each generation to get a sense of what they need to learn from the other side.

Given the broad range of ages involved in American politics today, there is a distinct role for cross-generational discussions, recently revealed through the 2008 election campaign, which featured strategies as diverse as The Great Schlep, which featured young Jewish voters engaging their grandparents in conversations about the 2008 election, and the increasing numbers of the Greatest Generation involved in the blogosphere. Many of these suggestions will be interactive to foster maximum engagement with the process of selfcraft, which I introduce in chapter 3. The end-of-chapter suggestions are intended to encourage *interdependent* political participation.

HOW TO TALK TO SOMEONE A LOT OLDER THAN YOU ABOUT WHY GERALDINE FERRARO SHOULDN'T HAVE BLOWN OFF RACHEL MADDOW AS A LIGHTWEIGHT OR ENEMY BECAUSE SHE SAW THE OBAMA GESTURE AS NONSEXIST

- Send them the link to Feministing.com so they understand that women under forty can be feminists who are committed to women's rights everywhere. You may already be linked to them through Facebook, Flickr, and YouTube, but go slowly if necessary.
- Send them the link to the Independent Women's Forum to give them an idea of a group that *really* doesn't agree with Gloria Steinem on women's rights.

- Together watch the "Believe in the Stars" episode of *30 Rock*, which expresses satirically the ridiculous logic of the Oppression Olympics.

How to talk to someone a lot younger than you about the bad old days without sounding like Dana Carvey's Grumpy Old Man (from *Saturday Night Live*) or worse, like your own mother!

- Do not, under any circumstances, start a sentence with, "In my day, we used to ..."
- Take them with you to see "9 to 5: The Musical."
- Watch *The Devil Wears Prada* together and rewind twice to watch and discuss the following scene:

> MIRANDA:
> Oh, I see, you think this has nothing to do with you. You go to your closet and you select, I don't know, that lumpy blue sweater for instance because you're trying to tell the world you take yourself too seriously to care about what you put on your back, but what you don't know is that sweater is not just blue, it's not turquoise, it's not lapis, it's actually cerulean and you're also blithely unaware of the fact that in 2002 Oscar de la Renta did a collection of cerulean gowns and then I think it was Yves Saint Laurent, wasn't it, who showed cerulean military jackets...and then cerulean quickly showed up in the collections of eight different designers and then it filtered down through the department stores and then it trickled into some tragic Casual Corner, where you no doubt fished it out of some clearance bin, but however that blue represents millions of dollars and countless jobs and it's sort of comical how you think that you've made a choice that exempts you from the fashion industry when in fact you're wearing a sweater that was selected for you by the people in this room ...from a pile of *stuff*.[63]

Notes

1. Martinez, Elizabeth. "Beyond Black/White: The Racisms of Our Time." *Social Justice* 20 (1993): 23.
2. NBC Universal, May 20, 2008, *The Today Show* Transcript, 3. Italics are the author's.

3. Author-generated transcript of YouTube video of Obama's speech. Accessed October 9, 2008.
4. "Dirt Off Your Shoulder" lyrics by Tim Mosly and Shawn Carter, 2003. The music video features multiple people making the same brush-off gesture Obama made during his comments, which Ferraro then mimicked on *The Today Show*.
5. What if, for example, the response had instead focused on exploiting the ally relationship (i.e., having these same black men push to extend the ballot when serving as voters or as elected officials)? My point is not that an alternative response was likely, but that alternatives did exist and were feasible, even if unlikely.
6. Grant, Judith. *Fundamental Feminism: Contesting the Core Concepts of Feminist Theory*. New York: Routledge, 1993; Hawkesworth, Mary. *Feminist Inquiry: From Political Conviction to Methodological Innovation*. New Brunswick, NJ: Rutgers University Press, 2006.
7. NBC Universal, May 20, 2008 *The TODAY Show*, Transcript, 3–4.
8. Steinem, "Women Are Never Front-Runners," *New York Times*, January 8, 2008.
9. Baumgardner, Jennifer and Amy Richards. (2000). *Manifesta: Young Women, Feminism, and the Future*. Quoted in: Kirkpatrick, Jennet. "Introduction: Selling Out? Solidarity and Choice in the American Feminist Movement." *Perspectives on Politics* 8 (2010): 241–45.
10. Steinem, "Women Are Never Front-Runners" *New York Times*, January 8, 2008.
11. Winter, Nicholas J. G. *Dangerous Frames: How Ideas about Race and Gender Shape Public Opinion*. Chicago: University of Chicago Press, 2008. See also Zatz, Noah. Beyond the Zero-Sum Game: Toward Title VII Protection for Intergroup Solidarity, 77 *Indiana Law Journal* 63 (2002).
12. This ignorance persists, just as most Americans don't know that the reason they have a weekend is due to the labor movement.
13. Schreiber, Ronnee. *Righting Feminism: Conservative Women, American Politics and the Future*. New York: Oxford University Press, 2008.
14. See Frankenburg, Ruth. *White Women, Race Matters: The Social Construction of Whiteness*. St. Paul, MN: University of Minnesota Press, 1994.
15. Banaszak , Lee Ann. "Women's Movements and Women in Movements: Influencing American Democracy from the Outside?" (2008). In Wolbrecht, Christina, Karen Beckwith, and Lisa Baldez, editors. *Political Women and American Democracy*. New York: Cambridge University Press. 2008, 91; see also Schreiber, Ronnee. *Righting Feminism: Conservative Women and American Politics*. New York: Oxford University Press, 2008, 111–13.
16. NBC Universal, May 20, 2008, *The Today Show*, Transcript, 3.
17. Staples, Brent. "Barack Obama, John McCain, and the Language of Race" *New York Times*, September 22, 2008.

18. Hawkesworth, Mary. *Beyond Oppression: Feminist Theory and Political Strategy*. New York: Continuum International Publishers Group, 1990, 165; italics mine.

19. Hollibaugh, Amber. "Sex to Gender, Past to Present, Race to Class, New to Future." *GLQ: A Journal of Gay and Lesbian Studies* (2004), 262.

20. Banaszak, "Women's Movements and Women in Movements," 89.

21. See Schreiber, *Righting Feminism*.

22. Ronnee Schreiber describes one such approach, "femball," in *Righting Feminism* (2008).

23. Schreiber, *Righting Feminism*

24. Fogg-Davis, Hawley. "Theorizing Black Lesbianism within Black Feminism: A Critique of Same Race Street Harassment." *Politics and Gender* 2(2006): 57–76.

25. NBC Universal, *The Today Show*, Transcript, 3.

26. Fields, Dorothy and Jerome Kern. "Pick Yourself Up" from the film *Swing Time*. Performed by Fred Astaire and Ginger Rogers, 1936.

27. Only two online posts on sites as diverse as *Spate* magazine (all things hip hop), *The Atlantic Monthly*, *The Chicago Tribune*, *The Washington Post*, and Bloggernista (an LGBT-oriented site) agreed with Ferraro's assessment that the gesture was sexist.

28. "A semi-contemptuous indifference toward Latinos—to focus on this one group—has emanated from institutions in the dominant society for decades. Echoing this attitude are many individual Anglos…if you bring up some Anglo's racist action toward a Latino, they will change the subject almost instantly to racism toward a Black person." (Martinez 1993, p. 24).

29. *Regents of the University of California v. Bakke*, 438 U.S. 265 (1978).

30. *Gratz v. Bollinger* 539 U.S. 244 (2003).

31. Martinez, "Beyond Black/White," 23.

32. For example, Derrick Bell (2004) outlines the racial fortuity argument, which contends that absent political interest convergence independent of racial justice interests, integration-oriented change to the racial status quo is in grave danger.

33. Goldberg, David Theo. "Devastating Disasters: Race in the Shadow(s) of New Orleans." *DuBois Review* 3(2006): 84.

34. See www.protectmarriage.com/about; this site was established in support of Proposition 8, which would amend the California state constitution to outlaw same-sex marriage.

35. Ibid.

36. Banaszak. "Women's Movements and Women in Movements"; Schreiber *Righting Feminism*; Faludi, Susan. *Backlash: The Undeclared War Against American Women*. New York: Anchor Books, 1991.

37. www.iwf.org/campus; accessed October 24, 2008.

38. Schreiber, *Righting Feminism*.

39. Hendricks and Hendricks, http://www.huffingtonpost.com/kathlyn -and-gay-hendricks/relationship-politics-bod_b_137042.html, posted and accessed October 24, 2008.

40. Tatum, Beverly. *Why Are All the Black Kids Sitting Together in the Cafeteria? And Other Conversations About Race.* New York: Basic Books, 1997: 98.
41. See Hooks, bell. *Teaching to Transgress: Education as the Practice of Freedom.* New York: Routledge, 1994.
42. To be fair, I don't think that Martinez, given her other scholarship, would object to this extension of her original formulation.
43. Martinez, "Beyond Black/White," 25.
44. See, Fraga, Luis et al. "Su Casa es Nuestra Casa: Latino Politics Research and the Development of American Political Science." *American Political Science Review* 100 (2006): 515–21.
45. Cocco, Marie. "Misogyny I Won't Miss," *The Washington Post*, May 15, 2008, A15.
46. Cocco writes, "Would the silence prevail if Obama's likeness were put on a tap-dancing doll that was sold at airports? Would the media figures who dole out precious time to these politicians be such pals if they'd compared Obama with a character in a blaxploitation film? And how would crude references to Obama's sex organs play?" (Ibid.).
47. A recent British study has shown that males are four times more willing to steal someone else's idea at work and take credit for it than are women.
48. Brooks, David. "The Class War Before Palin," *New York Times*, October 10, 2008. Accessed October 27, 2008.
49. Warner, Judith. "Compassion Deficit Disorder," *New York Times*, August 7, 2008. Accessed October 28, 2008.
50. Hancock, Ange-Marie. *The Politics of Disgust and the Public Identity of the "Welfare Queen."* New York: New York University Press, 2004.
51. "Only slightly less extreme, because not quite as explicit, the libertarian pluralist motto of 'live and let live' licenses a surplus of possibility and opportunity for the affording few at the expense of the impoverished many. It might more accurately be replaced with the motto, 'live free or die,'...which can be interpreted as implying that those who cannot afford the freedom will be left to perish. There is, as commentators on euthanasia have long pointed out, a thin line between (social) killing and letting die. Between making live and letting die, as Foucault has put it in *Society Must Be Defended*, are histories whitewashed and refashioned, activist interventions restricted, the racial status quo resurrected, revived, (re-)fixed in place." Goldberg "Devastating Disasters," 85.
52. Crowe, David. "Katrina: God's Judgment on America" www.beliefnet. com; www.restoreamerica.com; September 2005; accessed October 28, 2008.
53. Fogg-Davis, "Theorizing Black Feminisms."
54. Frymer, Paul, Dara Strolovitch, and Dorian Warren. "New Orleans Is not the Exception: Re-politicizing the Study of Racial Inequality." *DuBois Review* 3 (2006): 37–57.

55. Ransby found that race, class, *and* gender played complementary roles in nonevacuation outcomes. Ransby, Barbara. "The Deadly Discourse on Black Poverty and Its Impact on Black Women in New Orleans in the Wake of Hurricane Katrina." *DuBois Review* 3 (2006): 215–22.

56. This "victimology" approach has been castigated by antifeminist frames of Concerned Women of America (CWA) and the Independent Women's Forum (IWF). Schreiber, *Righting Feminism*.

57. Obama also used this strategy in Indiana, but the famous players were the WNBA's Allison Bales and Tamika Catchings.

58. Rich, John and Gretchen Wilson. "Redneck Woman" Song lyrics, 2004. Performed by Gretchen Wilson.

59. Forman, Tyrone and Amanda E. Lewis. "Racial Apathy and Hurricane Katrina." *DuBois Review* 3(2006): 175–202.

60. Frey, William H. (2010). "Will Arizona Be America's Future?" http://www.brookings.edu/opinions/2010/0428_arizona_frey.aspx Accessed July 26, 2010. Myers, Dowell C. *Immigrants and Boomers: Forging a New Social Contract for America*. New York: Russell Sage Publications, 2008.

61. Harvard Institute of Politics, 2006.

62. CIRCLE Civic and Political Health of the Nation Survey, 2006.

63. Hedges, Peter, Howard Michael Gould, Paul Rudnick, Don Roos, and Aline Brosh McKenna. *The Devil Wears Prada*. Screenplay accessed June 11, 2008. (Italics mine).

2

INTERSECTIONALITY TO THE RESCUE

Exactly one week after well-known "shock jock" Don Imus called the Rutgers University women's basketball team "nappy-headed hos," he was fired by CBS News Radio. The controversy, which simultaneously characterized the women in sexist and racist terms, targeted a team that was runner-up in the 2007 National Collegiate Athletic Association (NCAA) women's basketball championship. That Scarlet Knights team included eight women of color and two white women. Women's rights and civil rights organizations immediately came to the Scarlet Knights' defense. National Organization for Women president Kim Gandy joined civil rights activists like Jesse Jackson and Al Sharpton to stand in solidarity with the National Congress of Black Women and the National Council of Negro Women to demand termination of Imus's radio show.

This moment of convergence—the simultaneous attention to race and gender—produced solidarity instead of the Oppression Olympics and its attendant Leapfrog Paranoia, Willful Blindness, Defiant Ignorance, Movement Backlash, or Compassion Deficit Disorder. Demonstrating the best of coalition politics, leaders of both communities acknowledged the *dual* causes of this episode—racism and sexism; sexism and racism. This analysis allowed for people who believe in either form of equality (or both!) to join in a unified effort to oust Imus. This moment of convergence, produced in part by the recognition of *Categorical Multiplicity*, a term I define later, represents a taste of what intersectionality can bring to our public discourse about race, gender, class, and sexual orientation in American politics.

Unfortunately, Imus's period of contrition included a $20 million contract settlement and a new contract with ABC Radio only months later. Clearly, Categorical Multiplicity is necessary but not sufficient to turn the page for good. Likewise, the call for attention to Categorical Multiplicity is a long-standing part of intersectionality research—but intersectionality doesn't end there. This chapter will outline five aspects of an intersectional approach to politics that can thwart the lure of the Oppression Olympics. In contrast to the debilitating Oppression Olympics, intersectional approaches provide new ways for the privileged to stand in solidarity, foster egalitarian coalition building among groups, and enhance our attention to complexity in politics. We will return to these factors in greater detail in chapters 4 and 5.

Most Americans recognize that race and class are socially defined concepts with little to no biological meaning. Gender and sexual orientation, on the other hand, remain categories with presumptions of biology implicated as justifications for how people are treated.[1] Intersectionality scholars analyze all four categories as social constructions that retain political influence far beyond any actual meaning of the biological, phenotypical, and chromosomal differences among us. Many scholars recognize this claim as a constructivist one—based on the conviction that humans cognitively construct the world around them in order to best navigate a complex society.

While intersectionality starts with this constructivist premise, it recognizes the material reality that these social constructions impose on us. Despite our best efforts we learn norms of racialized, gendered, classed, and sexualized behavior as children through observation and imitation of the adults to whom we are exposed, whether directly or virtually through the media. Although we live in a nation with a strong commitment to individual freedom, these norms interact to produce a web of patterned rewards for norm-conforming behavior and punishments for behavior that doesn't. While we might want that patterned reward system in place for certain criminal justice purposes (such as preventing rape, domestic violence, or murder), extending them beyond that domain socializes Americans into an acceptance of injustice and discrimination. Think of these intersecting behavioral norms as analogous to the threat that Morpheus and Neo discuss when they first meet in the movie *The Matrix*:

Morpheus: Do you believe in fate, Neo?
Neo: No.
Morpheus: Why not?
Neo: Because I don't like the idea that I'm not in control of my life.
Morpheus: I know exactly what you mean. Let me tell you why you're here. You're here because you know something. What you know you can't explain. But you feel it. You've felt it your entire life. That there's something wrong with the world. You don't know what it is but it's there, like a splinter in your mind driving you mad. It is

this feeling that has brought you to me. Do you know what I'm
talking about?

Neo: The Matrix?

Morpheus: Do you want to know what it is? The Matrix is everywhere.
It is all around us, even now in this very room. You can see it when
you look out your window or when you turn on your television.
You can feel it when you go to work, when you go to church, when
you pay your taxes. It is the world that has been pulled over your
eyes to blind you from the truth.

Neo: What truth?

Morpheus: That you are a slave, Neo. Like everyone else you were born
into bondage, born into a prison that you cannot smell or taste or
touch. A prison for your mind . . .[2]

In the movie the matrix rewards Willful Blindness and Defiant
Ignorance. From a twenty-first-century political perspective, so, too,
does an Oppression Olympics orientation attempt to force people to
pretend that race, gender, class, and sexual orientation don't exist
when individuals, groups, and institutions interact with each other
as if they do.[3] Intersectionality adds a daunting but critical layer of
complexity: not only do such categories have material effects, but the
categories themselves interact with each other, teaching us how to
overlook invisible norms and spotlight what is different as normatively dysfunctional. This chapter illuminates a path through the matrix by revealing the intellectual roots of intersectionality.[4]

> *"To combine gender with race, language, sexual orientation, concrete
> interpersonal relations, and a host of other dimensions of identity is no
> easy or uncomplicated thing. But it is from the recognition of this com-
> plexity and these contradictions that we must start."*[5]

CATEGORICAL MULTIPLICITY: THE FOUNDATION OF INTERSECTIONALITY

As I noted in the introduction, the idea that only the marginalized
dimensions of categories matter and the bias toward conceptualizing
categories as mutually exclusive for political purposes both contribute
to the Oppression Olympics. For example, the African American
women on the Rutgers team aren't black on Monday, Wednesday,
and Friday and female on Tuesday, Thursday, and Saturday. What
would they do about Sunday? Yet most analyses of American politics
proceed as if this is the case. This allows the privileged dimensions
of categories to which people belong to remain invisible norms, as we

saw in the cases of Hillary Clinton, Barack Obama, and Sarah Palin in the introduction.

Certainly, the mainstream sexism we observed in the 2008 election must be addressed. But we must also recognize the racism, classism, and homophobia within the gender equality community. Moreover, we must also address the sexism, classism, and homophobia in the civil rights community.[6] By acknowledging the role of Categorical Multiplicity, intersectionality scholars draw upon two of the most useful contributions of multicultural feminist theory: that multiple categories are significant, and due to the multiplicity of such categories, multiple sites of power need to be reformed.[7]

The "intersectional turn" builds on cross-disciplinary work by feminist scholars and activists of color around the world. The impact of an intersectional approach to race, sexual orientation, gender, and class as analytical categories has emerged from over fifty years of scholarship.[8] Originally formulated as a personal identity-laden theory, early intersectionality theory focused solely on the identities of women of color. African American feminist theorists such as Patricia Hill Collins, Joy James, bell hooks, and many others articulated a both/and identity to locate black women's sociopolitical situation as one that is, variously, "doubly bound" or featuring "multiple jeopardies." This claim, evident across numerous disciplines of black women's studies, evolved from the both/and claims of eighteenth- and nineteenth-century writers such as Maria Miller Stewart and Anna Julia Cooper.

Latina and Asian American feminists have also made similar claims about the multiplicity of identity and claimed an inseparability of race, gender, sexuality, and class in the lives of women of color. Gloria Anzaldua and Cherrie Moraga have similarly talked about the categorical multiplicity of Latinas' lives in a racialized context of hybridity termed *mestizaje*. These convincing claims in the U.S. context have been joined by postcolonial feminists who add the importance of North-South identity as a politically relevant category of analysis for women's international movements.[9] The impact of this work has been tremendous, filtering into more generalized academic and international human rights work. International feminist and United Nations (UN) nongovernmental organization (NGO) forums have gradually put issues of intersectionality more centrally on their agenda.[10] Since then equality legislation in many countries as well as the European Union (EU) has moved from focusing on single category approaches to intersectional approaches. As well, Nobel laureate Amartya Sen's recent book, *Identity and Violence: The Illusion of Destiny* (2006), recognizes the role of multiple identities in civil wars and contexts of ethnic violence.[11]

The multicultural feminist claim of multiple jeopardies has traditionally been interpreted to mean that *some* women have a larger number of multiple marginalized categorical memberships that *therefore* deserve a larger share of the policy solutions. I call this logic the *additive oppressions argument*,[12] and it is easy to see where this logic leads—directly to the Oppression Olympics question of "Who has it toughest?" In addition to the normative concerns about the desirability or usefulness of such a debate, two specific problems emerge from the additive argument.

First, "adding on" race or other categories to claims of gender oppression falsely limits our attention to matters of quantity, ignoring the way that incorporating race, class, or gender into a single analysis *qualitatively* changes the characteristics of subordination.[13] Second, those steeped in quantitative empirical research have expressed serious concerns about the infinite quantity of possible categories and combinations thereof. Slicing the group of women or men into ever thinner, more politically isolated slivers is of particular concern in majoritarian political systems where numbers matter.[14] The additive oppressions argument creates significant obstacles to framing claims in a way that brings people together rather than drives them apart.

In contrast, intersectionality theory uses Categorical Multiplicity as a way to recognize that race, class, gender, and sexual orientation all can represent *equal but not identical* threats to the values of freedom and equality embraced by all Americans. For example, earlier I mentioned the role of biology in constructions of gender and sexual orientation. Interestingly, these biological justifications have cut both ways—to thwart gender equality (women are "naturally" weaker and more nurturing) and to promote lesbian/gay/bisexual/transgender (LGBT) equality (LGBT identity is genetic, not a choice). This example clearly demonstrates the assumption that multiple categories function identically isn't tenable under all circumstances; we will address this reality in subsequent dimensional discussions later.

So the question isn't "Is America *more* racist or *more* sexist?", which leads us to Leapfrog Paranoia and Willful Blindness. Instead, intersectional approaches to categorical multiplicity focus on illuminating the ways in which categories emerge as politically relevant based on processes operating at multiple levels—the self, the group, and government/society. This conceptualization changes, in other words, the first order question to something like: How do racism, sexism, classism, and homophobia interact and emerge to threaten our democracy in twenty-first century?[15] We will return to this point when we discuss *Time Dynamics*. Intersectionality research has stepped away from the assumption of a priori equal quantitative weight of the categories in research outcomes without stepping away from the central belief that such categories must be addressed in empirical research.[16] Yet as we saw in the case of the response to Don Imus, mere recognition of multiple categories is necessary but not sufficient for substantial societal transformation. Beyond identity politics, beyond the number of categories we discuss, the character of the relationship among these categories is also important. Intersectionality theory has expanded beyond late-twentieth-century multicultural feminist theory to address this political reality.

CATEGORICAL INTERSECTION: THE CENTRAL METAPHOR OF INTERSECTIONALITY

I've mentioned that categories of race, gender, class, and sexual orientation all present equal but not identical threats to our democracy as one nation with liberty and justice for all. Work produced by intersectionality researchers has characterized the relationship between categories in a variety of ways. Faced with the incompatibility of the *additive oppressions approach* with existing civil rights jurisprudence, legal theorists like Kimberle Williams Crenshaw,[17] Mari Matsuda, Adrien Katherine Wing, Patricia Williams, and Margaret Montoya identified numerous gaps in the American and international legal frameworks left unaddressed after mid-twentieth-century movement activism on behalf of women and racial/ethnic minorities. Within the legal domain, these women argued that a gap persists between the lived experience of women of color and the opportunity for legal remedy against discriminatory pay structures, work rules, or protection from domestic violence. Their convincing explanations of a relationship among political categories of difference such as race, class, and gender preserved the claims for justice based on Categorical Multiplicity, but on substantively different grounds than multicultural feminist theory. *Categorical Intersection* emphasized the invisibility of women's lived experiences in a legal system that constructed race and gender as mutually exclusive.

Characterizing the relationship between categories as intersectional rather than additive turned these scholars away from the Oppression Olympics and toward the possibilities for transformative politics. Crenshaw, recognizing this "tendency to treat race and gender as mutually exclusive categories of experience and analysis,"[18] coined the metaphor of intersecting streets to describe the legal location of women with multiple marginalized identities.[19] Each category is taken to be an intersecting "vector," and society occurs at the point of intersection for all people.[20]

Figure 2.1 displays the original metaphor, herein called "Content Intersectionality," because of its emphasis on three central categories of difference as substantively, not simply analytically critical to U.S. politics. More specifically, each of the roads in figure 2.1 has the same color and shape because, particularly in the legal arena due to the role of signals and spillover across movements, each category has been construed to require not simply *equal*, but more importantly *identical* legal remedies.[21] Content intersectionality has focused primarily on rendering the invisible visible—that is, enlightening the world about the lives of people (primarily women to date) who politically, socially, and/or legally exist at the intersection of race, class, and gender. Yet as intersectionality as an analytical framework has gained popularity, two central shifts have emerged, based on a deep theoretical and jurisprudential engagement with Crenshaw's original metaphor.

In the twenty-plus years since the landmark interventions of multicultural feminists like Gloria Anzaldua and Patricia Hill Collins

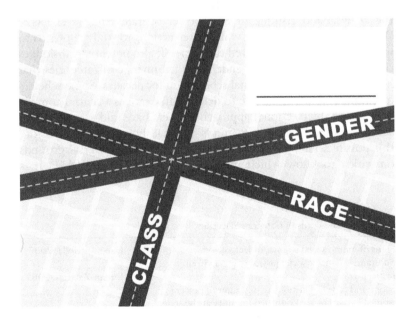

Figure 2.1   Content Intersectionality.

and Crenshaw's original metaphor,[22] intersectionality research has progressed to more explicitly include class and sexual orientation along with the initial categories of race and gender identified by Crenshaw and others.[23] The two-dimensional intersecting street metaphor must now accommodate this change in Categorical Multiplicity. We might first want to just add more streets—instead of a two-street intersection, we'd presume more of a British-style roundabout image. Unfortunately, this move is flawed because it violates the spirit of Crenshaw's original formulation, which emphasizes the indivisibility of multiple categories in our lives by removing the intersections completely. It is indeed impossible to be only white on Mondays, only gay on Tuesdays, and so forth.

So how might we capture the power relationships that exist along the North-South spectrum in international or transnational contexts? How might we account for religion or disability as categories of difference? In her forthcoming article and recent book, Rita Dhamoon quite helpfully walks through the multiple images and metaphors that have emerged from the serious consideration of additional categories and cites several standards for selecting the relevant categories within any particular political context for study. Table 2.1 lists several of them.

Dhamoon notes that all of the standards of choice are driven by the analysis and critique of how power operates and its effects.[24] While this step of selecting which intersections to study allows us to incorporate previously ignored categories, it also potentially dislodges the hegemony of the race-gender-class triumvirate of categories that have dominated intersectional scholarship for decades. Some scholars question this turn as a move to delegitimize race as a central component of the intersectional approach. Others have said similar things about gender. Dhamoon reminds us that however unsatisfactory this possible outcome might seem, "there are no universal grounds on which to know which interactions should be studied."[25] It is

Table 2.1 Standards of Category Selection

Signs of injury, social stigma, or lack of access	Garcia-Bedolla, 2007
Substantive issue of social justice (e.g., environmental justice)	Jordan-Zachary, 2007
Scope and target of critique (e.g., center of power in women's rights or civil rights community at the state, national, or transnational level)	Brah & Phoenix, 2004

important to note that the absence of universal grounds does not give us license to engage in Willful Blindness, Defiant Ignorance, or even Compassion Deficit Disorder, but instead recognizes that as political contexts vary, so, too, does the relevance of certain categories. To talk about race in India, for example, is not nearly as legible as talking about caste. Further, to assume that caste is simply a proxy for race in India also presents a host of problems for research design or policy prescriptions, whether methodological, in terms of validity or theoretical, or in terms of conceptual clarity.

Nevertheless, the central benefit of content intersectionality is its ability to make the "invisible" visible. It produces historically, politically, and socioeconomically accurate information that has several benefits. Canadian public health scholar Olena Hankivsky argues that intersectionality has "the potential to…in the final analysis, contribute an important conceptual advancement in expanding policy discourse in relation to social justice."[26] In this regard, we can think of intersectionality as a justice-oriented analytical tool.

If we are committed to that part of the U.S. Pledge of Allegiance to the flag that says, "with liberty and justice for all," then in addition to our focus on the invisible—overcoming Willful Blindness, Defiant Ignorance, and Compassion Deficit Disorder in the process—we must also attend to Movement Backlash, another aspect of the Oppression Olympics. By reframing the intersection as a dynamic center of both invisibility and hypervisibility, we can expand intersectionality's utility as an antidote to the Oppression Olympics.

Visibility for marginalized groups and individuals, particularly from a political or public policy perspective, is contingent and mediated by what I have elsewhere called a "politics of disgust." Welfare recipients, undocumented immigrants, prison populations, and terror suspects are usually identified with often disturbing *in*accuracy by authorities based on their memberships in multiple intersecting categories: single, poor, black, mothers; Latino/a working-class Spanish speakers; black and brown working-class men; young Arab American men, respectively. The perversion of democratic attention in a politics of disgust involves elites using a warped version of such populations' public identity as an ideological justification for outrageously invasive public policies. Second, among these subsets of larger groups, elites' power in a communicative context of gross inequality—their bigger microphones and megaphones—make contestation and relationships with logical allies difficult to the point of impossibility. Most ironically, for these intersectionally disadvantaged groups, sometimes the best one can immediately hope for *is* invisibility. The panopticon[27] of surveillance, to use Benthamite and Foucauldian terms, often features egregious and intense Movement Backlash.

Consider the following examples: The 1960s and 1970s activism of the National Welfare Rights Movement led a 1980s President Ronald Reagan to lay the economic ills of the United States at the feet of the Cadillac-driving "welfare queens"—a fabricated image. The successful push for the federal-level Immigration and Reform Control Act (IRCA) of 1986 was countered by states like California, which passed Proposition 187 in 1994 after immigrants were targeted as the cause of California's recession. While sadly, scapegoating is nothing new, the idea that such groups are *intersectionally* identified through a justice-oriented focus on power is new, and such efforts have met with varying levels of success.

In his recent analysis of intersectional court claims, Francisco Valdes found that among nine different categories of intersectional claims, only those that exclusively involved protected classes got relief from the courts. The remaining challenge for advocates is the larger set of cases where claimants were members of both protected and unprotected classes. In such situations the court's logic subsumed claimants' protected status (e.g., one's race) under their unprotected status (e.g., their class). Valdes's finding is a clear example of how the legal structure fosters or facilitates Willful Blindness to a claimant's own privilege (a clear link to the final dimension of intersectionality discussed later). In matters of legal strategy, claimants are incentivized to downplay or ignore their privilege. Valdes contends that while this juxtaposition reveals the continuing dysfunction of the U.S. legal system, it also provides a road map for future strategic litigation.

Along with Hankivsky and Dhamoon's work, Valdes's analysis demonstrates that Categorical Multiplicity and Categorical Intersection are by now the most well-known aspects of intersectionality theory among scholars. However, three additional tenets are emerging from the latest intersectional research. The first of these is attention to *Time Dynamics*.

TIME DYNAMICS

In a recent keynote speech, Crenshaw adjusted her metaphor from a pair of intersecting streets to a consideration of how the Grand Canyon evolved. Instead of streets, rivers have flowed in such a way as to craft the Grand Canyon, and rivers still flow therein, but not as they did thousands of years ago. The "intersectionality canyon," as it were, includes both the dynamic, time-oriented aspects embodied by the rivers that run through it and the institutional rock formations that change ever slowly based on the rivers' flow. *Time Dynamics* focuses on the river-based aspects of the metaphor.

Intersectional attention to recent presidential candidates in the introduction revealed that there are no pure victims. Therefore, we must acknowledge *both* where disadvantage yet remains *and* where privilege has emerged. Acknowledging the changing demography of the United States in the twenty-first century,[28] Time Dynamics refers to the idea that the membership of the privileged group and the disadvantaged group are not static throughout United States history. Unlike pluralism, which assumes that everyone has an equal chance at any point in history to land in the privileged or disadvantaged group, the Time Dynamics aspect of intersectionality recognizes the changes in the river's path over the course of time *and* humans' and their institutions' ongoing complicity in such changes at any point in time.

In light of the critiques of standpoint theory, scholars have argued for a more fluid, contingent approach to thinking about categories of race, gender, class, and sexual orientation. As we learned in the introduction, everyone is not either black or white;[29] moreover by 2025 more than half of all families will be multicultural.[30] A more fluid approach to race as a category is needed in the twenty-first century. Theorist Cristina Beltrán also argues for greater attention to time-based contingencies in race and sexual orientation categories: "Put another way, theorists of *mestizaje* must retain an attentiveness to historical specificity and inequality *in tandem with* an increased awareness that all human subjectivity is plural, contradictory, socially embedded and mutually constitutive." (emphasis mine)[31]

Time Dynamics recognize: *first* that tremendous progress has been made by excluded groups in American politics. If no progress had been made, Movement Backlash wouldn't exist. If the chance for additional progress didn't exist, Leapfrog Paranoia would never emerge. Thus, the *second*, more controversial claim of Time Dynamics directly challenges the Defiant Ignorance practiced by excluded groups: pretending such progress hasn't occurred, whether rhetorically or strategically, is false and disingenuous. The third, less controversial but equally important recognition confronts the Defiant Ignorance of groups with power: evidence of progress made does not necessarily equal *all* of the progress that needs to be made. Together the claims suggest that preexisting policies may have outlived their usefulness and need to be replaced with a better mousetrap to accurately reflect a twenty-first-century political reality.

Time Dynamics breaks down Defiant Ignorance on all sides of the political community, which makes it more difficult and controversial than Categorical Multiplicity or Categorical Intersection, because entrenched elites on opposing sides of policy debates have to let go of the "pretending not to know" posture. Chapters 3, 4, and 5 will wade directly into this controversy by calling for a shift from calls for public service to a call for "deep political solidarity." This aspect of intersectionality contributes directly to the potential for counter-intuitive coalitions that are egalitarian and have the power to transform politics. Instead of asking *whether* the other position is right according to your side's standards, the question instead is "How is the other side right?"[32] At that point dropping the Defiant Ignorance can slowly, carefully, begin.

Figure 2.2 reflects the shift from content intersectionality in its more static, limited form to a more dynamic, process-oriented image of intersectionality. This aspect of intersectionality theory also addresses the pragmatic reality of generation gap politics in the twenty-first century by acknowledging the dynamic nature of privilege and disadvantage without ignoring the role of *either* historical patterns *or* humans' ability to intervene in their own lives. The political ramifications of the current generation gap emanate from

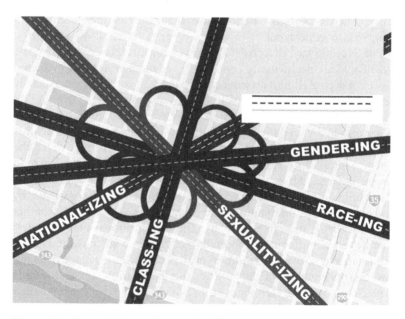

Figure 2.2   Dynamic Content Intersectionality.

the dually troublesome overestimations made by each end of the generational divide: the Baby Boomers, who tend to overestimate the importance of history,[33] holding on tightly to it as the reason for political action or inaction; and the Millennial Generation, who overestimate the irrelevance of history, dismissing the old ways as dust that can be swept out of the house without making anyone sneeze. Time Dynamics is possibly the most difficult but also potentially the most productive aspect of intersectionality theory.

DIVERSITY WITHIN

Following Don Imus's statement, Rutgers coach C. Vivian Stringer held a press conference to introduce the world to the women Imus had impugned. Designed specifically to confront the characterization of "hos," the women were dressed in business attire and spoke about their academic pursuits in an effort to take back their power to define who they were, instead of allowing Imus and his producer Bernard McGuirk to do it for them.[34]

Expanding upon the commonplace idea that "not all stereotypes are true of all group members," intersectionality theory demonstrates the *Diversity Within* all groups to combat mainstream stereotypes from both outside *and* within the group itself.[35] More specifically, Diversity Within emphasizes how intersecting categories produce subgroups within the groups, who often have divergent political agendas.

For example, within the group of African Americans, no one would dispute that television mogul Oprah Winfrey and former National Basketball Association (NBA) star Michael Jordan are not disadvantaged in the same way as unemployed African Americans living on the south side of Chicago, based on the intersecting category of socioeconomic class. Indeed, scholars of African American politics have long argued that African Americans share a sense of "linked fate" that can transcend politically relevant distinctions like class and gender in political attitudes and behavior.[36] Yet while linked fate may persist among black political attitudes, it does not significantly affect black political participation.[37]

Unfortunately, our political and public policy discourse is not always sufficiently nuanced to capture this complexity. Thus, subgroups of populations remain disadvantaged, with broad debate focusing on why exactly such diverse outcomes exist, overlooking the commonsense reality that many long-standing policies were designed to benefit a specific slice of a group (like middle-class blacks or white women) based on the assumption that what was good for this slice was good for the entire group.[38] Building on the idea that there is no pure victim, Diversity Within recognizes the differential power relationships and multiple centers of power in American politics.

The late political theorist Iris Marion Young attempted to reconcile the recognition of within-group diversity for practical politics, asking the question, on what grounds, then, can women claim to speak for women as a group? This question has emerged over the past twenty years not simply in response to women of color charging second-wave feminists with racism, but among conservative, independent, and moderate women who state that the feminist movement doesn't speak for them. So it's more than an idle question.[39]

We can't always spin our wheels, Young concludes, searching for what we have in common, because there will always be the chance that someone will be excluded.[40] But if that's the case, then how do we form groups to get things done politically? Young recommends we think of race or gender categories as "serial collectives."[41] When we think of women as a serial collective, there is no requirement that we must all have an identity-based something in common; a shared relationship to a material object and the social practices in relationship to it is all that's necessary.[42] If we think in terms of serial collectives, we set aside the paralyzing question of what we must have in common before we can speak and focus instead on what we can do to change our world.

Drawing upon the work of Jean-Paul Sartre, Young highlights the way in which politically, we can think of women as analogous to commuters taking the bus. Commuters need not all be a specific race, gender, class, or sexual orientation, of course, but they do share a relationship to the commuter bus[43] and the practices that are associated with it—including its route (over which they have little direct control), whether it's on time (something they may or may not have some control over), and how far they choose to ride (something they have more but not complete control over).

Surveying the variety of cars and buses and other forms of transportation, we can envision the degree to which individuals forming groups is a matter of choice *and* opportunity; in other words, where individuals have embarked and elected to follow the journey of the bus itself. Prior to embarking, potential riders represent a serial collective—a collection of individuals with the potential for group action. Once embarked, however, the individuals have elected to "link their fate"[44] with those of their fellow passengers, however temporarily, episodically, or contingently (e.g., solely for the purposes of arriving at a destination). The members of this collective may spend most days never actually thinking of themselves as a "group," until something specific happens—like the bus has an accident or doesn't show up at its scheduled stop one day. There may then be a specific block of time where commuters join together to address some specific task, like finding an alternate route to work or school.

Intersectionality's commitment to addressing extant inequality focuses our attention on the process by which the task is defined and achieved. Too often, a small subset of the serial collective decides among themselves what the task at hand should be, under the assumption that their decision sufficiently covers the entire group. Yet this agenda-setting process falsely assumes that what's good for them is what's good for the entire group. Intersectionality scholars have proposed new and different ways to set the agenda for the collective.[45]

Once that associated task is completed, they can then elect to dissolve the collective (and return to daily life as an individual commuter), or they may choose to remain together as a nonpolitical entity (socially saying hello, playing card games on the bus during the ride) or as a formally organized political entity (forming a Straphangers Campaign or Bus Riders Union).[46] Again, the future of the group is to be set by more than the privileged members of the collective. At any particular time some, one, or all may attempt to veer "off-road" in order to reach their intended destination, and may bump into items on the sides of the streets—buildings, parking meters, or other vehicles. The final aspect of intersectionality speaks to these risks and returns us to Crenshaw's new metaphor of the Grand Canyon. It focuses on the seriality of categories like race, class, sexual orientation, and gender to examine the dynamic relationships across individual and institutional levels of analysis.

INDIVIDUAL-INSTITUTIONAL INTERACTIONS

Crenshaw's original intersecting streets metaphor was deeply American in the sense that it was tied to a modernist sense of "progress" that is deeply deterministic and limiting. Using streets as proxies suggests that only two directions, forward and backward, exist, with little attention to where the road begins or ends. Theoretically, this limitation highlights the need to add the Time Dynamics dimension for historical specificity. Pragmatically, limiting politics to either forward progress or backward regress facilitates the entrenchment of political positions, making compromise and bipartisanship ever less likely in the twenty-first century. What if we could create a space for moving sideways instead of simply backward and forward? Luckily the intersectionality canyon metaphor alleviates some of these issues without losing the central points that remain so valuable to a twenty-first-century political context.

Whether intersecting streets or rivers crossing, intersections are sites of motion. Those who might get "stuck" in the intersection may be able to turn around and go home or return to the riverbank, but far too frequently their ability to act on such a choice is constrained. The *Individual-Institutional Interactions* dimension of intersectionality allows for the idea that race, gender, class, and sexual orientation are constructed and enacted at multiple levels—the individual, the group, and the institutional. In other words, the institutions are the rock formations created within the depths of the Grand Canyon. They are created by the rivers and the winds, worn away and built up after decades and centuries. Importantly, such rock formations are created in such a way that anyone traveling down or across the river must navigate any prevailing winds to avoid colliding with them. From a pragmatic political point of view, the depths of such canyons provide a more accurate sense of the amount and duration of effort required to completely dismantle systems of oppression like racism, sexism, homophobia, and classism without rendering them ahistorical phenomena.

The complexities of these Individual Institutional Interactions occur on multiple political planes: the organizational, intersubjective, experiential, and representational.[47] If we continue to use Crenshaw's metaphor and place a justice-seeking group in a craft to navigate the river, we can then fully embrace the serial collective agency that Young embraces, as each person has in some way elected to get on the boat (in however contingent a manner), but in doing so they recognize the route, the presence of rock formations (which we can suggest represent political institutions), and the presence of other vehicles (which we can suggest represent other groups both similar to and distinct from our focus group), as three semipermanent and dynamic forces with which those in our original rivercraft must contend, a fact largely out of their control. In other words, agency exists in embarkation and throughout the journey, but in ways that carry risks of close calls, crashes, and confrontations with other passengers and rock formations.

I've deliberately used the word "craft" rather than specify a type of vehicle to indicate the mutually constitutive roles of both Diversity Within and Time Dynamics in traversing the river in any particular direction. While some may have access to either a yacht or a Jet Ski to get from point A to B, others may only have a piece of driftwood

INTERSECTIONALITY TO THE RESCUE

or a river raft to navigate the same journey. What is an open question and subject for politics, however, is which craft will best navigate that section of the rivers' crossing and for whom. This new metaphor allows us, therefore, to contend with the ways in which individuals and groups contend with multiple centers of political power and institutions, particularly regarding what is common to both the Grand Canyon and intersectionality: prevailing [political] winds at any point in time.

Most recent intersectional work recognizes that the categories of race, class, gender, and sexual orientation shape *both* individuals' relative locations within political systems *and* macro-level phenomena such as international human rights compliance standards.[48] This move to embrace a full commitment to the focus on Individual-Institutional Interactions sheds light on the organization of political power more generally.[49] Thus, political power is not presumably located in *either* structures *or* individuals alone, and it flows in multiple directions instead of remaining static.

Unlike prior analytical approaches to race, gender, class, and sexual orientation, intersectionality recognizes that power should not be conceptualized in a zero-sum framework. The zero-sum framework contributes to the Oppression Olympics. Intersectionality's focus on relational power highlights the dynamic interactions and distributions of power within and between individuals and groups, institutions and nation-states.[50]

The Individual-Institutional Interactions element of intersectionality theory also avoids viewing the structure as undifferentiated power that completely dominates the individual's ability, or vice versa. All too often in U.S. politics, public policy debates are grounded in disagreement as to the cause and thus the locus of agency and accountability—in government policies and practices (aka structure) or in citizens' individual behaviors. One common area where such discussions focus either on systemic or on individual explanations is the role of fathers in poor households. Liberals focus on the systemic causes of absentee fathers—unemployment, poor education, and poor availability of a social safety net. On the other hand, conservatives focus on the role of personal responsibility among the fathers themselves. If we were to set aside Defiant Ignorance in an intersectional framework, we would acknowledge that there is an interaction between individuals and institutions that points us toward reform of both elements rather than just one or the other. Yet without setting aside Defiant Ignorance, there is no room for this higher-order conversation in our broader American political discourse.

The complex interactions between individuals (as *both* individuals *and* members of groups) and the institutional practices, norms, and structures produce the culture in which we live. More often than not this interaction is neither neat nor unidirectional in its influence. As we know, cultural production is a dynamic process that involves elements of opportunity for liberation and oppression at multiple levels of analysis. It is in fact possible that even as individuals are exercising their freedom to participate in American cultural discourse the cultural impact at the group or institution level reinforces the oppression of their compatriots. This tension continues to haunt U.S. political discourse, which tends toward the reductionist and the polarizing rather than toward complexity and nuance. For example, presenting oneself as the "anti-nappy-headed ho" plays into multiple dominant norms of respectability and uplift ideology that disciplines women athletes of color into cookie-cutter images predesigned for them.[51] We will continue this discussion of complexity using two examples in the next section.

ANALYZING AMERICAN POLITICS FROM AN INTERSECTIONAL PERSPECTIVE

Shifting from earlier figures, which emphasize specific content categories, figure 2.3 illustrates the relationships between all five aspects of what I term "paradigmatic intersectionality." Only when brought together do all five aspects of intersectionality effectively address the dilemmas posed by the Oppression Olympics.

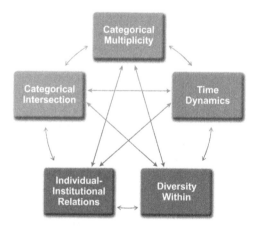

Figure 2.3   Paradigm Intersectionality.

Intersectionality takes seriously race, gender, sexual orientation, and class as analytical categories rather than just as identities.[52] Why? If we focus solely on race as an identity, we are limited to identity-based policy solutions that get bogged down in debates about the legitimacy and humanity of the individuals themselves, which ignores the role of institutions in shaping politics and provides an entry point for Compassion Deficit Disorder or Defiant Ignorance. The previous section on Individual-Institutional Interactions, however, taught us that we can't simply focus on the structure in response. Intersectionality's approach to politics can illuminate new ways to think about long-standing debates such as affirmative action and multiracial identity.

Focusing on gender, race, class, and sexual orientation as identities ushers in the reification of lived experience,[53] which often leads to paralyzing claims of "uniqueness," "incommensurability," and the dreaded Oppression Olympics. Using sexual orientation, gender, class, and race as analytical categories accepts the lived experience of people without making it a condition of group formation, epistemology, or agenda setting, further opening opportunities for deep political solidarity.

This expansion beyond the limits of identity politics in no way dismisses identity as irrelevant or downright pernicious, as some advocates of colorblindness do. Instead the work opens up space for the first benefit of intersectionality: creating diverse coalitions that are nonidentity-based but may still generate identity-based benefits. Intersectional approaches neither eschew identity nor remain mired in it. Multiple planes of interaction (the organizational, intersubjective, experiential, and representational)[54] and Categorical Multiplicity open up avenues of agency without ignoring the role of Individual-Institutional Interactions.

Take, for example, the news media's long-standing overdependence on single black mothers as prototypes of welfare recipients.[55] Intersectional analyses can certainly describe this problem, but it can also offer innovative solutions. A twentieth century identity politics laden solution might be civil rights driven: getting more black faces in our newsroom to counter this overdependence. Not only is that an indirect solution to this particular problem, one strategy to achieve it, affirmative action, has been eviscerated by the Supreme Court in recent years, thanks in part to Movement Backlash. Part of the twentieth-century approach to this problem would also pour most resources into defending and attempting to resuscitate the rollbacks of affirmative action programs at the state and federal levels. A noble effort but again, is it the most appropriate allocation of resources for this particular challenge?

A twenty-first-century intersectional analysis instead comprehensively attends to Time Dynamics and Individual-Institutional Interactions in order to identify an unlikely and previously unidentified site of action for welfare activists: the Federal Communications Commission (FCC), whose decisions about consolidation of media ownership can dramatically affect the diversity of images portrayed of women on welfare.[56] Here they might encounter new and largely counterintuitive allies in an effort to more accurately represent their stories and change the size of their microphone relative to the very large ones carried by political elites.

This kind of simultaneous attentiveness to Time Dynamics and Individual-Institutional Interactions follows in the footsteps of many scholars, including Iris Marion Young in her thinking of categories as serial collectives. Unfortunately, Young followed twentieth-century practice by discussing only one category, gender, in depth. Intersectionality integrates *all* of the analytical categories as interlocking categories of difference.[57]

Returning to the example of the Rutgers University Scarlet Knights, black female athletes endure a tremendous amount of surveillance and pressure[58] to conform to a "black lady" public image[59] that is simultaneously liberating (from the "nappy-headed hos" stereotype) and constraining (preventing complete autonomy of personal expression, including its heterosexism). Significantly, such athletes experience that pressure from coaches who are themselves often black women. Time Dynamics improves Young's original formulation by acknowledging the accrual of power over time by multiple centers of power, and Diversity Within recognizes the multiple centers of power as sites of struggle for the power of self-definition.

Whether through U.S. census categories; discriminatory policies like segregation, detention, and internment; or incentive-driven policies like affirmative action, government and its agents play a significant role in the access we have to freedom of identification and equality of opportunity in the United States. One final example of the relationship among the five prongs of intersectionality can illuminate the need for all five aspects in American political discourse. Millennial Generation–driven identity movements like the multiracial movement have sought complete freedom of self-identification in all aspects of their lives. Often this goal has been challenged by civil rights leaders who see it as a threat to hard-won gains for African American representation that is currently targeted by Movement Backlash. From the perspective of Categorical Multiplicity and Time Dynamics it is important to recognize the politically charged practice of "passing" and its legacy as part of the resistance to the idea of a multiracial identity and its goals.

First, attention to Categorical Multiplicity, Categorical Intersection, and Time Dynamics would draw our attention to the role of gender in the multiracial movement. When the mothers of mixed-race children in the United States were primarily slaves, there was little if any activism to reclassify these children as "mixed" rather than as the legislatively mandated "black." In the twentieth century, as greater numbers of white mothers have become involved in the multiracial movement,[60] the push for a "mixed," "biracial," or "multiracial" identity choice has emerged from multiracial citizens and their parents. This move has garnered resistance from communities of color who envision the shift as a move to share in the spoils of whiteness, like those who long ago passed into whiteness. Without a significant commitment to antiracism, it is difficult if not impossible for the multiracial movement to contest this belief, sparking a closing of ranks to protect allocations of resources tied to the census, like the 2000 and 2010 "Check the Black Box" U.S. Census campaigns targeting African Americans, Afro-Caribbeans, and African immigrants.[61] Far from influencing just the interpersonal identity domain, the multiracial movement has successfully altered the administration of the U.S. Census for all Americans and shifted Census-driven debates over allocation of resources toward a discourse that accepts their perceived reality of who they are. My point here is not to challenge multiracial people's agency to self-identify but to reveal the institutional impact of their activism and pinpoint possible obstacles to solidarity. In conjunction with the Time Dynamics element of intersectionality theory, Individual-Institutional Interactions focus on the idea that just as history (whether recent or centuries ago) plays a dynamic role in explaining the status quo, so, too, do government and cultural institutions play a shifting role in the political odds of a new politics.

Recent research on multiracial identity also laments the hegemony of African American and white parentage as a dominant prototype used to define the agenda of all multiracial individuals, a troubling legacy of the black-white paradigm's dominance of race-relations discourse. Clearly there is Diversity Within the multiracial community, which must be acknowledged in building models of identity development, agendas for political action, and egalitarian coalitions. What is perhaps most relevant to the discussion here is that an intersectional analysis that attends to *both* Time Dynamics *and* Diversity Within better helps the movement than a unitary model. Fuller recognition of Diversity Within and Time Dynamics by the movement itself might counter the image of the movement as one seeking its own share of white privilege, reducing the likelihood of sparking the Oppression Olympics. Without an intersectional analysis, much of the complexity required for full consideration of these issues drops out.

Each political debate—representations of welfare recipients and the multiracial census movement—gains deeper clarity from the five dimensions of intersectionality theory. The intersectional approach can be applied to policy debates of all kinds, as we will see in chapters 4 and 5. But before analyzing each case study, let's examine the benefits of the twenty-first-century intersectional approach.

BENEFITS OF PARADIGM INTERSECTIONALITY

While intersectionality theory started in identity politics, it has not remained there.[62] Identity politics cannot transform the United States on its own; institutional change beyond identity politics is critical to twenty-first-century politics. Attention to the five prongs of the intersectional approach—Categorical Multiplicity, Categorical Intersection, Time Dynamics, Diversity Within, and Individual-Institutional Interaction—directly challenges the Oppression Olympics. Specifically, it offers us three hallmark contributions to our politics in the twenty-first century, each of which will be explored in the case studies to come.

A unitary approach (e.g., focusing on race *or* gender) cannot handle the complex processes of self-integration that must take place in order to avoid harmful, antisolidarity actions like self-deception,[63] which undergirds the Willful Blindness, Defiant Ignorance, and Compassion Deficit Disorder elements of the Oppression Olympics. As I've noted throughout the chapter, intersectionality forces a direct confrontation with Willful Blindness and Defiant Ignorance through attention to Time Dynamics and Diversity Within to directly confront the role that privilege plays in all Americans' lives. There are no longer any pure victims in our political context. In the absence of any pure victims we must examine new ways to stand in solidarity with each other as individuals who are simultaneously marginalized and privileged. Chapter 3 will take up this directly by examining the individual-level preparation necessary to pursue deep political solidarity.

Second, I've also mentioned throughout the chapter that the intersectional approach provides the chance for new kinds of counterintuitive coalitions. Turning the discussion away from zero-sum questions using Categorical Multiplicity and Categorical Intersection eludes the threat of Leapfrog Paranoia. Along with such a turn, confronting Willful Blindness and Defiant Ignorance will facilitate the eradication of Compassion Deficit Disorder, as apathy is confronted as the exercise of privilege that it is in these contexts. Similarly, new domains for attention to the roles of gender, race, sexual orientation, and class are revealed by the attention to Diversity Within and Individual-Institutional Interactions. The political agendas of marginalized groups and their allies are transformed based on a different approach to the process by which the agenda is set and ultimately new kinds of egalitarian coalition building within as well as between groups to achieve such an agenda. We'll examine these more egalitarian coalition-building opportunities with regard to the issue of same-sex marriage in chapter 4.

Last but certainly not least, throughout the chapter there has been an emphasis on complexity that is often challenging for mainstream portrayals of American politics. Returning to *The Matrix*, recall that Morpheus's offer to Neo of a choice between the red pill (of liberatory knowledge) or the blue pill (to remain mired in Willful Blindness and Defiant Ignorance) is one that only Neo can make for himself; it cannot be forced upon him. Similarly, this book is addressed to those who have elected to take the red pill, who are open to the complexity and nuance that are rarely in evidence throughout most U.S. public discourse. For those of us interested in and committed to justice, the causal complexity of our political context is not something that can be avoided in the twenty-first century. Attention to intersectionality provides a structured way to engage this complexity without being as reductionist as past approaches. We will see this attention to complexity throughout the rest of the chapters.

HOW TO TALK TO SOMEONE A LOT OLDER THAN YOU ABOUT INTERSECTIONALITY

- Watch *The Matrix* (again, if necessary) with the purpose of analyzing the similarities between the matrix and the complexity of intersectionality as a tool to fight the Oppression Olympics. Tell your older folks that, like Morpheus, all you offer is the truth.
- Watch the Oscar-winning *Crash*. Do you see any troubling kinds of omissions with regard to Individual-Institutional Interactions in terms of the messages taken away about racial/ethnic prejudice?

HOW TO TALK TO SOMEONE A LOT YOUNGER THAN YOU ABOUT INTERSECTIONALITY

- Watch *Up in the Air*, with special attention to the interaction between Natalie (Anna Kendrick) and Alex (Vera Farmiga) for an example of how attention to Time Dynamics can bridge the generation gap to talk about contemporary issues.
- Read Mark Warren's book, *Fire in the Heart: How White Activists Embrace Racial Justice*, together to examine generational differences in becoming a racial justice activist. How could a paradigm intersectional approach have made a difference for his argument?

NOTES

1. Hawkesworth, Mary. "Confounding Gender." *SIGNS: Journal of Women and Culture in Society* 22 (1997): 687–713.
2. Wachowski, Larry and Andy (1996). *The Matrix*, original screenplay, 33–35.
3. The challenge to the constitution of and relationships between categories in politics should not be confused with a post-structuralist challenge questioning the very viability of such categories, a position McCall terms "anti-categorical." McCall, Leslie. "The Complexity of Intersectionality." *SIGNS: Journal of Women and Culture in Society* (2005): 1773.
4. There is a very good reason for doing so, even at the risk of "reification" of the term intersectionality. There is a significant amount of semantic slippage—chicana studies, black feminist studies, and Asian American women's studies are all often assumed to fall entirely within the rubric of intersectionality research, when in fact intersectionality and feminism (of any variant) in particular are not synonymous terms. My logic here is similar to the point that not all women and politics scholarship qualifies as feminist, nor all race politics as nationalist. While there are numerous sympathies, of course, this kind of semantic slippage obscures the very richness of the content that has so greatly shaped intersectionality: the multivocality for which intersectionality is known. For this reason, the next part of the chapter is dedicated to achieving analytical clarity. Both the semantic slippage and citations across disciplines and content populations suggest that this kind of work has taken place in multiple locations simultaneously, often unbeknownst to scholars immersed in their study of a specific intersectional group. Some scholars even go so far as to claim an exclusive origin for intersectionality in the specific group they study. Though it is beyond the scope of this chapter to demonstrate at length, the origins of intersectionality are multiple and intersecting.
5. Calhoun, Craig. *Critical Social Theory*. Cambridge, MA: Blackwell Publishers, 1995, 186.

6. Dara Strolovitch notes that in this day and age most social justice organizations agree that this is important work. However, "intersectionally disadvantaged" groups still fall through the cracks in terms of getting their political needs onto the agenda. Strolovitch, Dara. *Affirmative Advocacy: Race, Class and Gender in Interest Group Politics.* Chicago: University of Chicago Press, 2007. See also Cohen, *Boundaries of Blackness,* 1999, for analysis of homophobia in the African American communities and see Seidman for analysis of racism in the LGBT community.

7. Intersectionality's focus on these two contributions of multicultural feminist theory occurs in light of critiques advanced against its other tenets. For example, the idea that women of color have a unique standpoint approach has produced a vast array of work focused on the cases of women who endure "multiple jeopardies." This content of knowledge improves our global political literacy and improves the chances of developing effective policy ideas. However, the paralysis the claim of uniqueness produces for wide-scale political action hurts our attempts to undermine the Oppression Olympics, which thrives upon the assertions of "incompatibility" and "uncompromising" political postures. In particular, the claim that women of color have a unique standpoint that is distinct from and largely incommensurable with standpoints of other women has been criticized as impermissibly vague and paralyzing. [See, e.g., Maynard, Mary. "Race, Gender and the Concept of 'Difference' in Feminist Thought." In Bhavnani, Kum-Kum, editor. *Feminism and Race (Oxford Readings in Feminism).* New York: Oxford University Press, 2001. Zerilli, Linda M. *Feminism and the Abyss of Freedom.* Chicago: University of Chicago Press, 2005.]

8. Mary Hawkesworth lists the many areas in which intersectionality has already contributed to our knowledge: "Working within and across a range of disciplines, feminist scholars of color have demonstrated that attention to intersectionality changes understandings about the social construction of subjectivities, the materialization and stylization of bodies, the identities of desiring subjects, the designation of desirable objects, patterns of desire, sexual practices, gendered performances, the terms and conditions of sexual exchange, the asymmetries of power in public and private spheres, the politics of reproduction, the distributions of types of work, the organization of domestic activity, the divisions of paid and unpaid labor, the structures of the formal, informal and subsistence economies, the segregation of labor markets, patterns of production and consumption, terms and conditions of labor exchange, opportunities for education, employment, and promotion, the politics of representation, the structures and outcomes of public decision-making, the operating procedures of regulatory and redistributive agencies, the dynamics of diasporas and decolonization, the potent contradictions of globalization, war-making and militarization, and women's manifold resistances against the oppressive forces structuring and constraining their life prospects." Hawkesworth, *Feminist Inquiry,* 209.

Most of the research Hawkesworth lists is content-based scholarship about women who reside at the intersections of race-, gender-, class-, and sexual orientation-based marginalizations. Its achievements are analogous to the contributions made by Pateman's *The Sexual Contract* and Mills's *The Racial Contract* to social contract theory. For our purposes it is also important to note that this kind of intersectional work broadens our knowledge base about intergroup relations, justice, and democracy in particular. In "The Complexity of Intersectionality" Leslie McCall also notes briefly in a footnote the vast loci from which the term and framework emerged—fourteen different works from at least four different genres of theorists.

9. They also point out the importance of other sociopolitical divisions, including (dis)ability status, rural/urban, nomad/settled, and probably most importantly, inclusion/exclusion in global market relations.

10. Yuval-Davis, Nira. "Intersectionality and Feminist Politics." *European Journal of Women's Studies* 13 (2006): 193–209.

11. Ibid.

12. See Barvosa, Edwina. *Wealth of Selves: Multiple Identities and Mestiza Consciousness and the Subject of Politics.* College Station, TX: Texas A&M University Press, 2008, 77–78; and Weldon, S. Laurel. "Intersectionality." In Goertz, Gary and Amy Mazur, editors. *Politics, Gender and Concepts: Theory and Methodology.* New York: Cambridge University Press, 2008.

13. Maynard, "Race, Gender and the Concept of 'Difference' in Feminist Thought," 125.

14. Young, Iris Marion. *Intersecting Voices: Dilemmas of Gender, Political Philosophy and Policy.* Princeton: Princeton University Press, 1997, 20.

15. This more nuanced question genuinely considers the answer an open empirical question, which could mean at some point that these categories may shift in relevance for American politics.

16. Intersectionality can carry out the promise of both/and constructions of multicultural feminist theory without falling victim to the additive language embedded within multicultural feminist thought. It takes this claim seriously through its pursuit of analyses that have consciously avoided such attempts at dissociation. Earlier scholars like Cathy Cohen, Michelle Tracey Berger, Nancy Naples, and Ange-Marie Hancock have engaged in this effort through case-based, content-related research of a specific intersectional population through attentiveness in design to the contingencies of categories based on the dynamic aspects of their production and/or the acknowledgement of the diversity within such groups, whatever the categorization strategy. Changing the first-order question allows intersectionality to achieve the potential of select multicultural feminist claims without the concomitant pitfalls. See also Yuval Davis, "Intersectionality and Feminist Politics" and Weldon, "Intersectionality" for further concrete steps in this direction.

17. It is Crenshaw who is thought to have first coined the term "intersectionality," though these premises were percolating in several different disciplinary domains.

18. Crenshaw, Kimberle Williams. "Demarginalizing the Intersection of Race and Sex: A Black Feminist Critique of Antidiscrimination Doctrine, Feminist Theory and Antiracist Politics." *University of Chicago Law Review* 139 (1989).

19. According to an unpublished manuscript by Heath Fogg-Davis (2006), this formulation has been encapsulated in the law by Canadian courts.

20. Other two-dimensional images have also been utilized to illustrate the operation of such categories at the micro-level; see Dhamoon, Rita. *Identity/Difference Politics: How Difference Is Produced and Why It Matters.* Vancouver: University of British Columbia Press, 2009.

21. See Meyer, David and Steven Boutcher, "Signals and Spillover: *Brown v. Board of Education* and Other Social Movements." *Perspectives on Politics* 5 (2007): 81–93. Here I am referring to the strategic litigational practice of arguing similar standards of scrutiny for suspect classes like race and gender.

22. Despite numerous reproductions of her two seminal articles, Crenshaw has not yet published revisions of her original metaphor.

23. While in this book I focus on four categories in American politics, it is clear that other political contexts may or may not draw our attention to these categories. For that reason, I'm emphasizing the logic of intersectionality over the content of categories examined. Other scholars have explored categories of national/citizenship status, (dis)ability, and religion in analyzing U.S. politics.

24. Dhamoon, Rita. "Considerations on Mainstreaming Intersectionality." *Political Research Quarterly*, March 2011, 26–28.

25. Ibid, 26.

26. Hankivsky, Olena. "Gender vs. Diversity Mainstreaming: A Preliminary Examination of the Role and Transformative Potential of Feminist Theory." *Canadian Journal of Political Science* 38 (2005): 977–1001.

27. Proposed first as a prison arrangement by Jeremy Bentham, the term panopticon refers to a form of constant observation or surveillance. Michel Foucault later built upon this idea, expanding it beyond a prison architecture to encompass all of Western society.

28. Blackwell, Angela Glover, Stewart Kwoh, and Manuel Pastor. *Searching for the Uncommon Ground: New Dimensions on Race in America.* New York: WW Norton and Company, 2002, 48–49.

29. Martinez, "Beyond Black/White."

30. Nielsen Wire. "The United States in 2020 in a Very Different Place," (July 2009). Accessed January 31, 2010.

31. Beltran, Christina. "Patrolling Borders: Hybrids, Hierarchies and the Challenge of Mestizaje." *Political Research Quarterly*, 57 (2004): 606.

32. Shapiro, Edward, M. D. Talk Delivered at the "Living, Loving, and Voting Conference," Austen Riggs, October 17–19, 2008, Stockbridge, MA.

33. See Andrew Sullivan, "Goodbye to All That: Why Obama Matters." *Atlantic Monthly*, December 2007.

34. Yet as I noted at the start of this chapter, this window of opportunity was narrow and attenuated in space and time by sociopolitical structures within which black female athletes must navigate their lives. Indeed, one member of the team, Kia Vaughn, reportedly sued Imus for slander and defamation of character, contending that the team's abundant success was compromised by having to respond repeatedly to the controversy (AP, 8-15-07). She later dropped her lawsuit (AP, 9-11-07) after multiple media outlets lambasted her for it.

35. This concept addresses what Cathy Cohen has termed "secondary marginalization." Cohen, *Boundaries of Blackness*.

36. Dawson, Michael. *Behind the Mule: Race and Class in American Politics*. Princeton, NJ: Princeton University Press, 1994, Shingles, Richard D. "Black Consciousness and Political Participation: The Missing Link." *American Political Science Review* 75 (1981): 76–91.

37. Frasure, Lorrie and Ange-Marie Hancock. "Black Politics after Obama: Preliminary Results from the Collaborative Multiracial Political Study." Unpublished manuscript, 2009.

38. In *The Politics of Disgust: The Public Identity of the "Welfare Queen,"* Hancock identifies this psychological correspondence bias as the "failure of representative thinking." In *Affirmative Advocacy* Strolovitch empirically demonstrates the failure of social justice groups to represent intersectionally disadvantaged subgroups of their constituencies.

39. See Schreiber *Righting Feminism*.

40. Young, *Intersecting Voices*, 12.

41. Ibid, 13.

42. Ibid, 24.

43. Ibid.

44. I use these words in direct homage to the long trajectory of work on African Americans' group consciousness and sense of politically linked fates.

45. Strolovitch, *Affirmative Advocacy*, 218; Yuval Davis "Intersectionality and Feminist Politics." 205–6; see also Matsuda, Mari. "Beside My Sister, Facing the Enemy: Legal Theory out of Coalition." 43 *Stanford Law Review* (1991).

46. The Bus Riders Union is a Los Angeles-based group that describes itself as "a multiracial, working-class-based membership organization operating at the intersection of mass transit, the environment and public health, and civil rights." It was formed in 1992 and remains active in 2010.

47. Yuval Davis "Intersectionality and Feminist Politics," 198.

48. Several intersectional scholars have attempted to illuminate the ways in which an intersectional paradigm crosses the hegemonic, disciplinary, structural, and interpersonal domains. Both Berger and Hawkesworth examine how the analytical categories of race and gender interact with

facially neutral institutional practices (such as congressional seniority and the single-payer health care system) while simultaneously attending to and moving beyond the actual experiences of black women as black women in political contexts. Berger, *Workable Sisterhood*; Hawkesworth, Mary. "Congressional Enactments of Race-Gender." *American Political Science Review* 97 (2003): 529–50.

49. Garcia-Bedolla, Lisa. "Intersections of Inequality: Understanding Marginalization and Privilege in the Post-Civil Rights Era." *Politics and Gender* 3 (2007): 238; see also Collins, Patricia Hill. *Black Feminist Thought: Knowledge, Empowerment and Consciousness*. New York: Routledge, 2000, and Yuval Davis, "Intersectionality and Feminist Politics."

50. This more complicated analysis of power acknowledges the multi-directionality of power and opportunities for agency identified but left underdeveloped in multicultural feminist thought.

51. See Cohen, in press, for further delineation of this impact.

52. McCall, "The Complexity of Intersectionality;" Yuval Davis, "Inter-sectionality and Feminist Politics," 2006.

53. Yuval Davis, "Intersectionality and Feminist Politics," 197.

54. Ibid, 198.

55. Gilens, Martin. *Why Americans Hate Welfare: Race, Media and the Politics of Anti-poverty Policy*. Chicago: University of Chicago Press, 1999; Mink, Gwendolyn, editor. *Whose Welfare?* Ithaca, NY: Cornell University Press, 1999; Hancock, *The Politics of Disgust and the Public Identity of the "Welfare Queen."* New York: New York University Press, 2004.

56. Using similar logic about creative, counterintuitive coalition-making Cohen proposed a gay-straight alliance of welfare recipients and queer rights advocates based on the common challenge both groups present to the heteronormative structure of American family politics. Cohen, Cathy J. "Punks, Bulldaggers and Welfare Queens: The Radical Potential of Queer Politics." *GLQ: A Journal of Gay and Lesbian Studies* 3 (1997): 437–65. While this example is located within identity politics as a domain, it acknowledges sexual orientation as an analytical category rather than as a content binary of gay/straight, rendering the argument intersectional.

57. What does this shift imply for theory? First, deploying analytical categories (rather than the identity of "woman" or "black") provides a way to decode meaning and to understand the complex connections among various forms of human interaction, but in a meticulously con-textualized and historically accurate manner. Scott, Joan. "Gender: A Useful Category for Historical Analysis." *American Historical Review* 91 (1986): 1070; Hawkesworth, *Feminist Inquiry*.

Bringing together multiple categories of analysis in a similarly criti-cal and nuanced way distinguishes intersectionality as a meta-theory of race, class, gender, and sexual orientation.

58. Foster, Kevin Michael. "Panopticonics: The Control and Surveillance of Black Female Athletes in a Collegiate Athletic Program" *Anthropology and Education Quarterly* 34.3 (2003): 300–23.

59. Collins, Patricia Hill . *Black Feminist Thought: Knowledge, Empowerment and Consciousness*. New York: Routledge, 2000.

60. Williams, Kimberly. *Mark One or More: Civil Rights in Multiracial America*. Ann Arbor: University of Michigan Press, 2006.

61. In 2000 prominent media personalities Tom Joyner and Tavis Smiley collaborated on the You Count! Campaign to encourage blacks to fill out the form and check only the Black box. In 2010, the National Coalition on Black Civic Participation's 2010 Unity Diaspora campaign has targeted immigrant residents of African descent from the West Indies and the African continent.

62. Burack notes the continued commitment for black feminist theorists to an identity politics site of struggle, despite the challenging "politics of authenticity" produced by in-group essentialism fostered by reification of lived experience. Burack, Cynthia. *Healing Identities: Black Feminist Thought and the Politics of Groups*. Ithaca, NY: Cornell University Press, 2004.

    Although contemporary black feminists attend to this matter in a refreshingly reflexive way, the loci of such concerns maintain their focus upon identity politics. The politics of authenticity can be debilitating for a black feminist politics of empowerment, drawing people into a web of endless discussions of what constitutes "authentic" black feminist standpoint(s). The result is the stagnancy that Linda Zerilli, Naomi Zack, and others so roundly critique. Second, the inward turn can thwart creative coalition building. Bernice Johnson Reagon notes that while valuable, spaces for "just us" cannot provide all of the sustenance we as human beings seek. Moreover, as Crenshaw and others have demonstrated, structural limitations in jurisprudence and public policy create very real barriers to the relief sought by black women qua black women. Changes to such structures, deeply embedded in mainstream political and legal culture, require coalitions for change based on more than shared identity. Intersectionality opens up these assumptions and in so doing opens up opportunities for counterintuitive coalitions. One unintended consequence of this turn illustrates the point: the passionate claims of "double binds" and "multiple jeopardies" that emphasized the marginalization of black women in a way that alienated their struggles from those of black men and white women. In the quite legitimate quest to carve out a political space for themselves, black women were faced with a gender gap and backlash in the black community that persists today. It is not that black feminists were wrong to make claims passionately and publicly, but the resulting backlash has been problematic, as black men have used that public passion against them, at times joining mainstream constructors of black women to call them "angry," among other pejorative terms.

63. Barvosa, *Wealth of Selves*, 141.

3

From Public Service to Deep Political Solidarity

"Helo: I don't know, I...I keep doing it...I keep ending up on the wrong side of everything. You know, maybe Tigh's right. Maybe I want it that way. What if I'm flying a desk not because I'm good at it, not because I'm the right guy for the job, but because it's the right punishment for the guy who crosses the line and everybody knows it? Maybe I belong in Dogville..."[1]

So you think you'd like to stand in solidarity with a justice-seeking group. But do you know what you've signed up for? What kind of resources might a person need beyond their personal desire to stand in solidarity? The answers to these questions are particularly important, because standing in solidarity is distinct from other good deeds like political tolerance, altruism, or public service.[2]

In keeping with the goals of this book, this chapter speaks to individuals who want to end the Oppression Olympics. Not everyone may choose to engage in acts of solidarity. But many Americans, particularly younger Americans now coming of age in the most racially diverse generation in history, have basic political tolerance mastered. While many yearn for the next step, recent evidence suggests they have not yet figured out how to link their increased tolerance to specific policy changes to enhance freedom. Chapters 4 and 5 will analyze two specific cases of this evidence; this section defines solidarity as a distinct political behavior and examines the resources often used in performing it. Speaking solidarity or thinking solidarity is not the same as standing in solidarity, and the distinction has direct political effects.[3] Like the rest of this book, the focus here is on *action*.

In chapter 2, I argued that the components of intersectionality can combat the Oppression Olympics by revealing a path to solidarity. Unfortunately no *Matrix*-like red pill exists to prepare us for the deeply personal, political, and emotional challenges that working toward solidarity can pose. But there are fictional and real-life figures who can help us examine the sociological, psychological, and political dimensions of individual solidarity in the twenty-first century. The fictional characters of Karl "Helo" Agathon and Dr. Gaius Baltar from *Battlestar Galactica*, along with real-world twentieth-century exemplars Hannah Arendt and W. E. B. Du Bois, can illuminate how individuals can overcome the Oppression Olympics by mentally preparing for and engaging in deep political solidarity.[4]

DEEP POLITICAL SOLIDARITY: BEYOND TOLERANCE

The word solidarity originates in the French language with a simple definition: *unity of purpose*. Solidarity has been used as the name of an anticommunist liberation movement in Poland, a means for crafting a labor union identity that can supersede cleavages of race and ethnicity,[5] and as evidence that regional movements for equity represent the next wave of transformative politics.[6] But what *is* solidarity? Affirmative definitions of solidarity are rare; even more rarely is solidarity examined as a behavior or a set of behaviors that can test the limits of even the most seasoned activist's patience and commitment. All too often solidarity is left to be conflated with related phenomena such as political tolerance, altruism, and public service.

This section will therefore distinguish deep political solidarity from these other concepts. Solidarity as a political concept varies in three key ways from related concepts such as political tolerance, altruism, and public service, all of which have been studied in depth and lauded in normative political terms. Solidarity involves a distinct principle of justice, a distinct emotional foundation, and a distinct normative ideal regarding power relationships, all of which we will examine briefly here. Moreover, the chapter defines a specific type of deep political solidarity that is consistent with the paradigm intersectional approach outlined in chapter 2. Put more succinctly, deep political solidarity extends far beyond "I voted for Obama" as evidence of being racially progressive, or "I voted against California's Proposition 8" as evidence of progressive views on sexual orientation.

Deep Political Solidarity ≠ Political Tolerance

For a number of historically relevant reasons, empirical attention to America's cleavages along lines of race, gender, and sexual orientation have historically focused on reduction of personal prejudice and increasing aggregate levels of political tolerance. Given the ideals expressed in America's founding documents, measuring political tolerance traditionally tests our individual commitments to those democratic ideals—like freedom of speech or religion. Since most of us would have no problem granting such freedoms to those we agree with, studies of political tolerance have repeatedly sought to examine the extent to which a person would guarantee rights to groups they *dislike* the most. The larger question here is "What is the very least we are willing to give those we vehemently disagree with?" This question sets aside larger questions of justice for a more limited discussion of minimal standards of inclusion in the democracy. That is, whether the distributive logic associated with American ideals results in substantively just outcomes is a question outside the sphere of political tolerance studies, for the most part.

Over the last fifty years, most scholars agree that Americans have become significantly more tolerant of groups with whom they disagree. And yet we know that many inequalities of race, gender, and sexual orientation remain. Solidarity is more directly attuned to questions of justice than tolerance is. The primary principle of justice undergirding solidaristic relationships is equity, which can involve correctives or supplements to the extant law in order to achieve it. When citizens frame their relationship to each other as interdependent and one focused on communal sharing, it may be plausible to agree that "No Child [should be] Left Behind," or that, as then-candidate Barack Obama told Samuel Wurzbacher (aka "Joe the Plumber"), "sometimes we've got to spread the wealth around."

This cohesive ethic of equity, interdependence, and communal sharing is at the heart of deep political solidarity. Far too frequently such individual beliefs have very little impact at a broad national level, especially in terms of producing long-term or deep political solidarity. In fact, we may believe U.S. national politics involves far too many "every man for himself" market-oriented relationships or too many deferential unequal authority relationships. In other words, we can certainly think of today's political arena as involving multiple types of relationships, with communal sharing, the one associated with solidarity, occurring most *rarely*. Instead, tolerance has become the gold standard of political ideals, trotted out whenever someone issues a mea culpa for offending a group. We will examine the ramifications of making tolerance the gold standard rather than the point of entry into our democracies throughout the rest of the book.

What more might be asked of a democratic citizenry beyond tolerance? With the benefit of a century's hindsight, having lived through a twentieth century rife with multiple world wars and genocides, it is clear that the increase in political tolerance doesn't necessarily protect people from harm, even in democracies. In the late twentieth century, contemporary social theorists like Charles Taylor and Michael Walzer have focused on theories of "mutual recognition" as a step beyond tolerance to protect democratic rights and liberties for everyone.

Mutual recognition is possible when there is a shared moral appreciation of political values like political freedom.[7] Taylor focuses on the common values at the heart of recognition and the identification of cultural practices to reinforce them, while Walzer proposes a narrow swath of government practices that can build a culture of empathy among diverse sets of citizens,[8] presumably to facilitate such recognition. Like nineteenth-century social theorist Emile Durkheim,[9] Taylor and Walzer's arguments are contingent upon the presence of a community that recognizes itself as sharing a set of common values. Thus, theories of mutual recognition seek a level of universality across human beings based on shared values. This has been a rich area of research, to be sure, but intersectionality theorists have outlined the growing limits of universal pursuits when conceptualized in this way.[10] The presumption of common values cannot be assured in a rapidly changing twenty-first-century world of multiple and overlapping allegiances. Deep political solidarity can keep a diverse society egalitarian and its citizens safe from rampant discrimination.[11]

Deep Political Solidarity ≠ Altruism

Though Walzer shares much in common with Taylor, his focus on creating a culture of empathy creates a foundation ripe for solidarity, rather than a more limited facilitation of altruism. Kristen Renwick Monroe suggests that altruism includes a spectrum of behaviors that are "intended to benefit another, even when this risks possible sacrifice to the welfare of the actor."[12] Solidarity, in the tradition of social theorist Emile Durkheim, focuses on the "commitment to some kind of mutual aid or support," based on perceived common characteristics or perceived equality.[13] The mutuality of support is different from altruism. Whereas Monroe elides the distinctions between empathy and compassion as emotional resources for altruistic behavior,[14] to repeat such a move here would prevent conceptual clarity between altruism and deep political solidarity. The distinction between emotional foundations of empathy and compassion is also potentially important politically as a buffer in political contexts of fear or distrust, as I discuss in the final chapter of this book.

In *On Revolution* (1963), theorist Hannah Arendt dismisses the democratic potential of compassion due to its circumscribed applicability:

> Compassion, by its very nature, cannot be touched off by the sufferings of a whole class or a people, or, least of all, mankind as a whole. It cannot reach out farther than what is suffered by one person and still remain what it is supposed to be, co-suffering. Its strength hinges on the strength of passion itself, which, in contrast to reason, can comprehend only the particular, but has no notion of the general and no capacity for generalization.[15]

Arendt notes here that pity and compassion are troubling emotional foundations for politics.[16] Moreover, in practice, politics grounded in pity and compassion often lead to paternalism and the motivation to do "for" rather than "with." Due to its limited purchase in larger contexts, compassion is easily pervertable into pity, a mere sentiment with no potential for solidarity. For Arendt, neither pity nor compassion has any role in politics, because it compresses the space for politics to actually occur.[17] While compassion is an "organic" feature of humanity, it is susceptible enough to perversion that it is an unreliable building block for solidarity politics. Thus, one of the very reasons for the existence of the Compassion Deficit Disorder element of the Oppression Olympics is the political bankruptcy of compassion.

Indeed, as recent twenty-first-century events have shown, Compassion Deficit Disorder toward ongoing, recognizable, fixable problems has compounded tragedies that emerge from natural disasters. Both the publicity and consistency of action required for solidarity make a politically navigable foundation of empathy more useful than the compassion that underlies altruism.

For that reason among others, solidarity is grounded in empathy. The emotion of empathy calls for the inhabitance of another's predicament on *their* terms—a move that can lead to the transformation of an unequal political relationship into a more egalitarian one.[18] This is distinct from the pursuit of commonality often used as a foundation for politics—this isn't "we're more alike than we are different," or "we've all had loss in our family—you lost your mother and father, and I remember losing my pet hamster or goldfish." Instead, solidarity, cultivated by what Arendt called "world-travelling," implies more than just tourism. It involves sharing a conscious desire for a different world.

Empathy as the foundation also, somewhat counterintuitively, allows us to preserve what Arendt called "the space between us," to engage in politics with a certain sense of detachment. If we consciously want a different world—a world without female genital surgeries, or honor killings, or domestic violence, or poverty, we must be truly committed to working ourselves out of a job, in the way that Jonas Salk, when he discovered the polio vaccine, eventually worked himself out of treating polio patients.[19] While all of this seems logical, it is all too easy to allow one's self-identity to get so wrapped up in the struggle or movement that allowing the transformative outcome to occur becomes nearly impossible.

Deep Political Solidarity ≠ Public Service

Public service is what we've all been indoctrinated to believe is the appropriate response to individual or structural inequality. In contexts of acute need, like the immediate aftermath of the Haitian earthquake or the Thai tsunami, this may be the superior path, because it assists the person or family in need of service by addressing a pressing need—food in a famine, shelter after a storm, medical aid, tutoring, or literacy. But public service, through its dependence on compassion and altruism, does not fundamentally transform the political relationship between the two parties involved.[20] One remains the rescuer, and the other the "aid recipient," suggesting a relationship involving norms of gratitude, inequality, and obedience. Further, the fundamental structural politics of a situation—like the North-South relationship between the United States and Haiti—is left generally untouched by public service. Often people of all political stripes complain that people remain dependent across generations and blame the system of public service for keeping people dependent. But they are holding public service to a standard it is not designed to meet, because the public-service framework is not contingent upon transforming the relationship between aid provider and aid recipient into one of communal sharing, which would be emblematic of solidarity.

Of course, public service is also popular partially because it is deeply apolitical—that is, we can agree across ideologies or parties that we should morally commit to helping the less fortunate who are "victims" (setting aside for the moment the politics surrounding such definitions). For example, not many people around the world said publicly that we shouldn't provide any help to the victims of the 2010 earthquake that ravaged Haiti, the 2011 earthquake in New Zealand, and the combination of earthquake and tsunami in Japan. The common emotions that underlie such commitments to service include sympathy, compassion, pity, and even righteous indignation at the conditions people are forced to contend with.

Granted, in a triage situation, transformations of power relationships may not be possible. However, there are many other contexts where unfulfilled potential for transformation exists. Solidarity is frequently difficult or unfamiliar because it's often confused with public service in common parlance. While normatively desirable and beneficial for a broad range of reasons, public service is neither necessary nor sufficient for wide societal transformation in the direction of social justice. The lack of transformative power relationships in public service illustrates some of its qualitative distinctions from deep political solidarity. Recognizing that solidarity and public service are not synonymous is particularly important in order to ensure the potential for successful coalitions and wide social transformation can emerge.

Defining Deep Political Solidarity

Humanitarian aid is often critical to human survival. Such altruistic public service is often billed as something that is deeply fulfilling, and often is on some level despite any personal risks Monroe and other scholars rightly identify as consequences of altruism. But the benefits of deep political solidarity are distinct from those of public service and altruism. Moreover such benefits belie the simplicity of the original "unity of purpose" definition of solidarity. The relationships between society and solidarity are broad and complex. We now know from the previous sections what solidarity *isn't*; in this section we will develop a definition of deep political solidarity as an individual-level phenomenon; chapter 4 focuses on deep political solidarity at the group level.

Psychologists have determined that every individual has a set of predispositions for prosocial behavior—their term for solidarity.[21] Far from a nebulous normative concept of political theory, evolutionary biologists believe that solidarity is a kind of behavior that evolved over time in humans to serve particular evolutionary functions.[22] Both groups and societies depend heavily on people's willingness to engage in prosocial behavior, and neuroscientists have confirmed that emotions like empathy create the foundation for it.[23]

Our initial solidaristic tendencies are linked to both age and personality characteristics. As we will see in a later part of this chapter, threats of punishment are a likely risk of solidary behavior. Children are less likely to engage in solidaristic behavior because their moral judgment calculations tend to emphasize whether or not punishment may follow.[24] Early adolescents, like most teenagers you know, are more focused on social conformity, and judge adherence to social norms as morally good with little attention to the legitimacy of said norms. To date, developmental psychologists have found that only adults (of any age) are capable of comprehensively using abstract ethical rules as a basis for either moral judgment or solidaristic behavior.

We've all seen enough romantic comedy or reality TV to know that mismatches between behavior and situations usually occur when two people have vastly different ideas of what their relationship is. Beyond individual-level personality traits, the situational context also helps to provide the opportunity to engage in solidarity. The mental model, or set of ideas a person has about the sort of relationship they think they're in, serves as a frame for the interactions they have.[25] Once an individual settles on their perception of the relationship, the potential for solidarity or some other behavior becomes clear. For this reason, explicitly setting a communal sharing standard for the relationship among the individuals involved is key to future solidarity. Without terms and practices explicitly set and implemented, it is easy to fail to develop this kind of relationship. The importance of the early steps in the relationship helps to explain why public service frames of relationships leave the inegalitarian dynamic between individuals intact, thereby failing to foster deep political solidarity.

Of the four possible relationship frames that psychologists have observed—communal sharing, equality matching, market pricing, and authority ranking—only two produce solidarity.[26] A perceived relationship of *communal sharing* tends to produce *strong solidarity*, while *equality matching* tends to produce *weak solidarity*. Neither market pricing nor authority ranking produce solidarity.[27] Weak and strong solidarity vary in terms of both the expected sacrifice to be made by each party and distributional norms of equality that guide the relationship. We'll return to this relationship perception in our discussion of Helo.

While most of us have these predispositions for solidarity, we don't have much political or societal infrastructure, much less any instruction manuals for how to exercise such predispositions. As a result, most of these predispositions get channeled into public service or are left unused. This particular point, lack of use, is relevant to the potential for the development of deep political solidarity because neuroscientists confirm that the emotions like empathy that often lead to solidarity remain a step slower in traversing the brain than negative emotions like fear or anger.[28] On the bright side, however, as with many forms of physical exercise, repeated acts of solidarity facilitate the speed and ease of the brain's engagement in future solidary behavior, much like the way that riding a bike eventually becomes something we can access quite easily once we've learned how.

Even among adults, however, predispositions to solidarity vary based on situational contexts and personality traits. People who are more extroverted, agreeable, conscientious, and open to change are more likely to engage in solidary actions. Although we each have a different predisposition for these personality traits, countless self-help books are correct—you can become more extroverted, agreeable, conscientious, or open to change through consistent practice. Parents can help their children do the same thing within their age-related capacities, and teachers and coaches can help their students and athletes develop strengths in these areas as well. So if you want to stand in solidarity but know you are an introvert, don't lose faith!

We can stand in solidarity more frequently and better than our parents did. For that reason "strong" or what I call *deep political solidarity* is the focus of this book. In terms of individual acts, deep political solidarity at the individual level involves active, public *demonstrations* of ten different qualities vetted in the psychological and sociological literature, which are noted in Table 3.1.

Here we can see that tolerance (via **Open-Mindedness**) and **Altruism** are but *two* of the *ten* elements of deep political solidarity. They are therefore necessary but *not* sufficient components of our solidarity definition—in reality, solidarity is far more comprehensive. It's easy enough for most of us to do one of these acts at a time. The trick with deep political solidarity is that you must do most of the

Table 3.1   10 Acts of Deep Political Solidarity

Altruism	Assistance in times of need
Consideration	Avoidance of offense and effective resolution of conflicts
Cooperation	An interest in the common good
Cultural Empathy	Ability to recognize and empathize (not pity) with feelings, thoughts, and behaviors of members of different groups
Emotional Stability	Tendency to remain calm in stressful situations
Fairness	A distributive logic of equity
Flexibility	Ability to adjust one's familiar ways of acting in response to the demands of new and unknown situations; a tendency to see new situations as a challenge
Open-mindedness	Open and tolerant attitude toward members of different cultural groups and different norms or values
Social Initiative	Tendency to take the initiative and approach other persons
Trustworthiness	Avoiding breaches of implicit or explicit agreements

acts simultaneously to overcome many of the obstacles to building intersectional coalitions. Failure to do so, as we will see in chapter 4, can have disastrous results. But for now, the next section will examine how paradigm intersectionality (Categorical Multiplicity, Categorical Intersections, Diversity Within, Time Dynamics, and Individual-Institutional Interactions) and deep political solidarity work together in a fictional context. We'll consider the *Battlestar Galactica* characters of Helo and Baltar as two people with similar political status yet utterly different predispositions for deep political solidarity.

> *"What science fiction should be is a look at ourselves, an examination of humanity." Ronald D. Moore*[29]

Helo and Baltar: The Good Soldier and the Antitragic Hero

On March 20, 2009, the reimagination of the 1970s science fiction drama *Battlestar Galactica* reached its highly anticipated conclusion. "BSG," as the five-year-old contemporary series was known, shared its predecessor's premise: following a coordinated surprise attack on their home planets, the last twelve tribes of humanity embarked on a journey in search of a fabled thirteenth, what the older series, in a deep male voice, characterized as "a lonely quest for a shining planet...known as EARTH."

The contemporary series quickly transitioned to a Cylon occupation of Caprica, the planet at the center of humanity's power, after Cylons destroyed all but one of the space-roving battlestars that were assigned to protect the human race. Cylons are robots created by man who evolved into undistinguishable human-looking models from which multiple copies (rather than clones) are produced, ostensibly through the Cylon belief in "rebirth."[30] Culturally BSG has come to represent a twenty-first-century meditation upon many classic questions we continue to grapple with: the line between humanity and the products of human creativity, as well as the struggle between the ethics of human existence and the exigencies of human survival. The series's show-runner and executive producer, Ronald D. Moore, acknowledged the political reflections BSG may incite: "Our goal is both mirror and prism through which to view our world. It attempts to mirror the complexities of our lives and our society in turbulent times... Our goal is to examine contemporary culture and society, to challenge (and sometimes provoke) our audience, but not to provide easy answers to complex problems."[31] There have been at least three books that have seriously engaged with the connections between

BSG and politics,[32] and the United Nations sponsored a conference to explore the human-rights themes undertaken in BSG.

In no way are Moore and BSG's analysts the first to recognize the connection between science fiction and politics.[33] Legal scholar and critical race theorist Derrick Bell has consistently used science fiction techniques, particularly elements of time travel,[34] to offer a dark and incisive critique of the racial status quo in the U.S. As Susan Burgess notes, "Consistent with the parameters of tragedy, the heroes of Bell's story who resist oppression are doomed to fail due to the consequences set in motion by the [U.S.] founders' fateful decision to constitutionalize slavery."[35] Like Moore, Bell's approach leaves the final decision to the audience: "to stay and work within the parameters of contemporary constitutional discourse or to leave in order to explore alien worlds that may offer new and exciting possibilities."[36]

Thus BSG follows a long line of literary and popular science fiction that is markedly serious and attentive to the most vexing questions of politics. Over its five-year story arc, which garnered ten Emmy nominations, BSG has confronted the ethics of treason, suicide bombing, intergroup relationships, friendship, and justice. Like the best works of science fiction scions Octavia Butler, Orson Scott Card, and George Lucas, executive producer Ronald D. Moore and his team created a dark world, often Manichean in its discursive premise. Each episode, however, served to reveal the complexity underlying the presumptively simple Manichean dilemma, often imbuing individual character choices with implications for all that survives of humanity—41,401 people by the middle of the third season. In this way BSG connected fans with multiple expressions of humanity that reflect the complexities of the human condition, which are explored throughout this chapter.

Helo and Baltar: two characters, two polar opposite reactions to the end of humanity as they know it. How can it be that two people within the same situation display different levels of solidary behavior? We know, of course, that individuals are different and come to any situation with their own personalities, predispositions, and perceptions of the context. As we saw in the previous section all three elements, when combined, make determining the likelihood of solidary behavior significantly more likely. For this purpose we will focus initially on the first interaction between Helo and Baltar in the opening miniseries.

Who Is Baltar?

Brilliant scientist Dr. Gaius Baltar, or "Baltar," as he is known to most of the humans, has been reimagined by Moore as an infinitely twitching, complex character whose villainy is less pure evil and more tragic antihero. Baltar, played evocatively by British actor James Callis, is both a world-famous scientist and, unbeknownst to Helo, a notorious womanizer who envisions himself as "fated" to be long-suffering. His self-concept as a long-suffering, tragic figure is at complete odds with what the audience knows to be the facts of Baltar's life.

In chapter 1 of the miniseries that began this run of BSG, Baltar becomes involved with a stereotypically beautiful woman we later find out is an enemy Cylon, a heretofore unknown "skin job" type of the machine/species. In his narcissistic[37] attempts to extricate himself from discomfort when she tells him she loves him following one of their numerous sexual encounters (his verbal response: "Are you serious?"), he enters a quasi-relationship with her. It is a desperate mollification ploy, one with which dramatic audiences are all too familiar. This ploy, however, gains her entry into other areas of Baltar's professional life, ultimately producing access to the defense department's mainframe codes she will need to destroy virtually all of human government. Fulfilling the real-life Plato's prediction about the tyrannized person's fate, Baltar becomes a traitor long before the audience knows him to be a character of unlimited egocentricity, vanity, and lust.[38]

But Baltar's response to the discovery of his role in the attack potentially moves us away from fiction's often tragic determination. Rather than interpreting this turn of events as just desserts for faking love or karmic retribution for his womanizing,[39] Baltar integrates these facts into his own self-absorbed, sexualized identity.[40] To Baltar, his unwitting role in the Cylon attack fits into his own self-concept as a tragic hero, resolving the horror of having contributed to the obliteration of humanity by fusing it with his own tragic fate. Thanks to Callis's wink-and-nod portrayal of the character, the audience is not duped into thinking that Baltar *is* in fact a tragic hero, nor do they despise him completely.[41] Baltar's conviction that his fate is universally tragic—his own Willful Blindness to his privilege even as he later becomes president of Cylon-occupied Caprica—borders on the absurd. Later in the series Moore and his team mock Baltar's willingness to take himself seriously as a tragic figure with his self-reinvention as a religious figure, complete with underground radio broadcasts, self-styled prophetic visions, and a cultlike flock of mostly female followers.[42] They have created a parody of the tragic hero, and, as Burgess suggests about parody's impact more generally,[43] given the audience the opportunity to imagine alternatives to a predestined tragic outcome.

Through parody of the tragic hero, Baltar offers the audience a chance to imagine an alternative narrative practice in going "off-script." But it's Helo who provides an exemplar of an alternative itself. Only through Helo can we see ourselves as *both* privileged *and* disadvantaged, as the overwhelming majority of Americans are relative to each other. This intersectional consciousness, we'll see, is fully complementary with deep political solidarity.

Who Is Helo?

Helo's character trajectory differs greatly from Baltar's. Played equally brilliantly by Canadian indigenous actor Tahmoh Penikett, Karl "Helo" Agathon, a former electronic countermeasures officer and pilot, is the classic "good soldier," according to Moore.[44] Helo is rarely mentioned in studies of BSG beyond his reputation as the human who is married to the far more frequently analyzed Cylon Athena.[45] Although scholars overlook Helo, he is consistently ranked among the favorite male BSG characters despite his supporting role in the drama.

Chapter 4 of the miniseries brings Helo and Baltar together for the first time. As the last pilots leaving a decimated Caprica, flight partners Helo and Sharon "Boomer" Valerii decide to transport as many humans as possible to Galactica, the last surviving battlestar. But how does one choose the survivors? Helo and Boomer decide the fairest way to choose is to conduct a seat lottery.

Meanwhile, knowing that his unbridled lust for a defense contractor triggered the destruction of most of humanity, Baltar simply seeks anonymity and safe transport off of the now-occupied planet of Caprica.[46] Arriving at the ongoing seat lottery on foot, an old woman asks Baltar to read the lottery number on her slip to see if it matches the final number called by Helo. It does. Baltar's tense temptation to save himself by taking the last seat is cut short by Helo, who demands to know if he is Gaius Baltar. Knowing his guilty conscience (his verbal response: "What? I haven't done anything!"), Baltar hesitates until it is apparent that being recognized will favor him. It does.

Ever the good soldier, Helo voluntarily surrenders his own seat on the last transport to Dr. Baltar, telling his partner Boomer, "Look at those clouds and tell me this isn't the end of everything. What future is left is gonna depend on whoever survives ... Give me one reason why I'm a better choice than one of the greatest minds of our time."[47] What Helo missed while administering the lottery for seats on the transport was Baltar's voracious appetite for self-preservation.[48] As the joke goes, Twinkies, cockroaches, and Cher may all survive Armageddon in the real world, but in science fiction so, too, will Gaius Baltar. Boomer departs *without* Helo and *with* Baltar in tow.

In this scene Helo and Baltar display in stark relief the poles of self-interest and deep political solidarity. While both have similar levels of birthright privilege—male and Caprican (the most privileged of the twelve planets), Baltar displays lower levels of conscientious behavior—lying about love, withholding information until it's clear it will benefit him personally—than Helo does. What's more, in a single event (the seat lottery), Helo performs multiple acts that together exhibit deep political solidarity more broadly.

In deciding to take other humans with them, Helo and Boomer together display *Flexibility* recognizing that a new and unknown situation—the possible end of humanity—requires an adjustment of the familiar response (adherence to protocols that forbid unauthorized civilian transport). In distributing the scarce Raptor seats, they also decide to enact *Fairness* by conducting a lottery rather than use a more anecdotal process. Clearly the pair have strong *Altruistic* tendencies as well.

But Helo goes beyond these three acts to exhibit *Cooperation*, that interest in the common good, when he gives his own seat to the world-famous scientist who can contribute more to humanity. Whether Helo's belief in Baltar is empirically true given Baltar's apparent limitations is less important here than Helo's explanation of his motivation, as noted previously. As Boomer gets upset at the prospect of leaving her partner behind and attempts to reject Helo's decision, Helo remains calm in stressful situation, reflecting *Emotional Stability* even as he watches the Raptor take off. Thus by the conclusion of this single scene, Helo has enacted half of the behaviors identified by scholars as emblematic of deep political solidarity. The audience will later become familiar with Helo's position as a moral and sociopolitical conscience for humanity, culminating in a season-3 episode that cements this characterization. In this later episode Helo most clearly provides an alternative—certainly not the only one, but the one most relevant for our purposes, to enter the opening that the parody of Baltar as the antitragic hero provides.

Helo, Du Bois, and Double Consciousness

The political significance of Helo's personal predisposition to solidarity is enhanced by further attention to intersectionality in conjunction with deep political solidarity. A comparison of the fictional

Helo and the very real W. E. B. Du Bois's response to what Edwina Barvosa calls "identity conflict" demonstrates an intricate relationship between intersectionality and deep political solidarity that is relevant to twenty-first-century politics.

During his time on Cylon-occupied Caprica, Helo meets and falls in love with another copy of his flight partner, who reveals herself to be a #8 model Cylon, later named "Athena." Over the course of the series Helo returns to Battlestar Galactica and in subsequent episodes is promoted to executive officer (XO) of the ship.[49] In a season-3 episode entitled, "The Woman King," Helo in his new official capacity is assigned to manage an influx of Sagittaron refugees, a human tribe whose rural roots and traditional cultural practices offend the contemporary sensibilities of the other planetary tribes.

As mentioned earlier, Helo's tribe, the Capricans, are the sociopolitical elite; until the attack Caprica had been the location of the central government uniting all twelve human colonies and the center of human civilization. Earlier episodes allude to a complex relationship between the tribes: by this point in the third season, it is clear that Capricans' elite status has evolved largely at the expense of the Sagittarons. Thus, the status afforded Helo is simultaneously individual (as XO of the ship), group (he is a Caprican), and structural (he is part of a military institution in control during an ongoing state of emergency; he was also afforded all the prior structural benefits of his home location on Caprica).

At the same time, Helo is married to a member of the enemy Cylons and father to a daughter who is half human and half Cylon.[50] In this climate of military rule and state of emergency, Helo's loyalty to human survival is repeatedly questioned by his fellow officers and by President Laura Roslin.[51] As we saw with candidates Clinton, Obama, and Palin in the introduction, through choices he could control (like marriage and fatherhood) and many privileges he did not request (like his Caprican birth), Helo is multiply situated, demonstrating an analytical role for intersectionality dimensions of Time Dynamics, Categorical Multiplicity, and Diversity Within regarding categories of privilege as well as with respect to the disadvantaged memberships traditionally studied among intersectionality theorists (e.g., women of color).

The Sagittaron refugees are generally in the opposite location to Helo and the military elite[52]; their tenacious grip on centuries-old traditions and refusal of what the majority of humans considers the most basic of technological, social, and medical advances serve as justifications in the wider discourse for their low rank in the mostly accepted system of socioeconomic stratification.[53] As a medical epidemic breaks out among these people, Helo is forced to acknowledge both the pervasive prejudice and its potentially genocidal ramifications when he discovers a doctor in charge is withholding medication, allowing even the few treatment-seeking Sagittarons to die. The plot's primary dilemma centers on Helo's decision to report the crime.

When Helo brings the injustice against the Sagittarons to the attention of his superior officers, one—former prisoner of war Colonel Tigh—confronts him:

> "He [Dr. Roberts] is the only one who's had anything good to say about you in as long as I can remember. You may as well take whatever credibility you have left and chuck it out an airlock. You seriously want to stand up for these crazy frakkin' people? What is it with you? You just like being on the outside looking in, do you?"[54]

In recounting the events to his wife, Helo questions the costs of his principled stand in the statement that served as this chapter's epigraph: "What if I'm flying a desk not because I'm good at it, not because I'm the right guy for the job, but because it's the right punishment for the guy who crosses the line and everybody knows it?" The commanding officers' refusal to believe him and Colonel Tigh's veiled threats about career suicide present a stark challenge to Helo's sense of identity—who he has known himself to be conflicts directly with what others perceive him to be. This internal identity conflict, while clearly the result of multiple choices and situations that have occurred earlier in his life, prompts Helo to confront his own ambivalence about the marginality simultaneously imposed upon and chosen (but not always embraced) by him.

In lauding what Gloria Anzaldua called "cultivating a tolerance of ambiguity," Edwina Barvosa argues that ambivalence can play a role in helping individuals seeking to integrate identities that are socially constructed as mutually exclusive rather than intersecting.[55] In her analysis of the conflicts produced by such identities, Barvosa likens the ambivalence and ambiguity that follows to the malaise produced by what W. E. B. Du Bois termed double consciousness: "It is a peculiar sensation, this double-consciousness, this sense of always looking at one's self through the eyes of others, of measuring one's soul by the tape of a world that looks on in amused contempt and pity. One ever feels his twoness—an American, a Negro; two souls, two thoughts, two unreconciled strivings; two warring ideals in one dark body, whose dogged strength alone keeps it from being torn asunder."[56]

While in this statement Du Bois clearly speaks from a vastly differ-ent vantage point than Helo—he focuses on the *lack* of privilege he possessed in 1903—the ambivalence is just as palpable and occurs re-peatedly in his work. Thirty-seven years later in *Dusk of Dawn* (1940), Du Bois talks about the emotional outcome of his Harvard University years, which were tainted by experiences of the double consciousness for which he is now famous:

> Something of a certain inferiority complex was possibly present: I was desperately afraid of not being wanted; of intruding without invita-tion; of appearing to desire the company of those who had no desire for me. I should have been pleased if most of my fellow students had desired to associate with me; if I had been more popular and envied. But the absence of this made me neither unhappy nor morose. I had my "island within" and it was a fair country.[57]

At Harvard Du Bois made the choice to retreat to his island within, as a sociopolitical location from which he could contend with the identity conflict and the ensuing emotions without further harm or trauma. Confirming what Anzaldua and Barvosa argue, both Du Bois and Helo manage to transform the ambivalence into something politically productive for a later situation: deep political solidarity.[58]

Du Bois, writing from the location of relative disadvantage, uses the ambivalence and agency he does possess to develop a critical eye that can demystify the power relations between early-twentieth-cen-tury blacks and whites:

> Our work was easy, but insipid. We stood about and watched over-dressed people gorge. For the most part we were treated like furniture and were supposed to act the wooden part. I watched the waiters even more than the guests. I saw that it paid to amuse and to cringe ... I did not mind the actual work or the kind of work, but it was the dishon-esty and deception, the flattery and cajolery, the unnatural assumption that worker and diner had no common humanity. It was uncanny. It was inherently and fundamentally wrong.[59]

Du Bois's attention to the relational norms between servants and diners is striking, for he notes he "watched the waiters even more than the guests." Du Bois's analysis of relational power is compatible with more contemporary approaches to intersectionality. Though Du Bois cannot credibly be called an intersectionality theorist, close analysis of these moments of identity conflict shifts us away from prior schol-arship on Du Bois in this regard. The construction of black and white identities as mutually exclusive produced a singular norm of existence for whites[60] and another equally homogenous norm for blacks. In focusing our attention on these two homogenous norms, Du Bois provides further evidence of the perils of ignoring the intersectionality dimension of Diversity Within. That these black waiters were more than mere homogeneous stereotypes of black servility could not be conceived by white diners due to the "unnatural assumption that worker and diner had no common humanity," or in other words, an act of Oppression Olympics style Defiant Ignorance.

Similarly, Du Bois's interlocutors often focus on either his antiracist activism or his Marxist ideologies, as if Du Bois wrote solely from a single margin (e.g., racial disadvantage) to a single center (e.g., racial privilege) instead of linking them together.[61] Du Bois embraced Categorical Multiplicity long before "intersectionality" became a buzzword, in part because he was quite familiar with, if stingy with his public recognition of, the articulations of black womanhood put forth by Anna Julia Cooper and her compatriots who were his contemporaries.[62]

Du Bois's real-life attempts at solidarity are well known: cofounding the National Association for the Advancement of Colored People (NAACP), his close personal relationships and solidarity with Jewish writers and activists, and his ill-advised pursuit of solidarity with Mao Tse-Tung. That Du Bois pursued these paths of solidarity despite personality predispositions most charitably termed "unconducive" to solidarity[63] helps us recognize the potential that exists within all of us for solidarity.

Through Du Bois and Helo, we can see that the situations of both the relatively disadvantaged and the relatively privileged are intersectional in nature and share a susceptibility to identity conflict. Helo has a preponderance of privilege but experiences identity conflict when realities of his life are considered mutually exclusive (e.g., a human military officer and husband of a Cylon). Du Bois has a preponderance of disadvantage but also experiences identity conflict when realities of his life are considered mutually exclusive (e.g., an African American and a Harvard University student). These identity conflicts must be considered time-bound phenomena, as we know that nineteenth-century Harvard University is extremely different from the twenty-first-century Harvard, even as there remain worrisome continuities about race and class as categories of difference.

The identity conflicts experienced by individuals real and fictional provide a moment of opportunity, a break that draws a person's attention in ways that can create opportunities for solidaristic behavior.

Following moments or experiences of double consciousness, is there an avenue for a politically relevant resolution?

Using Helo as an exemplar, the next section highlights the role of intersectionality in an individual-level process of preparation to stand in solidarity with a justice-seeking group. By following the emotionally challenging responses of ambivalence and ambiguity to such moments of identity conflict in Helo's path, those of us with personality predispositions and/or personal preferences for solidarity can be empowered to take action in ways that also acknowledge the reality of intersectionality.

Preparing for Solidarity Step #1: Taking Inventory

"Why bother with such a process?" some may ask. Those seeking solidarity who come from the vantage point of privilege often want to just get started immediately, and see a process of personal preparation as not only a delay but wholly unnecessary, especially if they have been politically active before. Two brief examples illustrate why it's important to avoid rushing into solidarity.

In 1963 Hannah Arendt, by then a German Jewish émigré to the United States, published a broad critique of the U.S. civil rights movement for African Americans, criticizing in particular the movement's "use of children" as fodder for water hoses and police brutality. The critique, which lacked almost all attention to the history of civil rights struggles from an author whose careful attention to historical detail had been celebrated in other contexts, like her analysis of totalitarianism, made it nearly impossible for Arendt to engage in *Cultural Empathy* or *Trustworthiness*, two critical acts of solidarity, even after a long exchange with author Ralph Ellison. Arendt had largely shut off all possibility for deep political solidarity, not because she dared to criticize, but because she did so in the absence of having exercised Cultural Empathy, Trustworthiness, *Social Initiative*, or *Flexibility*.

More recently, Soheir Morsy, an Ethiopian feminist, analyzed the lack of trust between Western women and their counterparts in the South in efforts to eradicate female genital mutilation (FGM). "These are times now where 'the natives' know what is being said about them."[64] Effective egalitarian coalitions to end FGM between the North and South were delayed for close to twenty years based on numerous political problems that could have been solved with deep political solidarity among people who fundamentally agree about FGM.[65] Fifteen years later, in an era of Web 2.0, twenty-four-hour news cycles, and viral politics, the presumption of good intentions among the privileged have declined even further. Thanks to the Oppression Olympics and the political complexity facing the twenty-first century, standing in solidarity for wide social transformation is increasingly difficult to begin and challenging to pursue. Both examples suggest that the investment of time to prepare for deep political solidarity is time well spent.

In *Wealth of Selves: Multiple Identities, Mestiza Consciousness and the Subject of Politics,* Edwina Barvosa proposes a process she calls *self-craft* as a way to leverage intersectionality dimensions of Categorical Multiplicity and Categorical Intersections in conjunction with the ambivalence produced by identity conflicts. Ambivalence, Barvosa argues, provides the space for an individual to engage in self-inventory in order to reflect upon their own membership in groups that they strongly identify with. In such a reflective mode, the individual is "free" to feel both attachment and detachment to such groups.[66]

"Wait a second," you might say, "how can a person feel attachment *and* detachment to the same group?" Ambivalence changes a person's expectations about the benefits of group membership.[67] Rather than expect group membership to provide an exclusive sense of safety and belonging, ambivalence makes the character of the relationship between group member and group more ambiguous. This ambiguity can alleviate the intense obligation to present oneself according to rigid group norms, thereby destabilizing those norms. This not only improves a person's ability to be ready for solidarity by fostering general Flexibility (one of the ten dimensions of deep political solidarity), it affords an individual an opportunity to brainstorm in advance various responses "tailored to different occasions."[68]

Whether he is attempting to save Sagittaron lives, arguing against the commission of Cylon genocide, or trying to save his own daughter from her kidnapper, Helo's feelings run deep. As a good soldier Helo could have chosen to respond to Tigh's pressure to forget the Sagittarons with self-deception, which would involve denial of the ambivalence in order to preserve his military effectiveness. But self-deception functions dangerously like Defiant Ignorance because it requires active denial of the reality of disadvantage. So it's unlikely to serve as an effective tool *against* the Oppression Olympics. In fact, it could be particularly damaging politically if Helo or an individual has chosen self-deception regarding a closely held identity (like the notion of being a fair or unprejudiced person).[69] The revelation of the self-deception or the calling out of the hypocrisy will likely result in a vehement or impassioned denial, making solidarity even less possible due to the erosion of Trustworthiness (another of the ten elements of deep political solidarity).

Helo could also have chosen a response that Amelie Oxenburg Rorty has termed akrasia, "acting intentionally and voluntarily in ways that depart from what a person regards as their preferred course of action in that kind of situation."[70] An akratic response is the "easy" response because it is either the person's habitual response or the socially desirable response. In Helo's case, he could have engaged in a little Compassion Deficit Disorder, which would have allowed him to draw upon his Caprican status and personal career ambitions to take Tigh's advice and switch sides this time. He could have dropped his suspicions and left the Sagittarons to die, even telling himself justifications he's learned through years of socialization into the Caprican group about Sagittarons "deserving what they get."[71] But somewhere inside Helo would know that he was inconsistent in his commitment to equal treatment, a cost to a fully actualized person whose self-concept seeks consistency between talking the talk and walking the walk.

It's no surprise that the confrontation with Colonel Tigh affects him—it's a tangible conflict of identities that is intended to force Helo to choose one identity—member of the human race—over another—husband to a member of the Cylon "race." From Helo's perspective, ambivalence and ambiguity of group membership create a window of opportunity to take stock of his multiple privileges and select disadvantages, recognizing the good, bad, and ugly of such group memberships and their legacies.[72] Only acknowledging the ambivalence can put one on the path to selfcraft, and ultimately solidarity.

Though Barvosa briefly speculates on selfcraft's application to politics in the final chapter of *Wealth of Selves*,[73] it is beyond the scope of the book to fully consider selfcraft's political impact. In this section I want to focus on the first step of selfcraft: *taking inventory*. We've already noted that Helo has multiple identities, and described one of several occasions (the confrontation with Colonel Tigh) during which his identities are presumed by others to conflict. Helo's experience and ambivalent reaction to that pressure (his statement: "Maybe I belong in Dogville") provides an opportunity for reflection as well as two important tools to assist real-life individuals in positions of privilege to prepare to stand in solidarity.

Barvosa likens self-inventory to "the mapping of a city of bright thoroughfares and hidden neighborhoods ... It is the task of searching out and learning the history of the elements of one's subjectivity—our habits, schemes of thought and action—with attention to the politics and forced labor, and the possible atrocities and/or beauties involved in their construction."[74] The selfcraft inventory stage provides an opportunity to both examine one's own personality predispositions for solidarity and identify the not-so-pretty "schemes of thought and action" that require attention *prior* to standing in solidarity.

Research on development of individual intersectional consciousness reveals that an acknowledgement and appreciation of the Diversity Within dimension of paradigm intersectionality is crucial to the development of solidarity.[75] Intersectional consciousness is a set of beliefs and orientations toward action rooted in the need to account for multiple categories of difference in three ways: when considering the question of how the political world is constructed, when adjudicating among the possible remedies to pursue, and when deciding the appropriate strategies to achieve said remedies.[76]

Intersectional consciousness, when integrated with the inventory stage of selfcraft, begins to strengthen those neurological connections associated with solidary behavior. The process is one that requires a "city map" of the self that, unlike earlier consciousness-raising strategies, attends to multiple categories of difference and their intersections as part and parcel of oneself rather than developing consciousness along a single category (say, gender) that is deeply personal and a superficial or intellectual appreciation of others (e.g., race, sexual orientation, and/or class). This pursuit of intersectional consciousness during the inventory stage inoculates individuals in many ways against singular forms of consciousness that are particularly detrimental to group cohesiveness. Preliminary studies from Europe suggest that intersectional consciousness, when primed, improves one's ability to drop judgmental attitudes about Muslim women who choose to cover.[77] Thus, raising consciousness intersectionally rather than singly as part of the selfcraft process can prepare individuals to undertake the difficult work of deep political solidarity.

The selfcraft inventory stage also facilitates a self-assessment of the personality predispositions associated with solidarity. In addition to the Altruism, Cooperation, Flexibility, and Fairness demonstrated in earlier scenes of BSG, some of the traits Helo possesses in the exercise of his identities can be tied to an intersectional approach to deep political solidarity. His inventory process can trace the display of Emotional Stability to a pilot's tendency to remain calm in stressful situations, which can be the difference between life and death, a product of Individual-Institutional Relationships. (Helo was trained in a military institution.) This trait of Helo's, then, may have been grounded in his personality but was also primed and valued in his career as a military officer. Similarly Helo's life experience—the near-extinction of humanity—requires him to adjust upward whatever predisposition for Flexibility he might have just to survive.

Helo's confrontation with Tigh certainly provokes the ambivalence associated with identity conflict. From there, the ambivalence can move him into a period of reflection, toward an identity that taps these familiar aspects of himself, despite the challenges to his identities as a senior officer or human. Taking inventory to examine the origins of such traits in their entirety (that is, both the good and the bad) can further enhance Helo's predisposition toward solidarity, especially if he moves to the next step, discernment.

Step 2: Discernment

The step of discernment, as described by Barvosa, draws directly upon Anzaldua's metaphor of putting "history through a sieve." After taking inventory, individuals must enter a stage of *discernment*, where they think critically about all that they have learned. Where did that social norm I pressure myself to respect come from? Why do I subscribe to that stereotype, even a little, considering I know it's false? Where do I fit among the wealth of social forces and groups that swirl around and within me? When you take the time to keep the valuable nuggets of knowledge and beliefs and allow the rest to wash out into the current, you are involved in a process of discernment.

Although the term "discernment" may imply a religious or specifically Christian process, for the purposes of deep political solidarity, it is mostly a secular process, where a person engages with what they have learned through their own personal inventory. This process, if it does include a spiritual component, *includes religion as part of the inventory to be interrogated*, rather than locking the individual into an explicitly religious discernment process to conduct the inventory. As the Dalai Lama suggests in his book, *Practicing Wisdom*, "When we speak of which actions and states of mind need to be enhanced and which need to be discarded, we must choose and pursue the task intelligently. The faculty that generates this discernment is called discriminating awareness."[78]

The role of *"selbstdenken,"* or "thinking for yourself," cannot be underestimated in the secular discernment stage. It is critical to the preparation for solidarity. There will certainly be pressures to do otherwise, as Helo experiences with Tigh. Helo was not the first to experience such pressures. Like Helo and W. E. B. Du Bois, Hannah Arendt also experienced identity conflict, as her German and Jewish identities were socially constructed as mutually exclusive for most of her life. Nevertheless, when choosing to embrace the ambiguity of her own identity conflict, she was unrepentant in her replies to those who presumed she must repudiate one or privilege another of the identities:[79]

> What confuses you is that my arguments and my approach are different from what you are used to; in other words, the trouble is that I am independent. By this I mean, on the one hand, that I do not belong to any organization and always speak only for myself, and on the other hand, that I have great confidence in Lessing's *selbstdenken* for which, I think, no ideology, no public opinion, and no "convictions" can ever be a substitute.[80]

The process of personal discernment Helo engages in takes place off-screen. For those of us who do engage in selfcraft, it involves both the critical assessment as well as the rejection of acts of social subordination, not just in others but also *in ourselves*.[81] As many major religions note, we're very good at pointing out others' faults. Discernment helps us keep an eye out for the influence of the traditions and legacies—especially those we're a part of but no longer endorse—that affect our own thoughts and behaviors. While the inventory stage used intersectional consciousness as a way to address Categorical Multiplicity and Categorical Intersections, the discernment stage foregrounds Time Dynamics and Individual-Institutional Relationships, as one examines legacies and traditions emanating from multiple centers of power. Analyzing one's own complicity (explicit or implicit) in such centers of power also points out challenges that can be addressed in the final stage of selfcraft, Revisionary Living.

Step 3: Revisionary Living – Acting in Solidarity

Once an individual has taken stock and asked himself or herself the toughest questions, what remains is putting it into practice. "Having discerned and rejected one's own particular role in subordination,"[82] Helo must now find ways to practice and privilege the elements of himself that he does endorse in a way that might be challenged and involve lots of revisions of prior practices. But as with solidarity, the emphasis is on action. While Barvosa's attention is directed toward the self and self-directed behavior, using the case of Helo, I want to look at what deep political solidarity—behavior toward and with others—may look like following a process of selfcraft. As we will see, deep political solidarity is different from taking a class (or several) about a marginalized group or attending an event (or several) on their behalf. Intellectual knowledge may be helpful but it isn't sufficient for deep political solidarity; thus the commitment to Revisionary Living is critical.

Helo's actual behaviors are part of the last stage of selfcraft, *Revisionary Living*. We already know that Helo is a strongly altruistic personality from the miniseries, when he gave up his seat on the transport to Baltar. In the case of the Sagittarons, it is Helo's commitment to providing medical assistance that drives him to overlook the risk to his own career to ensure they receive proper treatment.

While Helo's discernment process as noted earlier takes place off-screen, several actions the audience sees later in the episode reveal that he, in fact, chose to think for himself, which allowed him to act in ways that could be characterized as solidarity. Helo's surreptitious visit to the medical bay to "see for himself" rather than depend on the medical reputation of the attending physician is reminiscent of Arendt's *selbstdenken* (thinking for oneself). In terms of solidarity, his action is also one kind of Social Initiative with which citizens of democracies with strong traditions of investigative journalism are familiar. But notice how Helo doesn't wait for a blogger or journalist to ask the right questions—he asks for himself and searches out the relevant data. Similarly, once he possessed the evidence, he didn't wait for a "critical mass" of people to sign on; he took the Social Initiative and spoke out (again) on his own.[83]

Armed with the evidence Helo displays a sense of Fairness, when he approaches his superiors about possible lack of treatment for a second time. He clearly thinks about the common good (Cooperation) when he contends that the Sagittarons have as much right to survival as any other human tribe, regardless of their cultural or religious beliefs. For that reason, Helo believes the Sagittarons deserve full medical treatment if they seek it, *no matter what their beliefs are or will be in the future.*

Helo's prior experiences also facilitate his practice of Cultural Empathy. When a mother approaches him about the treatment she sought for her now-dead son, Helo behaves as if he recognizes how difficult this step against her tribe's cultural norms must have been for her without lapsing into pity or paternalism toward her.[84] In response to her report of her son's death, Helo nods: "I'm sorry. That's a soma braid, right? You Sagittarons believe it's supposed to bring good health? Look, I'm sorry. [But] it's not enough. If you don't treat the disease it's fatal, okay?"[85] Contrast Helo's response with that of civilian Dr. Roberts, who was assigned to treat the refugees but does not understand and refuses to try to understand or empathize with the behaviors, thoughts, or feelings of this group: "I mean, what the hell am I supposed to say to her? 'Sorry ma'am, but if you would've just turned the corner a little sooner on your superstitious crap, we could've saved your son?'"[86]

Helo demonstrates an open and tolerant attitude toward the different tribes for two reasons: he is a member of a military with multiple tribes represented and the pretext of the series. His display of respect for difference stands in stark contrast to the typical human impulse. In the real world, emphasis on a collective identity that supersedes difference (a military or labor union identity, for example) is often the strategy of choice for dealing with difference. Yet research on intersectional consciousness illustrates another path: having an appreciation rather than a suspicion of Diversity Within can enhance activists' levels of solidarity with their groups.[87] Further, the fact that there are only 41,401 humans left anywhere in the galaxy might force the survivors to gloss over differences that were exacerbated in the past, just as Americans closed ranks in the immediate aftermath of Pearl Harbor and 9/11. But just as Pearl Harbor increased attacks and discrimination against Japanese Americans and 9/11 led to similar increases against Arab Americans, such a closing of ranks without attention to Diversity Within and Categorical Intersections can spark individuals to support the repeat of past mistakes instead of creating a different future.

Helo also extends the same Open-Mindedness as he approaches the doctor directly to determine whether he is appropriately treating the Sagittarons who are seeking medical care. He believes it's best to ask the doctor rather than jump to conclusions.

But there are more intersectional reasons Helo is open-minded that relate to social context and privilege. Helo can "afford" to be open-minded in some ways because of his place near the very top of the military leadership (second in command), his masculinity, and his own tribal identity (Caprican), which is the most cosmopolitan and privileged of the twelve tribes. While the risks he encounters are real and legitimate, they are not the same risks as Dualla, with whom he discusses the situation in a separate scene. Dualla, a far-lower-ranked female member of the military who herself is Sagittaron, is more like Du Bois in this regard. Solidarity emerges from the complex interplay of social, structural, and individual factors.[88] Without intersectionality, this complex reality of *both* privilege *and* disadvantage between differing locations would be overlooked or oversimplified.

Helo's behaviors, together indicating the presence of deep political solidarity, are evidence that he has chosen to think for himself instead of succumb to the pressures of sociopolitical norms that would result in injustice. This analysis is not meant to imply that Helo is perfect. But as a fictional character, Helo can assist in providing that "alternative narrative" that those who seek to stand in solidarity can pursue. In the real world, however, the selfcraft process is a difficult one, and not all those who profess solidarity either recognize the qualities of the commitment required or engage in any sort of rigorous process like selfcraft to prepare themselves. In the final section of this chapter we'll look at the risks of selfcraft.

Solidarity in the Real World Among Real People

In the course of reading this chapter it may seem like solidarity is fairly straightforward. On this view an individual can perform the ten acts of solidarity—Altruism, Cooperation, Trustworthiness, Consideration, Cultural Empathy, Social Initiative, Open-Mindedness, Fairness, Flexibility, and Emotional Stability—like some people would adhere to the Ten Commandments or the Golden Rule. But just as BSG could not resolve the complexity of humanity over a five-year television series run, deep political solidarity is not easily achieved after one or two episodes of Oprah's "Live Your Best Life" series or by simply reading this chapter. Both Hannah Arendt and W. E. B. Du Bois remained controversial figures throughout their long lives—accused alternately of being too radical or too conservative depending on the accuser and the year.

The last stage of selfcraft, Revolutionary Living, can produce deep political solidarity, but the process involves trial and error, and can be long, messy, and periodically repetitive.[89] For example, on a postelection panel featuring supporters of the successful mayoral campaign of Antonio Villaraigosa in 2005, activists Gilda Haas, Madeline Janis, and Anthony Thigpenn revealed a twenty-year history of conflicts, collaborations, honest conversations, and commitments to solidarity.[90] It is possible that the people you would like to stand in solidarity with may not yet want to stand in solidarity with you. Trustworthiness is often earned rather than bestowed. The people you would like to join you on the journey from your own privileged groups may not yet want to accompany you; as with physical flexibility, mental flexibility atrophies with lack of practice, no matter your age. For these and other reasons you may experience three specific fears as you move through the selfcraft process.

Like Helo, you, too, may confront a "fear of lost membership" as your ambivalence toward certain group memberships occurs.[91] While you are working to improve your Flexibility or Open-Mindedness, other individuals who are close to you may continue the pattern of thinking you seek to reject. Their reaction to your revisions, whether real or imagined, can threaten your commitment to practicing acts of solidarity. Whether it is family, friends, or more distant people you may want to stand in solidarity with, that rejection or just the threat of rejection can interrupt the process. Cultivating a healthy form of ambivalence toward being a group member and remaining in the moment can assist an individual in staying on a path to solidarity.[92]

Reverend Eric Lee is director of the Los Angeles chapter of the Southern Christian Leadership Conference (SCLC), the civil rights organization founded by Dr. Martin Luther King, Jr. Reverend Lee's support for lesbian/gay/bisexual/transgender (LGBT) marriage equality as a civil and human-rights issue has caused a stir in the African American faith community, of which he has long been a member. Both the national board of the SCLC and local faith leaders have persistently and explicitly withdrawn membership privileges in response to Rev. Lee's position, a not-so-subtle demand for him to comply with the heterosexist norms of their shared racial group instead of his stand in solidarity with the LGBT community. Chapter 4 will discuss the ongoing perpetuation of the idea that race and sexual orientation are mutually exclusive communities and categories of difference.

The second fear chapter 4 will engage with is the fear that we will lose our positive sense of self. When we are so conditioned to think of ourselves as either uniformly privileged or uniformly disadvantaged, we develop coping strategies to preserve our sense that we are worthwhile individuals. Eradicating Willful Blindness, Defiant Ignorance, and Compassion Deficit Disorder requires that we work through that pain rather than practice self-deception or akrasia. We must be willing to look at the shady parts of the city in our life map, not just the clean and shiny parts. Social Justice Leadership, a New York–based organization, suggests four signs of living the interdependence that is the foundation of deep political solidarity:

1. You are fully present for all interactions with others.
2. You take responsibility for your intentions and behaviors when interacting with others.
3. You listen to others deeply and actively.
4. You communicate authentically with others.[93]

Last, the move toward deep political solidarity can spark a fear that the baby will be thrown out with the bath water; that is, the positive elements of a particular group membership will be lost along with the bad. One of the reasons why intersectionality and selfcraft work so well together to produce deep political solidarity is their attention to complexity: complexity within (Diversity Within) and between categories (Categorical Multiplicity, Categorical Intersection); complexity in a given historical moment as well as over time (Time Dynamics); and complexity in terms of how categories like race, gender, class, and sexual orientation are shaped by individuals, groups, and institutions (Individual-Institutional Relations). Instead of the all-or-nothing, zero-sum thinking that produces elements of the Oppression Olympics like Leapfrog Paranoia or Movement Backlash, selfcraft conditions us to see the trees as well as the forest. Take the time for this journey using some of the reflection points below:

How to engage with someone a lot older than you about

- ### How to increase their Social Initiative skills:

  If their selfcraft process (or yours!) reveals that you should work on your level of Social Initiative, there are many different ways to do so. Beyond the stereotypical Stuart Smalley–like affirmations, "I'm good enough, I'm smart enough, and doggone it, people like me," there are games that help you train your brain that you can share with your older friends and family. Though the games are not guaranteed to provide psychological or medical benefit, you may be able to train your brain in a way that doesn't involve something hokey. One set of online games is available from Canadian psychologists Mark Baldwin and Stephane Dandenau: http://selfesteemgames.mcgill.ca/research/index.htm. The games help retrain the neurons to process negative feedback differently.

- ### How to think about Categorical Multiplicity, Categorical Intersections, and Time Dynamics:

  Use the following exercise to have them think about the ways in which different categories fit together in U.S. society while they were growing up:

  Using a pen and paper, ask them to insert the categories into various shapes and then redraw them in connection to each other. If there are categories they feel did not matter at all when they were growing up, they can leave them out.

Race/Ethnicity   Socioeconomic Class   Religion
Gender   Citizenship Status/   Disability Status
Sexual Orientation   Nationality

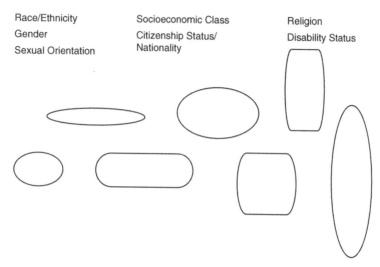

Figure 3.1 Exercise

While they are completing their first draft, complete one of your own. When they are finished, both of you should flip the paper over and repeat the exercise based on perceptions of how the categories would have related to each other in U.S. society during your parents' childhoods. Discuss the distinctions and examine how each of your inventories might be shaped by these diagrams.

- Convince yourself and your older folks that practice is indeed necessary, as with any skill or ability. Use reasons from *The Transformative Power of Practice* to help them embrace and interpret the realities of Revisionary Living. Authors N'gethe Maina and Staci Haines emphasize three central benefits of this type of intentional practice:

1. Practice is organized around your commitments. As Aristotle once said, "We are what we repeatedly do."
2. Practice lays bare all of our own resistance to change.
3. Practice begins to orient and shape how we show up in the world.

HOW TO ENGAGE WITH SOMEONE A LOT YOUNGER THAN YOU ABOUT

- **How to increase their Cultural Empathy:**

There was a time when people lived their lives with discretion and didn't show every aspect of their lives on YouTube, Facebook, or

Twitter. Instead of telling them this fact, *show* them how to flesh out the facts they've learned in history or political science classes with repeated and extended interactions that reveal the depth of diversity among people of different races, genders, and sexual orientations and how this varies from:

- Intellectual knowledge *of* a group
- Public service *to* a group

Remember that standing in solidarity occurs *with* a group. *Most importantly, show them how active listening to the other person should represent over 75 percent of the interaction,* instead of active texting or tweeting to let someone know who they are.

NOTE: If you find you are uncomfortable engaging with people of different groups, perhaps you should start with the online exercises listed earlier for younger folks to increase your Social Initiative.

- **A kick-start to conducting selfcraft step 1, Self-Inventory:**

  Together, use the self-inventory contained in Christine Pelosi's *Campaign Boot Camp*, which challenges someone thinking about running for office to sincerely reflect on their level of comprehensive knowledge of their political universe.

- **How to increase their Consideration:**

  Watch videotapes or DVDs of old political interviews in order to show your younger person different ways of engaging the issues other than loud character assassinations. Encourage them to think about how to engage differences of opinion in a way that leaves the opposite side with their dignity and full humanity intact.

NOTES

1. *Battlestar Galactica*, "The Woman King," Airdate February 11, 2007.
2. Public service and solidarity can share common ends, like a goal to end poverty. However, conflicts of interest between those who benefit in opposing ways from public service funding can thwart achievement of the ultimate goal. Those who have public service contracts and those who are public service clients can find themselves at odds as often as not.
3. Strolovitch, Dara. *Affirmative Advocacy: Race, Class and Gender in Interest Group Politics.* Chicago: University of Chicago Press, 2007.

4. Later chapters will focus on possible policy practices of solidarity (whether minimalist or maximal); but here the focus is on the personal—how individuals can cultivate deep political solidarity from a psychological, sociological, and ultimately a political action/activism perspective.

5. Kasinitz, Philip, John Mollenkopf, and Mary Waters, editors. *Becoming New Yorkers: Ethnographies of the New Second Generation*. New York: Russell Sage Foundation, 2004.

6. Pastor, Manuel, Chris Benner, and Martha Matsuoka. *This Could Be the Start of Something Big: Social Movements for Regional Equity Are Reshaping Metropolitan America*. Ithaca: Cornell University Press, 2009.

7. Honneth, Axel. *The Fragmented World of the Social: Essays in Social and Political Philosophy*. Albany: SUNY Press, 1995, 241.

8. Ibid., 245.

9. Ibid., 241. Durkheim considered commonality to be the factor that brings people together. See Crow, Graham. *Social Solidarities: Theories, Identities and Social Change*. Philadelphia: Open University Press, 2002.

10. McCall, "The Complexity of Intersectionality"; Barvosa, *Wealth of Selves*, 2008.

11. Fetchenhauer, Detleft, Andreas Flache, Abraham P. Buunk, and Siegwart Lindenberg. *Solidarity and Prosocial Behavior: An Integration of Sociological and Psychological Perspectives*. Groningen (Netherlands): Springer Science and Business Media, Inc., 2006, 3.

12. Monroe, Kristen Renwick. *The Heart of Altruism: Perceptions of a Common Humanity*. Princeton, NJ: Princeton University Press, 1996, 6–7.

13. Crow *Social Solidarities*, 6.

14. Ibid. 12–13.

15. Arendt, Hannah. *On Revolution*. New York: Penguin Books, 1963/1990, 85.

16. Arendt attributes the failures of the French Revolution to such factors as well. These theoretical moves occur prior to her analysis of what she considers the disastrous conflation of the political and the social, which has received far greater scholarly attention from political theorists.

17. Arendt, *On Revolution*, 86. This argument is related to but not dependent upon the larger claim Arendt pushes in the chapter entitled "The Social Question." I have concerns about that argument and deliberately decouple this assertion from the larger claim.

18. This could also potentially transform the nature of political coalitions as well.

19. This example also highlights the importance of attention to Time Dynamics, as without constant vigilance and expansion of health care polio has reemerged in several developing nations.

20. Both Arendt and W. E. B. Du Bois make this point. This kind of empathy, which can be defined as "the imaginative projection of one's con-

sciousness into the feelings of another person," is actually the converse of what Arendt later defined as "representative thinking", the projection of your reaction onto someone else's situation. In *The Politics of Disgust* I have critiqued the political ramifications of Arendt's representative thinking elsewhere, and its close correlation to what psychologists term "correspondence bias."

21. Fetchenhauer et al. *Solidarity and Prosocial Behavior*, 3.
22. Ibid, 4.
23. Immordino-Yang et al. 2009.
24. Fetchenhauer et al. 2006, 5.
25. Fetchenhauer et al, 4, 6.
26. Fiske 1991 quoted in Fetchenhauer, 10.
27. Instead, an "every man for himself" or a deferential status relationship emerges.
28. Immordino-Yang et al. "Neural Correlates of Admiration and Compassion," *Proceedings of the National Academy of Sciences* 106 (2009): 8021–8026.
29. Littlejohn, J. R. "A Sleeker Battlestar Galactica," www.usatoday.com, December 24, 2003, Accessed April 29, 2009.
30. Sharp, Robert. "When Machines Get Souls: Nietzsche on the Cylon Uprising." In Eberl, Jason, editor. *Battlestar Galactica and Philosophy*. Malden, MA: Blackwell Publishing, 2008, 26; Giardina, Natasha. "The Face in the Mirror: Issues of Meat and Machine in Battlestar Galactica." 2006. In Hatch, Richard, editor. *So Say We All: An Unauthorized Collection of Thoughts and Opinions on Battlestar Galactica.* Dallas BenBella Books, 2006, 49–50.
31. Quoted in Bell, James John. "An Army of One God: Monotheism vs. Paganism in the Galactica Mythos." In Hatch, Richard, editor. *So Say We All: An Unauthorized Collection of Thoughts and Opinions on Battlestar Galactica.* Dallas: BenBella Books, 2006, 253.
32. Cf: Eberl, Jason, editor, *Battlestar Galactica and Philosophy*; Potter, Tiffany and C. W. Marshall, editors, *Cylons in America: Critical Studies in Battlestar Galactica*; Hatch, Richard, editor. *So Say We All: An Unauthorized Collection of Thoughts and Opinions on Battlestar Galactica.*
33. Eberl, *Battlestar Galactica and Philosophy*, ix; see also Bell, "An Army of One God," 233–34; Roberts, Adam. "Adama and Fascism." In Hatch, Richard, editor. *So Say We All: An Unauthorized Collection of Thoughts and Opinions on Battlestar Galactica.* Dallas BenBella Books, 2006, 222; Blahuta, Jason P. "The Politics of Crisis: Machiavelli in the Colonial Fleet." In Eberl, Jason, editor. *Battlestar Galactica and Philosophy.* Malden, MA: Blackwell Publishing, 2008.
34. Burgess, Susan. *The Founding Fathers, Pop Culture and Constitutional Law: Who's Your Daddy?* London: Ashgate, 2008, 60.
35. Ibid, 59.
36. Ibid. 60.

37. Blahuta "The Politics of Crisis"; Koepsell, David. "Gaius Baltar and the Transhuman Temptation." In Eberl, Jason, editor. *Battlestar Galactica and Philosophy*. Malden, MA: Blackwell Publishing, 2008.
38. Loftis, J. Robert. "What a Strange Little Man: Baltar the Tyrant." In Eberl, Jason, editor. *Battlestar Galactica and Philosophy*. Malden, MA: Blackwell Publishing, 2008, 32–33; Roberson, Chris. "An Angel on His Shoulder." In Hatch, Richard, editor. *So Say We All: An Unauthorized Collection of Thoughts and Opinions on Battlestar Galactica*. Dallas BenBella Books, 2006, 32.
39. By no means are these the only possible reactions; my point is merely that there are alternative, equally plausible, interpretations of the events at hand.
40. Sharp, Robert. "When Machines Get Souls: Nietzsche on the Cylon Uprising." In Eberl, Jason, editor. *Battlestar Galactica and Philosophy*. Malden, MA: Blackwell Publishing, 2008; Roberson, "An Angel on His Shoulder."
41. In fact, he is one of the most analyzed and discussed characters.
42. Sharp "When Machines Get Souls"; Loftis "What a Strange Little Man."
43. Burgess, Susan. *The Founding Fathers, Pop Culture, and Constitutional Law: Who's Your Daddy?* London: Ashgate, 2008.
44. Indeed Moore revealed that Helo's original destiny in the miniseries had been to die, but the writing team changed the character's fate and kept Penikett for the full run of the series largely because, according to Moore, "We saw how he just popped on screen." Personal conversation, October 25, 2008.
45. During the rescue mission, Helo had no idea that his military buddy and flight partner, Sharon (call sign: Boomer), was a Cylon. After relinquishing his rescue craft seat, stuck living on Caprica during the Cylon occupation, Helo and another copy of Sharon fell in love and had a child together. I say copies for this reason because there are variations among them—similar to the way one can have multiple identical laptop computers but depending on the information downloaded to them they become no longer identical through interaction with their human users. Helo's original flight partner, "Boomer," returned to Galactica and attempted to assassinate Admiral Adama. His wife, "Athena," is a physical copy of the original "Boomer," but has pledged her loyalty to human survival (as well as Helo and their daughter Hera); she has not in any way attempted to attack the human race.
46. Cooke, Elizabeth F. "Let There Be Earth: The Pragmatic Virtue of Hope." In Eberl, Jason, editor. *Battlestar Galactica and Philosophy*. Malden, MA: Blackwell Publishing, 2008; Koepsell "Gaius Baltar and the Transhuman Temptation."
47. Battlestar Galactica, "Miniseries," Original air date December 8, 2003.
48. Loftis, "What a Strange Little Man"; Cooke "Let There Be Earth"; Koepsell "Gaius Baltar and the Transhuman Temptation"; Roberson, "An Angel on His Shoulder."

49. Helo received this promotion despite ongoing personal human prejudice regarding his Cylon life partner—and one who is physically identical to an attempted assassin. In fact, this was just the start of the trouble in his return; his highest superiors, Twelve Tribes President Roslin and Commander Adama, faked the death of his infant daughter, Hera, in order to avoid alerting the Cylons that a human-Cylon hybrid child had been born. These two events earlier in the series foregrounded Helo's struggle "to balance his very real loyalty to humanity's fight for survival with his equally real love for the Cylon mother of his child." (Sci-Fi.com website)

50. Here I wish merely to point out the cause of Helo's multiple status. I do not argue that Helo gains special insight about the Other simply by being married to a Cylon or having a child of dual identities.

51. Blahuta, "The Politics of Crisis: Machiavelli in the Colonial Fleet."

52. As is true on Earth, there are individual Sagittarons among the military elite, but as a group they are structurally situated at the bottom of the planetary hierarchy.

53. These systems are confronted occasionally, as when a labor dispute threatens the entire fleet, and Gaius Baltar, now an ex-president of the twelve colonies charged with treason and genocide, pens a book that inspires some of the lower tribe masses.

54. *Battlestar Galactica*, "The Woman King," Airdate February 11, 2007.

55. Barvosa, *Wealth of Selves*, 142.

56. Du Bois, W. E. B. *Souls of Black Folk*.

57. Du Bois, W. E. B. *Dusk of Dawn: Autobiography of a Race Concept*. Piscataway, NJ: Transaction Publishers, 1968/2002, 36; Du Bois's articulation of an "island within" as a sociopolitical location of "fairness" and, presumably, freedom is also present in *Darkwater* (1920) and *The Autobiography of W. E. B. Du Bois* (1968). His use of the words "island within" calls to mind the 1928 novel *The Island Within* by Jewish author Ludwig Lewisohn. More recently, there is a resemblance between Du Bois's island within and what Patricia Hill Collins calls the "outsider within" standpoint of black feminist thought. Collins defines the "outsider within" standpoint from the perspective of black female domestic workers, who are considered invisible for the most part by their white employers. This invisibility grants the women a unique lens with which to analyze their own situation, which Collins argues enables the achievement of several normative goals—including the demystification of power and the concomitant recognition that "one need not believe everything one is told and taught." Collins, *Black Feminist Thought*, 184.

58. This is another distinction between Helo and Baltar: only Helo is capable of both self-affirmation *and* critique (see Barvosa, *Wealth of Selves*, 206).

59. Du Bois, W. E. B. *Darkwater*. Amherst, NY: Humanity Books, 1920/2003, 127–28; Martin Kilson argues that Du Bois "fashioned an intellectual discourse that upheld and defended black honor," attacking

the presumption of white privilege that degradation of African Americans is somehow the birthright of whites (2000, 305). It also directly draws upon Lewisohn's book Island Within.

60. Indeed the scholarly focus on double consciousness has focused upon its political significance for the disadvantaged end of the spectrum, for the blacks, in this example, leaving few if any cues to the dominant group about possible change—for themselves or to the system.

61. See, for example, *Black Reconstruction* and *The Philadelphia Negro*.

62. There is, of course, wide speculation that his pro-feminist pieces were greatly influenced by Cooper and others, to the point where Du Bois was likely obligated under standard academic practices to cite them but did not. Carby, Hazel. "The Souls of Black Men." In Gilman, Susan and Alys Eve Weinbaum, editors. *Next to the Color Line: Gender, Sexuality and W. E. B. Du Bois.* Minneapolis: University of Minnesota Press, 2007; Griffin, Farah J. "Black Feminists and Du Bois: Respectability, Protection, and Beyond." *Annals of the American Academy of Political and Social Sciences.* 568 (2000): 28–40; James, Joy. "Profeminism and Gender Elites: W. E. B. Du Bois, Anna Julia Cooper and Ida B. Wells-Barnett." In Gilman, Susan and Alys Eve Weinbaum, editors. *Next to the Color Line: Gender, Sexuality and W. E. B. Du Bois.* Minneapolis: University of Minnesota Press, 2007.

63. Lewis, David Levering. *W. E. B. Du Bois, 1868–1919: Biography of a Race.* New York: Holt Books, 1994; Lewis, David Levering. *W. E. B. Du Bois, 1919–1963: The Fight for Equality and the American Century.* New York: Holt Books, 2001, Marable, Manning. *W. E. B. Du Bois: Black Radical Democrat.* New York: Paradigm Publishing, 2005.

64. Morsy, Soheir. "Safeguarding Women's Bodies: The White Man's Burden." Medical Anthropology Quarterly 5(1): 19–23.

65. Hancock, Ange-Marie. "Overcoming Willful Blindness: Building Egalitarian Multicultural Women's Coalitions." In Nnaemeka, Obioma, editor. *Female Circumcision and the Politics of Sisterhood.* Denver, CO: Greenwood/Praeger, 2007.

66. Barvosa, Edwina. *Wealth of Selves: Multiple Identities, Mestiza Consciousness, and the Subject of Politics.* College Station: Texas A&M Press, 2008, 155.

67. Ibid., 157.

68. Ibid., 156.

69. Ibid, 215.

70. Ibid, 122.

71. Chief Tyrol's comments on the same episode reflect this socialization in response to Helo's more sympathetic comment about the death of the sick Sagittarons: "Yeah well you'll get no tears from me. It's bad enough my gang's gotta sweat through their stench. I have a feeling one of these days we're gonna wake up in the morning, I'm gonna be really pissed 'cause we're out of meds, 'cause those frakkoids saw the light and now we gotta

share." *Battlestar Galactica*, "The Woman King," Airdate February 11, 2007.

72. This doesn't mean Helo couldn't have chosen self-deception, which would involve denial of the ambivalence, or akrasia—acting intentionally against your preferred response. Clearly the writers made the choice for him.

73. Barvosa, *Wealth of Selves*, 139.

74. Barvosa, *Wealth of Selves*, 177.

75. Greenwood, Ronni Michelle. "Intersectional Political Consciousness: Appreciation for Intragroup Differences and Solidarity in Diverse Groups." *Psychology of Women Quarterly* 32 (2008): 37.

76. Ibid. 38.

77. Greenwood, Ronni Michelle and Aidan Christian. "What Happens When We Unpack the Invisible Knapsack? Intersectional Political Consciousness and Inter-group Appraisals" *Sex Roles*, 59 (2008): 410.

78. His Holiness the Dalai Lama. *Practicing Wisdom: The Perfection of Shantideva's Bodhisattva Way*. Boston: Wisdom Publications, 2005, 64.

79. Though others saw them as impossibly conflicting, Arendt did not and said so repeatedly in her correspondence and in her celebration of Heinrich Heine: "Heine is the only German Jew who could truthfully describe himself as both a German and a Jew... he in fact put into practice that true blending of cultures of which others merely talked. One has only to remember how zealously assimilated Jews avoid the mention of a Hebrew word before gentiles, how strenuously they pretend not to understand it if they hear one, to appreciate the full measure of Heine's accomplishment when he wrote, as pure German verse, lines like the following praising a distinctively Jewish dish..."(JP 74–75). In *Men in Dark Times* (1955), political philosopher Hannah Arendt celebrates the ability to withstand the ambiguity and discontinuities in her portrait of Walter Benjamin. Lisa Disch (1994) notes that it is precisely the discontinuities in her own multiple identities that qualify her for the critical understanding she attributes to the conscious pariah (198). See also Ron H. Feldman's introduction, JP 47.

80. JP 250; italics in original.

81. Barvosa, *Wealth of Selves*, 178

82. Barvosa, *Wealth of Selves*

83. In another episode he also took the initiative when humans were contemplating the use of biological warfare against the enemy Cylons, speaking up and out to his superiors in spite of the normal chain of command.

84. Notably, Helo's cultural empathy isn't triggered by pity or compassion; in fact, in the scene Helo behaves more formally than we would expect someone who pities another to behave.

85. *Battlestar Galactica*, "The Woman King," Airdate February 11, 2007.

86. *Battlestar Galactica*, "The Woman King," Airdate February 11, 2007.

87. Greenwood, "Intersectional Political Consciousness," 37.

88. Ibid., 45.

89. Barvosa, *Wealth of Selves*, 180.

90. Pastor, Manuel, Chris Benner, and Martha Matsuoka. *This Could Be the Start of Something Big: Social Movements for Regional Equity Are Reshaping Metropolitan America*. Ithaca: Cornell University Press, 2009, 131.

91. Ibid., 189.

92. Barvosa, *Wealth of Selves*.

93. Social Justice Leadership. "Training Ethos: Five Core Principles of Effective Leadership for Social Justice." http://www.sojustlead.org/about/training-ethos. Accessed September 3, 2010.

4

SOLIDARITY IN *THE REAL WORLD* OF CIVIL RIGHTS, MARRIAGE EQUALITY, AND PROPOSITION 8

"The African American struggle demonstrated that as blacks gain ground, so do all others in this mosaic that is America."[1]

In 1992 MTV launched the reality television era with this simple introduction: "This is the true story of seven strangers, picked to live in a loft, and have their lives taped, to see what happens when people stop being polite and start getting real." The show, which remains a staple of MTV's programming almost twenty years later, features young people[2] from vastly different backgrounds (including people of color and lesbian/gay/bisexual/transgender [LGBT] cast members throughout the lifetime of the series) in order to tap audience interest in "getting real." While scholars doubt MTV's ability to adequately represent reality,[3] ongoing audience interest in the conflict often generated by serious topics like race (first gaining notoriety during season 1 in New York City[4]) and HIV/AIDS (which gained widespread notoriety during season 3 in San Francisco[5]) have provided a wide array of memorable moments that have become common themes throughout the show's history. Such moments, whether spontaneous or scripted versions of reality (or some mixture of both) have become increasingly rare over the lifetime of the series, but it is just those kinds of moments that originally earned the praise of critics and audiences alike. Yet *The Real World*'s representation of reality also epitomizes what many activists fear about diversity discussions left improperly framed and exploited for shock value.[6] In their line of work, discussions of diversity are often highly fractious and limiting, because the adults of the late twentieth century, whether Baby Boomers or Generation X, don't seem to know how to talk across lines of difference.

Enter the Millennial Generation. Born between 1981 and to 2000,[7] Millennials have grown up in the most racially and ethnically diverse United States to date. Most surveys of their civic engagement demonstrate that they are far more politically tolerant than their older counterparts.[8] This finding, though laudable, is unsurprising, because for most of the past sixty years, the United States has emphasized tolerance as the gold standard for dealing with difference. Producing a more tolerant generation, it has been widely and repeatedly argued, will lead to a twenty-first century that is postracial. Similarly, a more tolerant Millennial generation is expected to automatically and actively support full equality for the LGBT community. Given the expected demographic changes in the United States, Millennials are a critical voting bloc, second only to Baby Boomers by 2015. Chapters 4 and 5 examine Millennials as the more tolerant generation, to understand whether the logical connection made between increased tolerance and strong commitment to policy change on behalf of marginalized groups holds water. In this chapter we will examine the assumption that more tolerant Millennials are meaningfully different from older generations on the issue of same-sex marriage.

If Millennials don't have dramatically different political DNA than their parents or grandparents, then how are we going to get dramatically different results? If we find that Millennials are *not* as unique as their marketing agents suggest[9], then it's important to "stop being polite and start getting real" about assuming the inevitability of a "postracial society" or full equality for the LGBT community and focus on the kind of solidarity politics necessary for wide social transformation.

One way to get dramatically different results is to encourage every individual to pursue the selfcraft process and cultivate intersectional consciousness, as I discussed in chapter 3. Another way might encourage the cloning of people like Gilda Haas, Madeline Janis, and Anthony Thigpenn, who are just a few of many real-life (as opposed to "real world") examples of living deep political solidarity. A third way, often studied by scholars of political leadership, suggests that individual leaders can and have historically brought people together for a common purpose, as did Martin Luther King, Jr. or Harvey Milk during their respective eras, and as some predicted Barack Obama would during the 2008 campaign. But these individual driven approaches have several obvious limitations.

Such approaches ignore the fact that King, Milk, Haas, Janis, and Thigpenn are all embedded in groups that built coalitions within and between communities. It is these groups—whether formal or informal—that make movements go. Without groups that do things differently, the infrastructure for Millennials to accomplish what so many hope they will won't exist, preventing much of the broadscale change many of all ages claim to want.

I say "claim to want" because the second limitation of an individual approach focuses on the individuals involved. In an Oppression Olympics context of Movement Backlash and Compassion Deficit Disorder, many activists are deeply conflicted about how much they can "afford" to embrace Diversity Within and Categorical Multiplicity, two of the most common aspects of paradigmatic intersectionality, among and between their communities.[10] While many social justice organizations recognize this ambivalence about diversity as a problem,[11] many do not find the resources to resolve such a problem in terms of ranking it high on the agenda or allocating sufficient time, money, and human capital to the problem.[12] Interviews with group leaders reveal mixed messages; some have every intention of addressing the problem but face constrained resources,[13] and others, as I noted earlier, express a willingness to "set aside" issues of diversity in certain contexts for fear of destroying already fragile coalitions.[14] Coalition partners who are members of multiply marginalized groups encounter hostility. and threats to exit the coalition from their singular consciousness counterparts[15] when they raise issues associated with the "other" identity, and even receive advice from mentors to sidestep issues of race and issues of sexuality in the face of "larger" or "more pressing" issues.[16] Must this hesitancy persist in the twenty-first century? I argue that the answer is no.

Developing strategies to overcome this ambivalence is critical because the consequences of inaction continue to limit the chances for profound social transformation. By failing to account for Diversity Within, Categorical Multiplicity, and Categorical Intersection, the inaction of social justice organizations perpetuate what scholars term "secondary marginalization,"[17] the marginalization suffered by people holding multiple marginalized group memberships. For example, an LGBT person of color who experiences racism in the LGBT community or homophobia within their community of color experiences secondary marginalization from people who are marginalized like them in one way but are also distinctly privileged in another relative to the person, creating a power imbalance along another axis.[18]

Cultivating intersectional consciousness among individuals, as I suggested in chapter 3, will address the matter of hostility among individuals, but it won't necessarily reshape group-to-group relationships. For this reason chapter 4 discusses a case where deep political

solidarity must be cultivated beyond a select set of individuals—
reaching up to and including the group level. What would really happen if we "started getting real" when it comes to actually building
coalitions among and between marginalized groups?

If we start getting real with the epigraph of this chapter, where
would the conversation lead? We could certainly conduct empirical analyses to examine whether all have gained ground as African
Americans have done so. We spent a good portion of the last century doing exactly that.[19] But to "get real" about this issue in the
twenty-first century, we must also ask the "impolite" questions.
What if the more racially diverse Millennials aren't quite the progressive activists about LGBT issues we imagine them to be? What
does it mean when significant proportions of African Americans
continue to support barriers to equality for other groups within and
outside their communities, such as members of the LGBT community? Why do singular consciousness members of the LGBT community act as if their sexual orientation serves as a "get out of jail
free" card when it comes to issues of racism within and outside of
their own community?

Of course, these questions are deliberately worded as if they could
be part of a reality TV show. Setting such a provocative tone aside,
however, the ironies and controversies surrounding the passage of
California's Proposition 8 (hereafter "Prop 8") have simply reiterated
the preexisting need for an intersectional approach to race and sexual
orientation. Drawing on the concept of deep political solidarity I introduced in chapter 3, in this chapter I want to explore ways to build
deep political solidarity at the group level. How can we go further
than the minimalist "I voted for Obama" or "I voted against Prop
8" I discussed in the introduction? How, in the real world, do we put
tolerance in its proper place—as a point of entry into politics rather
than as a destination?

I first analyze data on Millennial voter attitudes about same-sex
marriage and then conduct an intersectional analysis of Prop 8 as a
case study using the five interactive dimensions of intersectionality
introduced in chapter 2. The purpose of both parts of chapter 4 is
to provide Millennials especially, but activists of all ages, the background and opportunity to look at marriage equality differently,
positioning the African American and LGBT communities as future
coalition partners *and* as groups with overlapping members. Thus,
following the analysis of the complex dynamics at play among and
between communities, I conclude by asking the question, where do
we go from here?

As I noted in the introduction, I selected same-sex marriage along with border policy as cases for analysis because they have become two of several issues that have emerged as gateways for political activism among various subsets of Millennials. For example, eight organizations were founded in the aftermath of Prop 8 by and for mostly LGBT Millennials in Los Angeles *alone*. Further, the issue of same-sex marriage has raised important challenges for coalition politics. Thus, the theoretical standards of judgment I use to move through the intersectional analysis are far from minimalist, which would only seek to preserve tolerance. They are instead geared toward solidarity: pursuit of a relationship of communal sharing (also known as interdependence) and an equity-driven principle of justice.

In a similar vein, it's important to note that in contrast to the well-known controversy same-sex marriage provokes among voters of all sexual orientations, a less well-known but equally passionate debate persists. Relative to the mainstream same-sex marriage debate, far fewer Americans know that: 1) the LGBT community continues to debate the merits of the outsize role marriage equality plays on the broader LGBT agenda,[20] including skepticism from a broad group of LGBT people of color;[21] and 2) many of these same critics are deeply skeptical about marriage equality's potential to serve as a fast track to full equality for LGBT members of a society.[22] I acknowledge this within-community debate where applicable because the tenets of intersectionality demand it, particularly in regard to the possibility of deep political solidarity in the future.

Millennials: The ATMs of Marriage Equality?

Curiously, as Millennials have become the cast members of *The Real World*, the political discussions have declined and the sexual escapades have increased on the show. Whether the cast members themselves or *Real World* producers are to blame is less the issue than recognizing the need to fully interrogate our assumptions about who can be counted on for deep political solidarity when it comes to marriage equality. The 2008 Collaborative Multi-racial Political Survey (CMPS) is the first multiracial and multilingual survey of registered voters across multiple states and regions in a presidential election. It recruited 4,563 voters in the 2008 election from eighteen states to participate in a telephone survey in the language of their choice, including 669 voters from California.[23]

Among California CMPS voters, 54.1 percent voted *for* Prop 8, while 33 percent voted *against* the proposed state constitutional amendment. Dividing the group into Millennials and their counter-parts, the voting results initially look promising among Millennials for marriage equality advocates: 52 percent of the Millennials voted *against* Prop 8, while only 41 percent voted *for* Prop 8.

While eleven points usually represents a comfortable victory in any election, additional tests demonstrate tremendous cause for cau-tion. A one-sample chi-square test was conducted to assess whether the apparent eleven-point difference across age groups is significantly different from what we should expect among Millennial voters based on the overall outcome of the election. Unfortunately, the effect of being a Millennial on an individual's actual Prop 8 vote was quite small. On a scale of 0 to 1, where 0 is no practical effect and 1 is a huge practical effect, the effect size is 0.15, far closer to zero than it is to one.[24]

California is neither the first nor the only state that has featured debates about same-sex marriage rights. The CMPS also asked a related question of all 4,563 respondents: Do you agree or disagree that the United States should have an amendment to the U.S. Constitution that bans same-sex marriage?[25] The chi-square results are consistent with those of California.

While only 36.5 percent of the CMPS voters overall agree with the ban (48.9 percent disagree overall), the effect of being a Millennial on this response question is even smaller than in California. The dif-ference between Millennials and older voters, using the same scale of 0 to 1, is 0.007.[26] Again, far closer to zero than to one. Moreover, disaggregating this question by race and ethnicity reveals that all four umbrella race groups of Millennials (African American, Asian American, Latino/a, and white) cluster around "neither agree/nor disagree" and "slightly disagree."[27] This additional evidence of weak support among Millennials is supplemented by the findings of the Pew Center for Research, which in its report, "Millennials: Confident, Connected and Open to Change," noted explicitly, "Their tolerance [on social value issues including what Pew calls 'gay marriage'] does not translate into outright approval."[28] Together, both the CMPS study, which surveyed a weighted sample of 514 Millennials, and the Pew Center study, which surveyed a sample of 527 Millennials, support the conclusion that Millennial voters are not the ATMs—Automatic Turn-key Messiahs—that some LGBT equality activists suggest they are,[29] particularly in a context of well-organized and effective opposition campaigns, fear-based advertising, and the polit-ical reality of a heightened public opinion threshold for many LGBT equality-oriented policies.

In a democracy, all you usually need in order to win any ballot initiative or election campaign is 50 percent + 1 vote in the final tally. The other half of the "demographic argument" favoring Millennials includes waiting for the older, more conservative part of the electorate to die off, thus increasing the percentage of Millennials in the voting pool. However, two recent studies of LGBT-friendly policies at the state level call that conventional wisdom into question when it comes to moving people on LGBT rights. Both authors found that public opinion must do more than *tilt* LGBT-friendly in order to generate policy change. For example, even when public support for changing the law is as high as *75 percent*, a prototypical statewide antidiscrimination housing policy has only a *50 percent* chance of passing into law.[30] In this current political climate, depending on a razor-thin distinction between Millennials and their older counterparts is politically perilous. Counting on demographic change among Millennials as either safe votes in the future or as a pool of future activists is not supported by the multiracial, eighteen-state voter sample of the CMPS.[31] Both the impact of being a Millennial versus part of the older generation and the weakness of support for marriage equality across a national sample suggest that the change will be achieved the old-fashioned way—using shoe-leather democracy to work for it, rather than wait for the passage of the older generation.

"THIS IS THE TRUE STORY" OF PROPOSITION 8

On May 16, 2008, the California State Supreme Court overturned California's Proposition 22, a statewide initiative that passed by a majority (61 percent) of voters in 2000. This initiative created a statute that read: "Only marriage between a man and a woman is valid or recognized in California." The court struck down the law, arguing that it violated the equal protection clause of the California state constitution.[32] This action, in effect, made same-sex marriage legal in California.

The celebration among advocates for same-sex marriage was tempered by an immediate announcement by their opponents of a push for a new statewide proposition, Proposition 8, which sought to amend Article I of the California constitution to include the previously unconstitutional language from Prop 22. While not common at either the state or the federal level, attempting to change the constitution is a perfectly legal response to a high-court decision if citizens or legislators disagree with the court's outcome. At the federal level, changing the constitution is subject to a high threshold, requiring a supermajority in order to ratify a change. In contrast, proponents of Prop 8 needed only a simple majority (50 percent +1) to amend the state constitution. With the introduction of Prop 8, both sides girded themselves for battle; concurrently, 18,000 same-sex couples took the plunge and got married between June and November 4, 2008. On November 4, 2008, the same night that the United States elected its first African American president, 52 percent of California voters also voted "Yes on 8," reinstituting the ban on same-sex marriages.

The irony, for marriage equality voters, set off a wide and bitter controversy, as CNN exit polls erroneously reported in the aftermath that 70 percent of African American voters in California voted in favor of Prop 8. According to a postelection voter analysis, in actuality 58 percent of African Americans voted for the passage of Prop 8, while 59 percent of Latinos, 49 percent of whites, and 48 percent of Asian American voters reported voting the same way.[33] Moreover, given the percentage of African American voters in California, it was statistically impossible for their votes to have been the difference in the vote on Prop 8.[34] Yet the CNN error lingered, as African Americans were widely perceived to be the cause of Prop 8's passage.

Prior to election day the Oppression Olympics were broadly visible in the black community, with Movement Backlash in full swing. Both sides of the African American community attempted to convert those likely Obama voters in the black community to their side for a vote on Prop 8. Obama had been dragged into the Prop 8 debate by Yes on 8 supporters who flooded black communities with misleading direct mail that suggested they had the presidential candidate on their side. No on 8 leaders managed to get a letter from Obama headquarters signed by the candidate reiterating his "No" position on 8, but left the dissemination of the letter and its message to the state National Association for the Advancement of Colored Peoples (NAACP), who received a budget of $200,000 for access to their mailing list and a one-time direct mail effort.[35]

Twelve days before the election African American religious leaders held dueling press conferences to broadcast their messages. Forty-seven pastors of predominantly African American and Latino congregations gathered in Los Angeles to share their support for Prop 8 and the movement to "Protect Marriage," using the very civil rights language coined by LGBT rights supporters to their own advantage, reframing who the real "victim" of the marriage debate was—children. Bishop Frank Stewart from Zoe Christian Fellowship of Los Angeles spoke candidly about claims of civil rights violations from gay advocates and reminded reporters that "children also have civil rights that deserve to be respected and not violated, and so do I as a parent and a grandparent."[36] Just a few miles away five African American and Latino leaders, including three pastors, stood inside the Lucy Florence Community Center in South Los Angeles on the same day to voice their opposition to both Prop 8 and the stereotype that African Americans are more homophobic than any other community. The difference in numbers and message was, of course, striking.

But what accounts for this striking difference? Part of the overwhelming advantage held by the Yes on 8 side in communities of color was based on prior reciprocal relationships established between the religious right and religious communities of color.[37] In 2008 the National Organization for Marriage (NOM), who helped lead the Yes on 8 charge, capitalized on preexisting relationships[38] between black churches and organizations from the religious right, like the Traditional Values Coalition, to partner with black megachurch pastors like Bishop Charles Blake of the West Angeles Church of God in Christ (COGIC) in Los Angeles. As the spiritual leader of the fifth-largest African American denomination in the United States, Blake incorporated language preventing same-sex marriages from ever being performed in COGIC institutions and instructed his flock through sermons about homosexuality that marriage is between a man and a woman.[39] The prevalence and depth of such relationships could not be matched, *largely because relationships of similar depth between African American religious organizations and LGBT marriage equality activists did not exist prior to 2008.*[40]

In lieu of such relationships the No on 8 campaign's approach to converting and turning out black No on 8 voters was predicated on two inaccurate assumptions about racial identity as a predictor of vote choice. First, several members of the leadership assumed, based on the damning evidence just presented, that African Americans were not worth the effort to organize because of their religion and their expressed resistance to framing marriage equality as a civil right. That is, some conflated African American resistance to the civil rights frame as resistance to marriage equality overall based on their presumed religious homophobia, failing to attend to the intersectional principles of Diversity Within or Time Dynamics.

Those who are familiar with the work on African American attitudes on marriage equality know that several researchers have noted the ineffectiveness of the "civil rights frame" for marriage equality among African American voters. The People for the American Way Foundation ran African American focus groups and discovered that marriage is constructed as a religious, not a civil practice among even the most ardent supporters of antidiscrimination.[41] The Arcus and Gill Foundations[42] collaborated on survey research that specifically explored African American resistance to the civil rights frame and found that African Americans use the term "civil rights" as an historical referent—not as an analytical concept. This usage practice is not unique to African Americans—we can make an analogy to the usage of the term "Holocaust" by the Jewish community. Just as the expression "Darfur Holocaust" or "Rwandan Holocaust" isn't really legible to the Jewish community because "Holocaust" is used as an historical reference, so, too, is "civil rights" for African Americans. So is marriage a civil right? Absolutely, under virtually any definition of the term. Will such language be legible to the masses of African Americans? Probably not.

Those who were more optimistic about African American attitudes veered to the opposite end of the spectrum and relied on an age-old stereotype: assuming a monolithic liberal ideology among African Americans that would logically include liberal attitudes on social issues like same-sex marriage because of the legacy of the civil rights movement in the 1960s. The logic is flawless—previous rights movements should support emerging ones. Moreover, it is the morally just thing to do.

Those more optimistic activists knew of the liberatory actions of historical civil rights church leaders like Martin Luther King, Jr.[43] and contemporary national figures like Jesse Jackson and Al Sharpton, but did not consider the ways in which an additional category of religiosity would complicate the presumed homogeneity of black voters. Religiosity, or how involved a person is with their faith organization, explained much of the variation among African American voters' positions on Prop 8, as those who attended services frequently were most likely to vote Yes on 8.[44] Thus, both the failure to attend to Diversity Within the racial community and the Time Dynamics of established relationships among groups hampered progress for the No on 8 organizers.

Following the election, the Oppression Olympics once again emerged with dueling accusations as the false CNN report took on a life of its own. African Americans were touted as the face of hypocrisy on equality and homophobia, and blamed for their Defiant Ignorance and a lack of solidarity with other movements for civil rights. The LGBT community was condemned for its Defiant Ignorance and lack of solidarity on matters of race and racial privilege, which was considered the root of the highly offensive superficial parallels to the civil rights movement. As we will see in the intersectional analysis that follows, the truth is not nearly as simple as the "black vs. LGBT" frame that emerges from the Oppression Olympics filter.

THE INTERSECTIONALITY CRITIQUE OF EQUALITY AS SAMENESS

Gender scholars' analyses of the marriage equality movement point out that attending solely to sexual orientation is neither theoretically sound nor politically prudent. How might attention to Categorical Multiplicity (the first dimension of paradigm intersectionality) change the approaches of the marriage equality groups seeking to build deep political solidarity with communities of color? In this section we will examine the way in which intersectionality challenges the political logic of "equality as sameness." Efforts to translate the legal logic of equality as sameness into politically potent frames in favor of marriage equality has largely failed in the African American community. A paradigm intersectionality analysis, which begins with deep attention to race and sexual orientation as processes of difference that require comparable depths of interrogation, illuminates the shift in the first-order question away from the Oppression Olympics style statement, "Gay is the New Black." In-depth attention to multiple categories of gender, sexual orientation, race, and class can empower marriage equality activists to step away from their uncritical dependence on arguments premised upon the logic of equality as sameness.[45]

Equality as Sameness: "We Are Just Like You, But for ... "[46]

Those who favor same-sex marriage rights often use the legal logic of precedent to ground their claims for marriage equality in public discourse. This strategy has included dependence on one famous and one not-so-famous legal precedent in which courts struck down state laws banning interracial marriage: *Loving v Virginia* (1967) and *Perez v Sharp* (1948).

In 1948 the California Supreme Court created one small stepping stone toward the nationwide invalidation of antimiscegenation laws that would eventually occur in 1967. *Perez v. Sharp* focused upon California's ban of interracial marriages between whites and other races, which had been in effect since California was admitted into the United States in 1850. Andrea Perez, a Mexican American woman who was classified for census purposes as white,[47] applied for a marriage license to marry her fiancé, Sylvester Davis, who was black. Writing for a 4–3 majority, Justice Roger Traynor concluded that these sections of the California Civil Code violated the equal protection clause of the Fourteenth Amendment to the U.S. Constitution. In so doing he held the state to the highest burden of proof—that such a law served a compelling government interest—ultimately concluding that the state of California's stated interests were not compelling at all.[48]

In 1967, when Chief Justice Earl Warren wrote the majority opinion for a unanimous United States Supreme Court in *Loving v Virginia*, *Perez* only received a footnote. Yet the facts of the case were similar. Mildred Jeter and Richard Loving got married in the District of Columbia, which permitted interracial marriages, and returned to their home state of Virginia only to be charged with violating Virginia's antimiscegenation law. In his opinion, Justice Warren was crystal clear:

> Marriage is one of the "basic civil rights of man," fundamental to our very existence and survival...To deny this fundamental freedom on so unsupportable a basis as the racial classifications embodied in these statutes, classifications so deeply subversive of the principle of equality at the heart of the fourteenth amendment, is surely to deprive all the state's citizens of liberty without due process of law. The fourteenth amendment requires that the freedom of choice to marry not be restricted by invidious racial discriminations. Under our Constitution, the freedom to marry or not marry, a person of another race, resides with the individual, and cannot be infringed by the state.[49]

Due both to its origins in California and the substance of the decision, same-sex marriage advocates who originally argued against Prop 22 contend that *Perez v Sharp* is a "landmark case" that provides ample evidence that marriage is a civil right to which all are entitled.[50] For them, however, what is most important about the case was Justice Traynor's conclusion that individuals have a right to marry the person of their choice.[51] Together *Perez* and *Loving* create a compelling precedent for marriage ban opponents to argue: 1) Marriage is a civil right. 2) Sexual orientation deserves the same level of protection as race when it comes to how states regulate marriage as a legal institution. Therefore, bans of same-sex marriage should be judged by the same yardstick as antimiscegenation laws. This legal logic is flawless—if we consider racial classifications odious, shouldn't we as a nation also consider sexual orientation classifications similarly odious? Many would answer yes to this question from a legal perspective, and it is at the heart of *Perry v Schwarzenegger*, the ongoing federal legal challenge to Prop 8 now making its way through the courts.

While this strategy has worked to some degree in the legal system,[52] it has had far less success in the larger political system, where it continues to be more controversial outside of the legal context. In her landmark work on intersectionality, Kimberle Williams Crenshaw distinguishes between structural (meaning legal, for our purposes) and political intersectionality.[53] While the basic premises of intersectionality remain the same in the political and legal contexts, they remain distinct contexts that potentially require different remedies. In the next section we'll examine the utility of the equality as sameness argument and its limitations in the broader political context.

Responses to civil rights frames of marriage equality and post-Prop 8 responses to media frames like "Gay Is the New Black" by straight and LGBT African Americans indicates trouble with the equality as sameness frame put forth by many advocates of marriage equality. Why, when removed from the legal arena, does this claim of equality as sameness and exchanging race for sexual orientation fail so spectacularly? While simply asking for comparably strict scrutiny to apply to classifications of sexual orientation makes sense as a legal strategy, its transition into the political world has caused more problems than it has solved. For those already privileged on multiple dimensions like race, class, or gender, being the "same" but for one difference (like sexual orientation) seems harmless at first glance, and tempting given its success in the legal arena for so many singularly identified groups. However, such an approach creates multiple challenges for building a movement and developing deep political solidarity. Exporting the equality of sameness argument has triggered a protective response to perceived cultural cooptation and missteps in representations that perpetuate stereotypes that the LGBT and black communities are mutually exclusive—the precise form of invisibility Crenshaw lamented in her construction of political intersectionality. Both outcomes can be avoided by greater usage of paradigm intersectionality.

Using Categorical Multiplicity and Time Dynamics concurrently in a paradigm intersectionality analysis illuminates why the civil rights frames of marriage equality and equality as sameness logic are resisted. Issues of cultural co-optation lie under the surface of many African American communities based on their prior group experiences with the mechanisms of co-optation that can lead to shallow politics and nonexistent alliances with the people whose ideas, histories, or practices are being borrowed or taken.[54] One site where this discourse continues is among African Americans who advocate more accurate or progressive representations of black masculinity and femininity in hip-hop culture. Author Kenyon Farrow takes both mainstream and so-called conscious rappers to task for allowing their music to be co-opted:

> None of these artists interrogate their representations of masculinity in their music, but merely perform them for street credibility. And for white market consumption.
>
> It cannot be taken lightly that white men are in control of the record industry as a whole (even with a few black entrepreneurs), and control what images get played. Young white suburban males are the largest consumer of hip-hop music. So performance of black masculinity (or black sexuality as a whole) is created by white men for white men. And since white men have always portrayed black men as sexually dangerous and black women as always sexually available (and sexual violence against black women is rarely taken seriously), simplistic representations of black sexuality as hyper-heterosexual are important to maintaining white supremacy and patriarchy, and control of black bodies.[55]

Though conversations about the co-optation of hip-hop are not as often concerned with homophobia as they should be, the cultural co-optation frame of the black public sphere remains chronically available to black voters, including black voters in California. Attention to Time Dynamics by chronicling recent California initiative politics can explain the ongoing sensitivity.

In 1996 California voters amended the state constitution by passing Proposition 209, which banned close to all affirmative action policies in the state of California. Entitled "The California Civil Rights Initiative" in a cynical attempt to lure less-informed voters (including many African Americans) to vote for it, the campaign featured Ward Connerly and others hijacking the civil rights language of Martin Luther King, Jr., resulting in the passage of the proposition.[56] These efforts were preceded in 1994 by immigrant rights activists of Latino and Asian American descent who framed their opposition to California's Proposition 187 as an attack on their civil rights as well,[57] and the proposition passed by majority vote. Now fast forward to 2008, only three presidential elections later, and another group, stereotypically perceived and visually represented as all white, used claims of civil rights to get African Americans to vote their way. In a cultural context where fear of cooptation persists, such a frame was doomed to fail.

Even without having Prop 209 clearly in mind twelve years later, black voters were treated to a Halloween display that received national attention for its violence against women in the West Hollywood enclave adjacent to Los Angeles. West Hollywood, a city widely known for its progressivism on LGBT issues, does not possess a similar reputation for racial progressivism in the black community. A gay male couple hung Republican vice-presidential candidate Sarah Palin in effigy a week before the United States had the opportunity to elect its first black president. The symbol of the noose has a profoundly negative association in black communities, and while no polling data about black response to the Sarah Palin effigy is available to date, this matter has been posited by black authors who support marriage equality as evidence that black communities interpret it as the "true feelings" of the LGBT community about African American civil rights. These authors suggest that framing marriage as a civil right is more than a conceptual conceit, issue frame, or lexical flourish. For black activists, use of the civil rights frame obligates a group to implement the core principles of the movement and to understand comprehensively the people and the history associated with it[58] prior to any expectation of solidarity in terms of votes.

Based on this brief exploration of Categorical Multiplicity and Time Dynamics, further examination of the risks of cultural co-optation and shallow civil rights politics are warranted. Comprehensive familiarity with multiple categories allows activists to foresee these risks in advance of their occurrence and to best decipher resistance—is it resistance to an issue frame (e.g., marriage is a civil right)? Or is it resistance to equality more substantially? Quite obviously marriage rights groups can't police Halloween displays, but understanding why a display featuring a noose has such a profoundly negative impact on a community where solidarity with the LGBT community is in a nascent stage can empower white marriage equality activists to work differently to educate their own racial communities in partnership with their communities-of-color counterparts.

Visually Representing the LGBT Community: Help or Harm?

The Real World created a stir during the San Francisco season when it aired the final episode of the season, which featured a commitment ceremony between castmate Pedro Zamora and his African American partner Sean Sasser. Since his death in 1994, a 2009 film, *Pedro* was written to commemorate Pedro's life by Dustin Lance Black, the Oscar-winning writer of *Milk*, a chronicle of Harvey Milk's life and untimely death. These visual representations of LGBT love and relationships are now joined by a host of reality shows, openly gay talk show host Ellen DeGeneres, and an MTV-owned cable network,

LOGO, that is committed to LGBT-friendly programming. In sum there are now many visual representations of the LGBT community. But how can we examine the more politically oriented representations? A paradigm intersectionality analysis of how the equality as sameness logic was visually mobilized on both sides of the LGBT rights debate will further reveal its double-edged political ramifications. In this section I extend the queer of color analysis introduced by Roderick Ferguson in order to examine how the equality as sameness logic is politically vulnerable to Defiant Ignorance and Movement Backlash. The next section then briefly articulates how attention to Categorical Multiplicity, Diversity Within, Time Dynamics and Individual Institutional Relationships can produce attention to complexity that can produce alternative frames of marriage equality.

The way a political issue is framed has long been demonstrated to influence public opinion. In this area of research, issue framing has both inter- and intraracial effects. From an interracial perspective, the social constructions of the people who are the subject of policy debates (whether welfare recipients, HIV/AIDS patients, immigrants, etc.) influence public opinion on policy remedies. Specifically, there are significant differences across racial groups on the "deservingness" of certain groups, and thus support of public policies on their be-half. More recently such effects have also been found intraracially, providing further evidence of Diversity Within racial groups. For example, issue frames of HIV/AIDS have been shown to shape the intraracial attitudes of African Americans toward black gay and bi-sexual men.[59]

The visual representations of LGBT rights have long struggled to fully represent the Diversity Within the community. Media accounts following the celebrated Stonewall Uprising greatly underrepresented people of color and transgender people who participated in the trans-formative resistance.[60] These struggles with representation, at times a result of exclusionary practice and at times part of the tyranny of the closet,[61] have been more recently the source of debate in the LGBT community and the material of political demonization within the evangelical Christian Community.

Two recent representations, one from each side of the marriage de-bate, prove instructive. In the 1990s, the Traditional Values Coalition produced a documentary targeting black church audiences entitled *Gay Rights, Special Rights*. It constructed the LGBT community as white and upper class, with sexual "preferences" deemed clearly at odds with the pure, chaste, Black religious folk.[62] Using scriptural references to the equality of sameness argument, the Christian right understood that Black religious communities, like many broader black communities, adopt more conservative social norms in a bid for the precise but false promise of assimilation and full inclusion previously denied to them.[63] This politics of respectability, closely tied for over a century to the concept of "uplifting the race" among African Americans, is alluring precisely because black communities also associate the concept of uplifting the race with the perception that the black family is an institution under attack from various threats—slavery, various agencies of child and family services, the prison-industrial complex, as well as the gang and drug wars. With fluency in this history, those pushing the anti-same-sex marriage frame position the struggle for LGBT people (represented as upper-class white gay males) as just the latest assault on the black family. This frame then cues the protective traditions of strength and survival in the face of group threat[64] in black discursive spaces and religious institutions, producing Movement Backlash.[65]

Compare this politically motivated documentary and its appeal to an equality of sameness frame on the dimension of religion to the journalistic intent behind a 2008 *New York Times Magazine* cover story featuring two young white upper-class males as the quintessential couple disadvantaged by gay marriage bans.[66] The largely positive story, complete with photos, also used the equality of sameness logic that legal advocates of LGBT equality promote. It is critical to note that both sides of the political spectrum represent those denied the right to marry as white, upper class, and male.[67] This ongoing misrepresentation of gay marriage as a practice for white upper-class males only creates two serious, ongoing obstacles. First, its coupling with the equality of sameness frame by the Christian right obliterates the new and far less intuitive equality as sameness frame articulated through a comparison of LGBT rights to the African American civil rights struggle. The second obstacle is similarly troubling: it continues to render the complex relationship many groups have to marriage as an institution and the ambivalence surrounding its use as a gateway to freedom. Together the two continue to perpetuate larger stereotypes in black communities that have been fanned by earlier operatives and can continue to swing votes away from LGBT-friendly policies. The next section of the chapter will demonstrate that the change in frame, not just the faces delivering the message, is critical.

The institution of marriage has been historically harmful to women as a group[68] and women are, of course, a major sector of the LGBT community. Also relevant for our purposes, heterosexual marriage has historically been positioned as an often impossible standard for the "inherently deviant" black family to meet, creating both a respect for the sexual norms of the dominant culture by those aspiring to assimilation and full inclusion[69] and an invisibility among those whose practices were neither heterosexual nor in pursuit of marriage.[70] The equality of sameness frame fosters Defiant Ignorance of the harms this frame can present to diverse members of the LGBT community, who relate to the institution of marriage in vastly different ways.[71] Attention to both Categorical Multiplicity, defined earlier as the development of comprehensive experiential knowledge of more than one category, and Diversity Within can counteract and prevent repetitions of past mistakes.

When marriage equality activists read analyses that focus solely on sexual orientation as a single, isolated cause for marginalization and fail to develop literacy and fluency with race, gender, and class they cannot adequately represent their entire community. African American LGBT activist Mattie Richardson articulates this difficulty:

> Every time white lesbian and gay leaders trot out some well-heeled homosexual couple who own their own homes, have six figure salaries, and live the American dream, they do violence to the numerous forms of intimate arrangements and loving parenting that do not conform to mainstream ideas. For example, not so long ago my partner and I accepted the challenge of caring for my teenaged nephew. During that time I had to interact with several state and local agencies that did not recognize us as a legitimate family even though I am a close blood relative...[72]

Attending to Diversity Within can reveal challenges like that articulated by Richardson, who does not personally *want* to get married. Further, attending to Time Dynamics in conjunction with Diversity Within can also reveal that the religious homophobia displayed in the African American community is connected to the *same* kinds of misrepresentations. In other words, the homophobia (and far too often it is *indeed* homophobia) is dependent on the same visual representation of homosexuality.

Advocating for marriage without attention to the negative impact of the equality as sameness logic reinforces the Defiant Ignorance and Movement Backlash elements of the Oppression Olympics. In discussing the same *New York Times Magazine* piece, feminist theorist Lori J. Marso argues that those who support same-sex couples' right to be married should "interrogate how the politics of marriage as legitimization of marriage...further entrenches not only consumerist but also (and even more troubling) very conservative sexual, as well as racist and class-based norms of bourgeois behavior."[73] Attending to Categorical Multiplicity, Time Dynamics, and Diversity Within can go beyond simply fostering greater knowledge among marriage equality groups to also help avoid pitfalls in the future. But not making mistakes isn't the goal of the LGBT movement—full equality is.

Intersectionally Leveraging *Loving* and *Perez*

As I noted in the introduction to this chapter, many justice-seeking groups and leaders express ambivalence about whether discussions about "race" are productive for coalitions. Similarly, discussions about "sexuality" receive the same reception. But engaging in meaningful discussions and joint activism to combat racism in the LGBT community and homophobia in the African American community is essential to forward movement. Rather than settle for the reflective glow of earlier movements, reconceptualizing how to frame marriage as an intersectional proposition will remove previous obstacles to the building of concrete alliances grounded in deep political solidarity. In contrast to the debilitating impact of the equality as sameness argument, prior intersectionality research has revealed that cultivating a practice of recognizing the ways in which the dimensions of paradigm intersectionality work simultaneously to create different patterns of vulnerability and relationships to power, and navigating that multiplicity and diversity, far from threatening the purity of purpose or health of the coalition, actually facilitated participants' "subjective sense of responsibility for each other" and their commitments to caring for particular identity groups.[74] Through group-based activities that cultivate Altruism, Consideration, Cooperation, Cultural Empathy, Emotional Stability, Fairness, Flexibility, Open-Mindedness, Social Initiative, and Trustworthiness deep political solidarity can germinate. But knowing how to avoid using the wrong frame is only part of the plan; in a majoritarian society cultivating allies and building egalitarian coalitions are not only desirable but also critical.

While the freedom of individuals to choose whom they marry articulated in *Loving* and *Perez* has intuitive appeal, a paradigm intersectionality analysis directs us to deepen our analysis to consider Categorical Multiplicity, Diversity Within, Categorical Intersections, Time Dynamics, and Individual-Institutional Relationships. One of the promised benefits of paradigmatic intersectionality is its capacity for revealing unlikely or counterintuitive coalition partners. This case study is no different; in this section I focus on cultivating straight African American women as allies using an intersectional rather than equality as sameness approach. This intersectional approach would examine the patterns of vulnerability and relationships to the state that affect straight black women's and the LGBT community's prospects for marriage.

Straight black women might seem far removed from a fight for LGBT marriage equality, until one recognizes that black women, who are mostly single, wield a considerable amount of aggregated power in the black community. Even if they are infrequently the pastors of churches, they are the backbones of most independent churches and sit on boards who hire (and fire) pastors. Collectively, their tithes often bankroll church activities—again, an economic power that is rarely used but nevertheless present. Last but certainly not least, young black women's turnout has not only grown substantially since 1972, but in 2000 and 2004 their turnout matched (statistically speaking) their young white female counterparts,[75] and black women of all ages consistently turn out to vote at higher rates than do black men,[76] even in the 2008 election, when black voter turnout spiked.[77] While the analysis of the CMPS demonstrated that we cannot *assume* that young black women are the ATMs of marriage equality, cocreating messages with black women's groups can build deep political solidarity, a broader and more reliable strategy than attempting to break the bonds that many major black religious leaders have with the religious right on this issue.

By no means is an alliance with single straight black women a magic bullet for the LGBT community's fight for marriage equality. Moreover, we can't assume that marriage is an equal priority across all races, sexual orientations, or ages.[78] But intersectionally leveraging *Perez* and *Loving* in the twenty-first century reveals why such women can be an as-yet untapped part of the solution. In order to examine the possibility, we will reframe the interracial marriage situation originating in *Loving* and *Perez* by applying Categorical Multiplicity, Categorical Intersection, Time Dynamics, and Individual-Institutional Relationships.

Instead of assuming that the 1967 Loving decision means the same thing to all people for all time, we must examine how the court's decision has shaped marriage rates and, more importantly, the intraracial debate about marriage rates of black women and black men.[79] While overall attitudes toward interracial marriage have become drastically more positive over time[80] among all races, some race-gender groups are more likely to participate in interracial marriages than others for a variety of reasons. Asian American women are most likely to marry outside of their race (40 percent), followed by 25 percent of Latinos of either gender and 22 percent of black men.[81] By contrast only 9 percent of black women reported marrying outside of their race.[82] Combine these recent findings with prior analyses, which demonstrate that between 1950 and 2000 the number of black women who are married dropped from 62 percent to 36.1 percent, and we begin to see a more complicated picture.[83]

There have been far too many academic and popular culture examinations of such statistics regarding black women's marriageability to chronicle here. Moreover, I don't mean to imply that black women are any more desperate to be married than any other part of the population. But part of the explanation for such low interracial marriage numbers among black women is the low numbers of black women who are married overall and the Pew Center's concurrent finding that family acceptance of interracial marriage drops by 15 percent when the person coming into the family is black (to 66 percent) versus another race.[84]

Armed with this information, how should groups seek to build bridges about "marriage equality for all" with single straight African American women voters? Instead of beginning with an equality as sameness frame that would feature an uncritical valorization of interracial marriage, it would pose a different question that opens a discussion that stops being polite and starts getting real: What unintended consequences did *Loving* have on African American women as a group, despite the fact that one of the original plaintiffs, Mildred Jeter Loving, was a black woman? Examining those unintended consequences by analyzing multiple categories in depth and the intersection of race, gender, and sexuality leads to the next "real" question: what unintended consequences did this decision have on the entire LGBT community?

Although intersectional framing avoids the pitfall of discussing *Loving* in rights-based language, which frames LGBT folks as seeking a golden ticket, the analysis is still capable of revealing straight privilege. It is still possible to view the Supreme Court's invalidation of the remaining antimiscegenation laws as an institutional change for straight whites and blacks only, given the institutional configuration and implementation of marriage rights in the years since *Loving*. What is distinct in this discussion is how this outcome is framed *as a political connector* of racism, sexism, and heterosexism, as LGBT activist Priya Kandasharma suggests:

> I would disagree with your assumption that love is actually at the foundation of the institution of marriage. Rather, I would argue that

marriage is a legal institution that is fundamentally about preserving property relations. Not only does the marriage contract have its historical roots in the ownership and exchange of women, but it has been a key mechanism though which material wealth has been kept within particular families. In addition, the centrality of anti-miscegenation [93] laws in U.S. history also demonstrates the ways that marriage has functioned to police racial borders and preserve white privilege.[85]

Discussing race and sexuality *together* instead of in an either/or framework allows both marriage equality and straight black women's groups to learn that race and sexual orientation are intertwined as intersecting phenomena that *simultaneously* convey *undeserved* privilege and stigma. It is recognition of the simultaneous privilege and stigma that facilitates intersectional consciousness at the group level in a way that inoculates the group from the anxiety and fear of the Diversity Within both groups, which further facilitates deep political solidarity.

It is only *after* conversations such as these are conducted *successfully* that messaging and other shared work can begin. I argue for successfully engaging in these *prior* conversations based, in part, on my experience in helping to produce thirty-eight two-minute public service announcements (PSAs) for the Courage Campaign, entitled, "The Wedding Matters." Executive producer Valerie Alexander did an amazing job of corralling about thirty couples, their families, friends, and clergy to talk about same-sex weddings that did occur in the brief window between May and November 2008. Based on prior research by the Courage Campaign, Alexander was encouraged to pursue an equality as sameness frame: "our weddings are just like everyone else—we cut the cake, we wanted our parents there," etc.— and many of the spots convey this point brilliantly.

But this equality as sameness frame again did not succeed with likely African American voters, even when the people presenting the frame were also African American. I showed a few of the African American–subject PSAs to a group of twenty-five likely African American female voters who were enrolled in an intensive course in political leadership.[86] The spot featuring a gay black male couple with the youngest of their five adopted children was most negatively received as "artificial"—from the aesthetics of the camera shot to the daughter seeming like she was coached to repeat the intended equality as sameness message. This spot garnered far more negative responses than an interracial female couple, where the African American wife, Karla, talked about how her Southern Baptist parents from Texas had told her they would not attend the wedding under any circumstances but in the end they came. Rather than focus solely on sexual orientation, Karla also talked about race; she talked about how her parents grew up in segregated South Carolina, and that made all the difference. The question for this audience wasn't what makes gay couples "just like us, *but for*" in terms of a wedding, nor were they trying to exchange being "gay" for being "black" but how Karla was both/ and—how racial identity and connections to the community were still salient in her family's lives even as she was out of the closet and getting married—connecting Categorical Multiplicity and Categorical Intersection.[87]

The mixed reactions to the Courage Campaign videos are an excellent example of why media frames should be derived from grassroots leadership. Social movement experts Manuel Pastor and Rhonda Ortiz agree: "While there is a tendency to think that this can be provided externally, it is important for groups to have their own capacities. It is also important that the 'frame' be derived from grassroots leaders rather than transplanted in by messaging experts who depend on focus groups rather than on the groups themselves."[88] The pair goes on to discuss research as a journey of shared inquiry into the processes that produce the conditions in which we live, demonstrating a larger purpose for the research than just getting the right message, a purpose that can include building deep political solidarity.

Through the process of analyzing unintended consequences and structural realities that go beyond any one group's control, single straight African American women, who have spent plenty of time analyzing their own situation, can understand better the structural barriers the LGBT community faces. For example, in chapter 2 I introduced the concept of serial collectives using the example of people waiting in line for the bus.[89] If we think about race, class, gender, and sexual orientation as *more* than the identities that we have as individuals—indeed, if we think of them as sociopolitical institutions that organize us into smaller chunks of a mass society, then we can see how people have the ability to plug into these collectives, *but in predetermined ways* that indicate attention to the complexity captured by the Individual-Institutional Relations aspect of intersectionality. In the states where laws and/or state constitutions define marriage as an institution for heterosexuals only, the serial collective of "married couple" is structurally unavailable to the LGBT community. That's not a bus they're allowed to ride, no matter what, as long as they identify and act publicly as lesbian or gay. Members of the LGBT community and their allies can choose to contest such laws, vote with their feet by leaving the jurisdiction, or do nothing at all. But the option of same-sex marriage in these jurisdictions is categorically unavailable. This unintended consequence of *Loving* interacts with other cultural narratives in the black community to make black LGBT people invisible, and has an impact on the entire community. Black women can thus assist in reframing same-sex marriage from a "threat to the black family" to an expansion of what we mean by black family.[90]

Similarly, LGBT folks can understand the unintended consequences of *Loving* affecting the structural barriers faced by straight African American women for marriage. Although straight black women are "free," according to *Loving*, to marry whomever they choose, other structural realities influence the abilities of these women to exercise that freedom—low rates of outmarriage among black women, far too many black men in prisons, and far too few in school. Certainly there is an important qualitative difference between having the legal freedom and exercising said freedom, but there are also a number of commonalities of limits on the freedom under consideration that can serve as a starting point for conversation.

These phenomena that individual black women must contend with are not simply present for them as single straight women who might be seeking a mate, but as mothers, sisters, aunts, and grandmothers. Similarly, the freedom to marry someone of the same sex may not affect all LGBT people in an identical way, but may have unintended consequences, like the trouble Mattie Richardson had with social services. An intersectional process of message identification that explores a theme of policy consequences, broadly defined, can foster a number of opportunities for solidarity—on marriage equality, yes, but also on prison reform, educational reform, social services reform, and presumably other issues.

The paradigm intersectionality analysis has provided one possible solution to the pitfalls of the equality of sameness legal logic so far. Intersectionally leveraging *Loving* can also help to prepare individual members of both groups to provide a more welcoming context for African American LGBT folks to come out fully as African American LGBT, not one or the other. The second outcome of a paradigm intersectionality analysis of Prop 8 reveals the invisibility of the African American LGBT community in an equality of sameness context—the exchange of "gay" for "black" is, as Crenshaw's original formulation of political intersectionality postulates, a barrier to obtaining the relevant social justice remedies. Using their blogs and public works as narratives, African American LGBT authors and activists are privileged here so as to allow them to speak for themselves. In so doing they speak to multiple centers of power, demanding reforms that acknowledge the political reality of their existence in both African American and LGBT communities.

INTERSECTIONAL INVISIBILITY AND HYPERVISIBILITY

There have been two black gay males on *The Real World*, the second of whom came out of the closet after his season ended. Anissa, the openly bisexual woman of color, was the only out woman of color on the program. All three presented distinct substantive representations of what it means to be a member of the African American and LGBT communities at the same time. An in-depth history of African American LGBT communities in the United States is beyond the scope of this chapter. Instead I focus my attention on black authors and bloggers focused on marriage equality debates, which means that long-celebrated black LGBT authors like James Baldwin and Audre Lorde are decentered in this particular chapter.[91] In this section I want to foreground the Categorical Intersection aspect of paradigm intersectionality in order to highlight LGBT African Americans' analysis of same sex marriage. As I noted in chapter 2, reframing metaphorical intersections as dynamic centers of both invisibility and hypervisibility expands intersectionality's utility as an antidote to the Oppression Olympics.

Foregrounding the analyses of the African American LGBT community provides further evidence of the interactive relationships between the dimensions of paradigm intersectionality and simultaneously provides tremendous evidence for why rendering the invisible visible is so incredibly important. Their analyses and critiques of marriage equality's oversized role on the LGBT agenda are reflective of qualitatively distinct relationships to the state. The interrogations and confrontations with multiple axes of power further mark the end of being polite in favor of honest conversation, with the ultimate goal of finding promising points of connection, collaboration, and coalition.

Discursive institutions within mainstream and targeted interest media perpetuate the intersectional invisibility of African American LGBT people by perpetuating a unitary, single category analysis of the same-sex marriage debate. Following on the heels of the controversy generated by the flawed CNN exit poll, a controversial headline in *The Advocate*, the self-described "leading gay news and entertainment magazine in the U.S." further perpetuated conflict. "Gay Is the New Black," the title given to white author Michael Jay Gross's article, again emblematized the hegemony of the equality as sameness legal logic in nonlegal discursive contexts. The one-to-one exchange coined by the headline was also reflected throughout the article; despite a nod to having black LGBT friends the argument positioned "gays" as exclusively nonblack and "blacks" as exclusively straight.[92] Referring to an earlier example in a non-LGBT media outlet, author Kenyon Farrow articulates the impact of such superficiality in the media and the invisibility it imposes upon him as a marginalized member of both communities:

> What struck me about the front-page story was the fact that all of the average Atlanta citizens who were pictured that opposed gay marriages were black people. This is not to single out the *Atlanta Journal Constitution*, as I have noticed in all of the recent coverage and hubbub over gay marriage that the media has been real crucial [*sic*] in playing up the racial politics of the debate.
>
> For example, the people who are in San Francisco getting married are almost exclusively white whereas many of the people who are shown opposing it are black. And it is more black people than typically shown in the evening news (not in handcuffs). This leaves me with several questions: Is gay marriage a black/white issue? Are the Gay Community and the Black Community natural allies or sworn enemies? And where does that leave me, a black gay man, who does not want to get married?[93]

Bloggers Derrick Mathis (U.S.) and Renee Martin (UK) explicitly reject the equality as sameness argument underlying "Gay Is the New Black," by exposing the underlying invisible norm of white privilege within its logic. Martin does so explicitly via revelation of Categorical Intersections that takes the competitive aspects of the Oppression Olympics head on:

> As long as there are those that are both gay and black, gay can never be the new black. It is white privilege that causes this issue to be framed in this way. Powerful white leaders in the gay and lesbian community have so over-valued whiteness that they have failed to see the racism that is inherent in this kind of organizing. No study can measure which is worse, because black gays and lesbians do exist.
>
> The GLB community frame organizing [*sic*] around a desire to achieve equality, but the question we fail to ask is equality for whom. The white elite of the GLB community do not seek equality with people of colour, they seek equality with white cisgendered heterosexuals, which is problematic. Continually we see the argument of "we are just

like you", however, the "you" in question is necessarily white, afflu-
ent and largely male. There is this sense that certain people are being
robbed of their ability to properly benefit from white privilege because
of homophobia.[94]

Allowing privilege to remain invisible facilitates the Oppression
Olympics because it permits superficial discussions that do not
address the connectivity of problems faced and distributions of privilege. Mathis, who shares the same complex differential perspective as Martin, goes further to lament the failure yet again of the
white members of his LGBT community to overcome their Willful
Blindness. "Gay Is the New Black" was also rejected by *Huffington
Post* blogger David Kaufman and ESPN/CNN contributing writer
LZ. Granderson. All of these authors reject the invisibility imposed
by the provocative claim, taking to Web 2.0 to demand recognition
that they are both/and, not either/or. Mathis and Kauffman in particular push the LGBT leadership to see the intersection and drop their
Willful Blindness in order to reduce the secondary marginalization
African American LGBT communities suffer due to white privilege
in the LGBT community. They demand, in its place, comprehensive
attention to the Diversity Within the LGBT community.

Yet the LGBT community is not the only one that perpetrates
invisibility. Black culture demands a "don't ask, don't tell" approach
to being a part of the community,[95] which at earlier points in twentieth-century history could have been seen as relatively tolerant, but
certainly not solidaristic. Ferguson argues that Harlem Renaissance
author Richard Wright's 1937 essay, "Blueprint for Negro Writing,"
conceptualized the white patron/black artist relationship in heteronormative terms even as he encouraged African Americans to "shirk
[their] bourgeois notions of progress."[96] Stories of Bayard Rustin,
architect of the civil rights movement's nonviolent strategies, being
asked to refrain from engaging in relationships with men are now
well established as causes for his erasure from popular histories of the
civil rights movement. In the African American community, LGBT
African Americans are subtly and overtly convinced to pursue a practice similar to what Asian American scholar Kenji Yoshino has called
"covering" in relationship to mainstream society.[97] Even if they come
out of the closet, they are told or warned to not "flaunt it"—that is,
LGBT African Americans should perform blackness exactly like the
rest of the community does. The community is willing to provide
conditional acceptance for LGBT African Americans—as long as
they are willing to "wear the mask" in their own racial community.

Tragically, there are also countless cases of violence (threatened and enacted) against black LGBT individuals within the black community, and their importance to the intellectual cause of African American Studies is similarly rendered invisible. The brutal murder of 15-year-old Sakia Gunn in Newark, New Jersey, has been under-theorized by black feminist theory's failure to grapple deeply with heterosexual privilege.[98] Similarly, reports of the 2009 suicide of 11-year-old Carl Hoover-Walker in Springfield, Massachusetts, following sexuality-based bullying by African American popular culture website Bossip.com generated multiple comments accusing it of hypocrisy in reporting on the death. Three comments were particularly emblematic of this trend:

> Yea bossip you guys are the main one making side jokes about gays, so don't act like you care now! You guys add to this problem we are facing today!

> Why all of a sudden bloggers are trying to give sympathy when THIS very blog put that little boy standing next to Bey [R&B star Beyonce] on blast because of the way he posed. This is the very ignorant shit that kids are exposed to. I have made many a comment about Bey but once that post came up, I didn't have anything to say because it's someone's child, brother, nephew, cousin, grandson, that people are making negative, uncalled for comments about because him and many other young boys don't act the norm. I feel for the parent of this innocent child that felt he had to take his own life in order to get away from the cruel taunting. There is no excuse for the school faculty not to take action once the mom complained. This is so sad. Rest in peace baby because GOD loves you know matter what!

> Aw bossip, don't try and act like you got a conscience all of a sudden. We all know You, [sic] and more than half your readers are just as homophobic as the ignorant children who tormented this boy. So spare me your fraudulent sympathy.

I cannot be certain of the racial identity of these commenters, but each of these comments carries the same message: Bossip contributes to the culture of homophobia in the African American community that allows tragic outcomes like this to occur. Perhaps more tragically, a search of traditional black publications like *Jet* and *Ebony* revealed they did not cover the suicide at all. This demand for "covering" and the threat of violence when blackness is not performed according to heterosexist norms imbues straight African Americans with heterosexual privilege that is both undeserved and embodied in institutions within and outside the African American community.

Acceptance of this privilege provides a tempting gateway for straight African Americans to assimilate into mainstream America,[99] but most often this gateway is not the path to full equality it is advertised to be.

The narratives I've analyzed in this section so far illustrate the claim that many LGBT African Americans do not feel completely accepted and represented in either the general LGBT community or the African American community. I also alluded to sets of historical "bleaching" practices in the previous section on visual representations of the LGBT community by anti-LGBT and LGBT communities alike, including the visual legacy of the 1969 Stonewall riots, a mobilizing flashpoint for the LGBT rights movement, that has typically been represented as an exclusively white uprising instead of the multiracial act of resistance that it was.[100] True to Crenshaw's original formulation of political intersectionality, LGBT African Americans disappear from calculations and representations on the LGBT and the African American agendas.

Yet as I noted in chapter 2, paradigm intersectionality constructs Categorical Intersections as a dimension with two distinguishing features. First the intersections involve hypervisibility as well as invisibility of those marginalized as the metaphorical intersections. Second, such intersections are dynamic sites of politics—that is, due to its engagement with the Time Dynamics dimension of paradigm intersectionality, neither visibility nor hypervisibility is a permanent status. The ramifications of this analysis suggest that the rite of "coming out" as LGBT, a practice first proposed in the 1860s, functions to produce both invisibility and hypervisibility for African Americans who come out and seek to live as full members of the LGBT community.[101] LGBT African Americans who do come out into the broader LGBT community do not just face invisibility; often they are hypervisible in LGBT enclaves that remain predominantly upper class, white, and male. This hypervisibility, particularly for gay black men, can repeatedly produce two experiences: reduction of one's entire identity to one's genitals (sexual objectification)[102] or social exclusion and discrimination based on race, which can include slow or no service in white LGBT-friendly restaurants and bars[103] and patterns of residential segregation that persist in LGBT enclaves.[104] Both have long historical records associated with being hypervisible in a nonblack context even as the men share sexual-orientation identities with their nonblack counterparts.

The narratives presented here and the dynamism of the intersections also suggest that LGBT African Americans have not simply endured such conditions in silence or in paralysis. They have spoken up and acted out to hold LGBT and African American leaders accountable for their relationships with the black LGBT community. In so doing, such authors "get real" by speaking to multiple centers of power, to which I now turn.

Speaking to Multiple Centers of Power

African American LGBT authors and activists suggest a kind of dual coming out that is just as politically potent but speaks to multiple centers of power with which they routinely grapple. ESPN sports columnist LZ Granderson, who is out of the closet, connects some of the aforementioned historical realities to present-day ones in Chicago and Atlanta:

> The line to get in [to The Prop House in Chicago] usually stretches down the block and unlike many of the clubs in Boystown and Andersonville, this one plays hip-hop and caters to men who may or may not openly identify as gay, but without question are black and proud...Bars such as The Prop House, or Bulldogs in Atlanta, Georgia exist because a large number of gay blacks—particularly those who date other blacks and live in the black community—do not feel a part of the larger gay movement. There are Gay Pride celebrations and there are Black Gay Prides.[105]

Mattie Udora Richardson echoes this reluctance to join the mainstream LGBT community and provides suggestions for how black LGBT folks should engage on equal footing with what is now commonly called "Gay, Inc."[106] in the blogosphere: "Until we as black queer people speak our own truths, what passes for gay rights will do very little for us. Let's not jump on the white lesbian and gay bandwagon without assessing our own political needs and goals."[107] Her colleague Marlon Bailey agrees: "Black queers should be highly skeptical of any movement where we are being asked to jump on the bandwagon because at the end of the day, we are not the ones who stand to gain anything."[108]

While the excerpts from Granderson, Richardson, and Bailey are addressed to the mainstream white upper-class LGBT center of power, authors Kenyon Farrow and Mignon Moore speak to the African American center for power, cueing especially the relationships of invisibility and hypervisibility LGBT African Americans face in the context of Individual-Institutional Relationships. As I noted before, Farrow takes not only select hip-hop artists to task but here notes how homosexuals who are black in this case are represented as threats to rather than full members of the black community:

> The song [DMX's "Where the Hood At?"] suggests that the "faggot" can and will never be part of the "hood" for he is not a man. The song and video are particularly targeted at black men who are not out of the closet, and considered on the "down low…" But it's not just "commercial" rap artists being homophobic. "Conscious" hip-hop artists such as Common, Dead Prez and Mos Def have also promoted homophobia through their lyrics, mostly around notions of "strong black families," and since gay black men (in theory) do not have children, we are somehow anti-family and antithetical to what a "strong black man" should be.
>
> Lesbians (who are not interested in performing sex acts for the pleasure of men voyeurs) are also seen as anti-family, and not a part of the black community. A woman "not wanting dick" in a nation where black dick is the only tangible power symbol for black men is seen as just plain crazy, which is also expressed in many hip-hop tunes…
>
> Black people are merely the unfortunate middlemen in an exchange between white men. We consume the representations like the rest of America. And the more that black people are willing to accept these representations as fact rather than racist fiction, the more heightened homophobia in our communities tends to be.[109]

Moore notes that activists and scholars alike believe that coming out in the black community can only help the cultural climate to improve further,[110] but doing so remains a daunting practice for those who wish to remain in churches and neighborhoods of African descent. In Los Angeles, Moore further asserts that local African American LGBT organizations focus more on relationships with the mainstream LGBT community than they do building bridges to the straight African American community, and so this intraracial work remains the challenge of individual LGBT African Americans rather than any systematic effort.[111] In other words, the results stop short of deep political solidarity.

LGBT African Americans don't focus on any single center of power exclusively, nor do they reserve their critiques for African American and LGBT elites only. Instead, a broader discussion of patterns of relationship to the state are just as incredibly important for setting the political agenda within the mainstream political system. In the same discussion of same-sex marriage where he cautioned against jumping on the bandwagon, Marlon Bailey alludes to multiple aspects of paradigm intersectionality: "I see this forum as a very important opportunity to begin to grapple with some of the complexities of same-sex marriage, especially when we begin to see it in the context of race, class, gender, and sexuality. Not everybody's relationship to the state is the same; therefore people's different investments in same-sex marriage or lack thereof should be discussed."[112] In this statement Bailey attempts to provide an intersectional frame of the marriage equality issue that is similar to the one proposed earlier regarding straight African American women—one that acknowledges shifting patterns of vulnerability and power and addresses the levels of complexity he sees in charting a path forward. His acknowledgment of the connection between Categorical Multiplicity and Individual Institutional Relationships gestures well beyond the equality as sameness lens that has been so politically problematic. Building upon this gesture it's important to think about the way in which his statement could be interpreted as an invitation to build deep political solidarity.[113]

None of these authors articulate any kind of desire to separate completely from either the African American or LGBT communities. Public conveyance of their thoughts are instead an invitation to collectively address the ways in which race, gender, class, and sexual orientation as categorical systems that simultaneously confer privilege and disadvantage shape the possibility of deep political solidarity not just between but within communities as well. The narrative analysis presented here cannot aspire to represent the entire African American LGBT community. Nevertheless, several sites for possible deep political solidarity have emerged in addition to same-sex marriage. Where might these overlapping groups go from here?

WHERE DO WE GO FROM HERE? BUILDING DEEP POLITICAL SOLIDARITY FOR GROUPS

One of the central dynamics of *The Real World* that has long since become a hallmark of reality television is the ever-present danger of conflict across lines of difference. Overcoming such emotional landmines is often a challenge that activists fear they cannot achieve because of the usual organizer's mandate to focus on similarity as a catalyst for collective action.[114]

And yet it is precisely the similarity—the infinitesimally small differences found between Millennials and their older counterparts—that points out the crucial need for marriage equality activists to find political solutions beyond passive demographic change. The paradigm intersectionality analysis conducted in this chapter revealed an irredeemable flaw in the political utility of the equality as sameness logic, an unlikely ally group with whom activists can intersectionally examine prior case law for building a functional alliance that recognizes difference, and a challenge to *both* the larger LGBT and African American communities to walk the walk with their African American LGBT brothers and sisters. This may seem like a daunting agenda, but engaging in solidarity politics effectively the next time can ideally reshape equality and access for a broad swath of people.

Is this a utopian vision of solidarity politics—to have the time, much less take the time, to engage in intersectional analysis, then deep political solidarity? Fortunately, many activists have already accepted the aforementioned challenges as a call to conduct solidarity politics differently, based on their experiences with intersectionality in practice, which involves eschewing evidence of tolerance or shared identity as proof of deep political solidarity. Native American feminist activist Andrea Smith learned the hard way that it is possible: "So then I learned from experience [a meeting nearly exploded in violence] that you can't assume allies with other communities of color...you have to go through the trouble of actually creating [alliances]."[115] Successful alliances overcome ambivalence about diversity as a threat by using standards of deep political solidarity and paradigm intersectionality to cultivate interdependence in intergroup relationships.

Deep political solidarity will involve comprehensive collaboration and comprehensive knowledge of communities—more than what's learned by reading the collected works of Martin Luther King, Jr., or having a black friend or partner, or voting for Obama. It will require more than having a gay friend or coworker or treating gay members of the family with more respect. From a paradigm intersectionality perspective, attending to Categorical Multiplicity requires more than lip service; to act as if the categories of race and sexual orientation matter equally but not identically demands knowledge of the nuances of multiple categories in equal depth as well.

Attending to Categorical Intersection requires dropping the premise that communities of color and the LGBT community are mutually exclusive. Moreover, communities of faith and the LGBT community are also not mutually exclusive. Categorical Intersections assist in building deep political solidarity through calls for holistic rather than partial views of individuals and groups in a way that can build a shared agenda that is the responsibility of *all* members of the community, not simply those who live at the intersections.

Previously successful alliances have used Categorical Multiplicity and Categorical Intersection among group members to recognize and legitimate multiple understandings of a specific political issue,[116] much like I have proposed multiple understandings of the impact of *Loving* here. In order to actually accomplish this, group members started with the group norm that defined difference as legitimate—that is, they stepped away from the logic of equality as sameness—and in so doing were able to undermine intragroup dynamics of in-group favoritism.[117] They next realized that those with relatively more power on one dimension had to critically rethink their standard operating procedures and develop such procedures through collaboration rather than by fiat.[118]

Categorical Multiplicity and Intersections interact with Time Dynamics to urge a process of shared inquiry that involves understanding history as it relates to the contemporary moment. Deep intersubjective knowledge of multiple categories means contending with the reality of secondary marginalization that emerges from lack of attention to Diversity Within and failing to recognize that patterns of Individual-Institutional Relationships can vary systematically in such a way that a single court decision or law can affect different subsets of communities differently. It seems self-evident, but acknowledging the five dimensions fully prevents reproduction of the Oppression Olympics and makes deep political solidarity possible.

To Gain an Ally, Be an Ally

It's important to remember that solidarity is distinct from public service and altruism. This paraphrase of Ralph Waldo Emerson's aphorism, "To gain a friend, be a friend," speaks perfectly to the points made by African American LGBT activists to their mainstream LGBT counterparts. Moving African Americans on marriage takes joint political work that cultivates a reservoir of deep political solidarity. Joint work on issues deemed relevant to African Americans by African American LGBT groups themselves would also make this possible.

As well, African Americans looking for proof of evidence of understanding from the LGBT movement can similarly abide by the exhortation. Straight African Americans can openly express concerns about sermons that frame LGBT people as external to the black community, and recognize the full identities of many LGBT African Americans who have been and continue to be incredibly important parts of black history (Time Dynamics). Moreover African Americans can push themselves to embrace their LGBT brothers and sisters in the Black community as full members of the community on their own terms, recognizing their agenda as an equally important component of the black agenda (Diversity Within). There are religious institutions all over the United States that embrace a both/and approach to faith—being LGBT or being an ally is compatible with many forms of Christianity and practiced by many churches. Find out how your group can learn more and do more as cocreators of this country.

Develop Coordinating Mechanisms

In 2000, as some of the oldest Millennials were in high school, LGBT educators and their allies responded to an emerging need for resources and information for students, parents, and teachers interested in forming groups to protect LGBT youth and to foster discussion about how to create a more tolerant climate for them. Now known as the Gay, Lesbian and Straight Education Network (GLSEN), it focuses on working with local chapters to provide educational resources for teachers, students, and parents who want to provide a more welcoming context. GLSEN is an example of an organization within a larger social movement focused on building tolerance. In order to make the leap to developing deep political solidarity, social movements that have successful coalitions develop coordinating mechanisms, organizations that provide a lab for formulating frames, succeeding and building upon what we know and plugging that knowledge into the brain centers of mobilizing organizations across categories.[119] But developing such mechanisms is dependent upon prior long-term relationships that one can't simply fast-track. For that reason, this chapter has emphasized the initial building blocks of deep political solidarity between groups.

December of 2010 was similarly a landmark moment, as President Barack Obama made good on a campaign promise to get Congress to repeal "Don't Ask, Don't Tell," a policy that barred LGBT members of the military from serving openly. This policy change, expected to be implemented in 2011, will reduce the number of discharges under this policy, which prior data showed disproportionately affected black female service members. Would an intersectional analysis have produced a broader coalition that would have more fruitfully prepared No-on-8 activists and straight black women to organize the black community for marriage equality? Would it have led to the repeal of "Don't Ask Don't Tell" any quicker? We can't possibly know. But we can examine another interesting turn in social movement organizing, which puts the LGBT community in the very position its use of the civil rights frame has traditionally put the African American community in.

Much of this chapter emphasized the complex challenge of attempting to borrow from prior movements. Ironically, December 2010 was simultaneously a disappointing moment for undocumented immigrants seeking to duplicate the end of term policy success of the LGBT community by having Congress pass the DREAM Act, which provides pathways to citizenship in exchange for pursuit of a college education or military service. DREAM-qualified student activists, those whose undocumented status would qualify them for the pathways to citizenship enshrined in the bill—pursuit of a college education or military service—have urged their fellow undocumented folk to "come out" as a "DREAM-er." Borrowing language directly from the LGBT rights movement did not persuade the Senate to pass the legislation, and the measure failed. But the use of "coming out" as a metaphor remains a key strategy of DREAM Act activists. The paradigm intersectionality ramifications of this political strategy remain to be seen.

The next chapter focuses on paradigm intersectionality and deep political solidarity from the perspective of public policy. Paradigm intersectionality, as we've seen, provides depth and nuance at the individual and group levels that is critical for the successful pursuit of social justice. The next chapter will demonstrate paradigm intersectionality's diagnostic capacities—specifically the possible challenges to deep political solidarity regarding immigration policy.

How to cultivate deep political solidarity among groups a lot younger than you are

- Gilda Haas has created an online alter ego, Dr. Pop, with a website that features a specific three-step process of group decision-making involving a speed dating exercise. The goal, according to Dr. Pop, is for the whole group to hear what is most important to each individual before they enter a decision-making process and make assumptions about what is most important. Each person spends two minutes one on one with every other person in the room. The entire three-stage process can be found at http://drpop.org/2010/02/3-exercises-for-group-decision-making/#more-324.
- Byron Hurt has produced a video, *Hip Hop: Beyond Beats and Rhymes* (2007), that has been widely acclaimed for its ability to analyze from the perspective of a hip-hop head (fan) the role that homophobia and misogyny play in contemporary hip-hop. This video talks to fans themselves about the images and lyrics and provides a wealth of opportunities for discussion. Pair this video with a broader discussion of *Loving* and unintended consequences of

larger actions to start groups thinking about how multiple interpretations of the same issue can produce solidarity, not simply
division.

- The People for the American Way produced a video about a successful collaboration of marriage equality activists in Ohio that
included African Americans, both secular and people of faith, at
the forefront of its efforts. The video, "A Blinding Flash of the
Obvious," is on YouTube. In particular, the thirty-minute video
allows African Americans to make connections to the civil rights
movement that are legible to the African American community
without triggering fears of cultural cooptation.

How to cultivate deep political solidarity among groups that are older than you are

- Learn more about the social constructions of black gay men in
the mainstream community by watching together the "Bomb
Shelter" episode of *Six Feet Under*, which draws upon this long-
standing social construction in a way that both considers the
narrative and turns it on its ear. Another source of social constructions of black gay men made by and for them is *Noah's Ark*,
a four-season series available on DVD and run on the LOGO
network. It is important to work through this carefully, perhaps
as an intentional practice for each of the individuals involved as
discussed in chapter 3.
- Gently offer the opportunity for older people to both consider
their practices and work through how they developed, and give
them a way to adjust their default practices. In their work *The
Transformative Power of Practice*, Social Justice Leadership's
N'gethe Maina and Staci Haines focus on the deconstruction of default practices. Because our default practices have often been shaped
out of difficult experiences when we had limited means of dealing
with and processing them, these practices often don't align with
our present-day values, politics, and/or what we most care about.
We can find ourselves acting and reacting in ways that make us
more difficult for others to trust, less effective in our work, or more
limited in our approaches to systemic change and movement building. Where once they were essential survival strategies, they may
now be problematic. Because they are so practiced and have now
become unconscious behaviors, we can feel like we have no way to
change them.

The good news is that we can learn to observe our default practices instead of reacting out of them immediately. We can learn other ways to take care of what they were taking care of—other ways to deal with conflict, power, and our own and others' emotions and need for safety. We can begin to purposefully take on practices that align with our values, to become organizers, leaders, and people who more embody or model the social visions we hold.

- For older people who are also people of faith, a program created by the California Council of Churches, "Living Lovingly: Talking About Marriage Equality from a Faith Perspective," focuses on small group discussions within individual congregations. Perhaps ironically, this document encourages a secular process of discussion and self-discernment rather than an other-inspired/directed religious process of judgment. This program encourages forgiveness and empathy for oneself in terms of past thoughts and judgments and courage to live differently in the future.

Notes

1. Blackwell, Pastor and Kwoh. *Searching for the Uncommon Ground: New Dimensions on Race in America.*
2. Originally the young people on *The Real World* were part of Generation X, but they are now Millennials based on year of birth.
3. Orbe, Mark P. Constructions of Reality on MTV's *The Real World*: An Analysis of the Restrictive Coding of Black Masculinity." *Southern Communication Journal* 64(1998): 32–47.
4. Episode 11 featured multiple verbal confrontations between Kevin, the African American male character on the show, and Julie, the white Southern female on the show, centering the audience's attention on the potential threat of violence from Kevin and Julie's discomfort with Kevin's continued presence in the home.
5. The San Francisco cast featured Pedro Zamora, a Cuban American gay male who had AIDS, and received an award from President Clinton for his work in AIDS education among young people. The last San Francisco episode featured Zamora exchanging vows with his partner, Sean Sasser. Zamora died one day after the final episode of the third season aired in 1994.
6. Greenwood, Ronni Michelle. "Intersectional Political Consciousness: Appreciation for Intragroup Differences and Solidarity in Diverse Groups." *Psychology of Women Quarterly* 32 (2008): 37; Pastor, Manuel, Chris Benner, and Martha Matsuoka. *This Could Be the Start of Something Big: Social Movements for Regional Equity Are Reshaping Metropolitan America*. Ithaca: Cornell University Press, 2009.

7. I am using the same time span as the Pew Research Center, which conducts well-regarded cross-generational research on social and political trends in the United States.

8. Taylor, Paul and Scott Keeter. "Millennials: Confident, Connected and Open to Change." Pew Research Center Report; Center for Information and Research on Civic Learning and Engagement (CIRCLE), 2010.

9. I say marketing agents because many pundits point to findings by public opinion researchers like the Pew Research Center, which reports that only 7 percent of Millennials surveyed say that their liberal/tolerant values are what make their generation unique (Taylor and Keeter, "Millennials,"12).

10. Pastor, Benner, and Matsuoka, *This Could Be the Start of Something Big*, 140; Blackwell, Pastor, and Kwoh, *Searching for the Uncommon Ground: New Dimensions on Race in America*.

11. Strolovitch, Dara. *Affirmative Advocacy: Race, Class and Gender in Interest Group Politics*. Chicago: University of Chicago Press, 2007..

12. Strolovitch *Affirmative Advocacy*.

13. Strolovitch *Affirmative Advocacy*.

14. Pastor, Benner, and Matsuoka, *This Could Be the Start of Something Big*, 102, 168–69. Blackwell, Pastor and Kwoh, *Searching for the Uncommon Ground*; they have also noted that facing these issues and fighting for them almost always falls squarely on their shoulders, a personally and professionally exhausting experience to repeatedly endure. Cole et al 2010; see also Barvosa, Edwina. *Wealth of Selves: Multiple Identities, Mestiza Consciousness, and the Subject of Politics*. College Station: Texas A&M Press, 2008.

15. Greenwood, "Intersectional Political Consciousness" Cole, E. R. "Coalitions as a Model for Intersectionality: From Practice to Theory." *Sex Roles* 59 (2008): 443–53.

16. Cole, Elizabeth R, and Zakiya T. Luna. "Making Coalitions Work: Reflections from the Margins of US Feminism," *Feminist Studies* 36.1: 71–98.; Stevens, Jacqueline. "The Politics of LGBTQ Scholarship." *GLQ: A Journal of Lesbian and Gay Studies* 10.2 (2004): 220–26, 222; see also Cohen, Cathy. *Boundaries of Blackness: AIDS and the Breakdown of Black Politics*. Chicago: University of Chicago Press, 1999.

17. I deliberately avoid quantitative language like "double" or "triple" minority in order to both avoid triggers of the Oppression Olympics and preserve the type of intersectional consciousness described in chapters 1 and 2—a simultaneous recognition of undeserved privilege and stigma within an individual, group, or community.

18. Cohen, *Boundaries of Blackness*; Strolovitch, *Affirmative Advocacy*.

19. Blackwell, Pastor, and Kwoh, *Searching for the Uncommon Ground*.

20. Willse, Craig and Dean Spade. "Freedom in a Regulatory State? Lawrence, Marriage and Biopolitics." *Widener Law Review* 11 (2005): 309–29.

21. Granderson, LZ (2009). "Gay Is Not the New Black" http://www.cnn.com/2009/POLITICS/07/16/granderson.obama.gays/index.

html. Accessed June 16, 2010; Richardson, Mattie Udora, Marlon M. Bailey, and Priya Kandaswamy. "Is Gay Marriage Racist?" Transcript of a Conversation at the New College of California, 2004; Farrow, Kenyon (2007). "Is Gay Marriage Anti-Black?" http://www.nathanielturner.com/isgaymarriageantiblack.htm. Accessed May 31, 2010; *Beyond Same-Sex Marriage: A New Strategic Vision for All Our Families and Relationships.* http://www.beyondmarriage.org, 2006; accessed June 2010.

22. Josephson, Jyl. "Romantic Weddings, Diverse Families." *Politics and Gender* 6 (2010): 128–34.

23. The CMPS contains 4,563 respondents who voted in the November 2008 election and self-identified as Asian, black, Latino, and white, and the study was available in English, Spanish, Mandarin, Cantonese, Korean, and Vietnamese. Respondents were offered the opportunity to interview in their language of choice.

    There are six states in the country where representative studies will yield robust samples of all four major racial groups. These states include California, Texas, New York, Florida, Illinois, New Jersey, and our state-wide samples range from 243 to 669 cases. In order to arrive at more nationally representative samples of each minority group, we added two supplemental states per racial group, including Arizona and New Mexico (Latinos), North Carolina and Georgia (blacks), Hawaii and Washington (Asians). Of these twelve states, three were considered political battle-grounds in the 2008 presidential election—New Mexico, Florida, and North Carolina. In order to examine multiracial politics in competitive and noncompetitive environments, we supplemented our sample with six additional diverse battleground states: Colorado, Michigan, Nevada, Ohio, Pennsylvania, and Virginia. As of the 2008 election, two-thirds of the national electorate is concentrated in these eighteen states. For Latinos, 92 percent of all registered voters reside in these states, 87 percent of Asian Americans, 66 percent of blacks, and 61 percent of whites.

24. $\chi 2$ (4, N = 107) = 7.814, $p < .10$; effect size is .15.

25. Do you agree or disagree that the United States should have an amendment to the U.S. Constitution that bans same-sex marriage?

26. $\chi 2$ (5, N = 514) = 15.119, p < .01; effect size is .007.

27. This question was a standard 5-point Likert Scale, where 1 = Strongly Agree [with the ban], 2 = Somewhat Agree, 3 = Neither Agree nor Disagree, to 5 = Strongly Disagree [with the ban]. For African Americans, the 95 percent Confidence Interval ranged from 2.99 to 3.53; for Asian Americans, the 95 percent Confidence Interval ranged from 3.34 to 4.01; for Latinos/Hispanics 3.07 to 3.54; and for white Americans 3.25 to 4.00.

28. 2010, 58.

29. Solomon, Marc and Geoff Kors. "Returning to the Ballot in 2010 vs. 2012" Press Release: http://www.eqca.org/site/pp.asp?c=kuLRJ9MRKrH&b=5190603. Accessed June 16, 2010.

30. Lax, Jeffrey, and Jason Phillips. "Gay Rights in the States: Public Opinion and Policy Responsiveness." *American Political Science Review* 103 (2009): 367–86, 376; Patrick Egan also notes that in votes on marriage directly, there is a persistent 3 percent undercount of likely ban supporters, who show up on election day and cast their votes against same-sex marriage supporters, speaking in part to the social response bias that can often undermine connections between public opinion reports of voter intentions and actual election results. Egan, Patrick. "Findings from a Decade of Polling on Ballot Measures Regarding the Legal Status of Same-Sex Couples." Unpublished study, 2010.

31. Citing John D'Emilio, Jyl Josephson puts it best: "There seems to be widespread expectation that demographic changes in the electorate will lead to change with respect to access to same-sex marriage…This may well be true in the states where access to marriage or to civil unions or domestic partnerships has already been achieved. But it does not give sufficient weight to the fact that the backlash to the marriage movement has also been quite successful, and that the institutional, political, and cultural change that [132] will be required for the inclusion of diverse families in the majority of states with state marriage bans and other antigay policies will require significant and sustained political organizing…" Josephson, Jyl. "Romantic Weddings, Diverse Families," 131–32.

32. *In re Marriage Cases*, 43 Cal. 4th 757 (2008).

33. Egan, Patrick and Ken Sherrill. "California's Proposition 8: What Happened, and What Does the Future Hold?" 3; See also Lee, Eric P. *Proposition 8: The California Divide.* Los Angeles: Heat International Publishing, 2009. The 58 percent seems more reliable given the quality of empirical analysis, but the national figures still remain daunting— according to national studies in 2004, 66 to 67 percent of African Americans opposed gay marriage. Spence, Lester K. "Episodic Frames, HIV/AIDS, and African American Public Opinion." *Political Research Quarterly* 53 (2010): 258.

34. An informal analysis by David Silver indicates: "If the exit polls are accurate, Proposition 8 would have passed even if no black voters had turned out. (African Americans voted in favor by a margin of 450,000, and the initiative passed by 500,000.) On the other hand, if 5 percent more white voters had rejected it, Prop 8 would have failed. Or if either Catholics or white Protestants hadn't voted, it would have been defeated by more than 500,000 votes. Without either weekly churchgoers or evangelical/born-again Christians, Prop 8 would have lost by more than a million votes…" private e-mail correspondence, November 12, 2008.

35. The $200,000 was for the most part, in this logic, a token effort but more winnable voters were considered to reside elsewhere in the electorate.

36. Brown, Sonja Eddings."Top African American Religious Leaders Join Apostle Frederick K. C. Price in endorsing YES on Proposition 8," http://www.protectmarriage.com/article/top-african-american-

religious-leaders-join-apostle-frederick-k-c-price-in-endorsing-yes-on-prop-8, October 22, 2008. Accessed June 5, 2010.

37. There is both legal and political evidence of a new antimarriage equality frame: Farrow (2007) discusses the video produced by the Traditional Values Coalition called "Gay Rights, Special Rights" targeting the African American religious community; Eyer (2010) cites Eskridge's chronicle of the evolution of the new frame in a legal context to its current incarnation, "no promo homo."

38. Lee, Eric P. *Proposition 8: The California Divide*, 92, 94, 97.

39. Postelection, Bishop Blake received the 2010 Marriage Protector award from NOM for "the steadfast witness of the Church of God in Christ in defending marriage as the union of husband and wife" in front of 20,000 African American female COGIC members and bishops. "NOM Honors COGIC Presiding Bishop Charles E. Blake and Mother Willie Mae Rivers," June 2, 2010. http://www.nationformarriage.org/site/apps/nlnet/content2.aspx?c=omL2KeN0LzH&b=5075187&ct=8421183, Accessed June 5, 2010. See also Moore, Mignon. "Black and Gay in L.A.: The Relationships Black Lesbians and Gay Men Have to Their Racial and Religious Communities." In Hunt, Darnell and Ana-Christina Ramon, editors. *Black Los Angeles: American Dreams and Racial Realities*. New York: New York University Press, 2010.

40. Characteristic of the attention to communities of color was the No on 8 campaign's last-minute hire of Javier Angulo as deputy director to organize Latino, African American, and Asian American communities eight weeks prior to the election. Understandably, Angulo could not work miracles in the two months prior to the election, particularly without adequate money or human capital.

41. Lee, Eric P. *Proposition 8: The California Divide*.

42. GLAAD. "Talking About LGBT Equality with African Americans" New York: Gay and Lesbian Alliance Against Defamation and Movement Advancement Project, 2010.

43. A deeper familiarity with King, for example, would reveal his long-standing desire for Bayard Rustin, the primary architect of his civil rights movement, to stay in the closet for the good of the whole movement. Rustin resisted, but ultimately lost the battle and was ousted from the organization.

44. Egan, Patrick and Ken Sherrill. "California's Proposition 8: What Happened, and What Does the Future Hold?," 6.

45. Marso, Lori J. "Marriage and Bourgeois Respectability." *Politics & Gender* 6 (2010): 145–53; Josephson, Jyl. "Romantic Weddings, Diverse Families," 132.

46. Josephson, Jyl. "Romantic Weddings, Diverse Families," 128.

47. I make this distinction because Perez did not attempt to "pass" for white nor did she, according to contemporary accounts, look white.

48. This conclusion sidestepped a standing United States Supreme Court precedent (*Pace v Alabama*) that might logically have resulted in the preservation of bans on interracial marriage.

49. 388 US 1, p.12

50. In re Marriage Cases; Lenhardt, Robin. "Beyond Analogy: Perez v. Sharp, Antimiscegenation Law, and the Fight for Same-Sex Marriage." *California Law Review* 96 (2008): 839.

51. Lenhardt, "Beyond Analogy;" In re Marriage Cases.

52. In a recent presentation, Francisco Valdes notes that intersectionality claims were successful only under conditions where petitioners were members of categories exclusively established by precedent as protected classes—mixes of protected and unprotected did not succeed in their claims.

53. Crenshaw, "Mapping the Margins."

54. hooks, bell. *Talking Back: Thinking Feminist, Thinking Black*. Boston: South End Press, 1989, 14.

55. He continues by calling the black community to task as well: "Black people are merely the unfortunate middlemen in an exchange between white men. We consume the representations like the rest of America. And the more that black people are willing to accept these representations as fact rather than racist fiction, the more heightened homophobia in our communities tends to be." Farrow, "Is Gay Marriage Anti-Black?" 2007.

56. Parts of Prop 209 were ultimately invalidated by the courts.

57. Ramakrishnan, Karthick. *Democracy in Immigrant America: Changing Demographics and Political Participation*. Stanford, CA: Stanford University Press, 2005, 119.

58. Lee, Eric P. *Proposition 8: The California Divide*, 87; see also Farrow 2007; Willse and Spade 2005.

59. Spence, Lester K. "Episodic Frames, HIV/AIDS, and African American Public Opinion." *Political Research Quarterly* 63.2: 266.

60. Meyer, Richard. "Gay Power Circa 1970: Visual Strategies for Sexual Revolution." *GLQ: A Journal of Gay and Lesbian Studies* 12 (2006): 441–64.

61. In the same article Meyers also chronicles both how gay men readers pushed for eradicated lesbian issues from their magazines as well as a mass mobilization requesting everyone to show up for a photo array, which did not garner much participation by LGBT people of color community.

62. Farrow, "Is Gay Marriage Anti-Black?" 2007.

63. See also Elizabeth Cole's work for citation of empirical evidence of variation in sexual conservatism based on race-gender group: "Intersectionality theory suggests that researchers must attend to differences within groups if their work is to shed light on the meaning of social categories. For example, Gonzales and Rolison (2005) developed a theory of sexual

capital, positing that social identity groups with relatively more social power will be freer to disregard hegemonic norms of sexuality. They found that white men's reported sexual activities and desires were least constrained by conventional morality, whereas black women's were most constrained. Their findings concerning social class also supported their theory. Gonzales and Rolison's approach and findings move beyond seeing sexuality in terms of a simple gendered double-standard to consider the ways that the forms taken by desire are affected by multiple dimensions of power and privilege." Cole, Elizabeth. "Coalitions as a Model for Intersectionality: From Practice to Theory." *Sex Roles* 59 (2008): 443–53.

64. See "Episodic Frames, HIV/AIDS, and African American Public Opinion," 262; Collins, *Black Feminist Thought*; Harris-Lacewell, Melissa. *Bibles, Barbershops and BET: Everyday Talk and Black Political Thought*. Princeton, NJ: Princeton University Press, 2004.

65. As Farrow noted earlier, it is also made plausible by other features of black political culture like hip-hop music.

66. Denizet-Lewis, Benoit. "Young Gay Rites." *New York Times Magazine*, April 28, 2010. Accessed April 28, 2010.

67. While these issues of visual representation are not limited to the marriage equality sector of the LGBT movement, they are no less pressing in this context.

68. Ibid.

69. Townsend, Tiffany. "Protecting Our Daughters: Intersection of Race, Class and Gender in African American Mothers' Socialization of Their Daughters' Heterosexuality." *Sex Roles* 59 (2008): 429–42, 434–35; Richardson, Mattie Udora, Marlon M. Bailey, and Priya Kandaswamy. "Is Gay Marriage Racist?" Transcript of a Conversation at the New College of California, 2004, 88.

70. Ferguson, Roderick. *Aberrations in Black: Toward a Queer of Color Critique*. Minneapolis: University of Minnesota Press, 2004.

71. Shane Phelan quoted in Josephson, Jyl. "Romantic Weddings, Diverse Families," 129; see also Willse and Spade, "Freedom in a Regulatory State?," 322; Cathy Cohen, *Boundaries of Blackness* for different examples of oversimplification involving African American responses to the HIV/AIDS crisis leading to secondary marginalization.

72. Richardson, Bailey, and Kandaswamy. "Is Gay Marriage Racist?"

73. "For Judith Butler, the question comes down to whether gays and lesbians should 'desire the state's desire' (2004, 105). Butler argues that when we ask the state to legitimate certain forms of intimate relations, we foreclose the feminist quest for a radical sexual culture and deepen the normalization that bourgeois culture promotes. Even while feminists can applaud that same-sex marriage has become a choice for those residing in certain states, we need to draw attention to how this makes the options outside of marriage become increasingly less respectable, or, as Butler would put it, unthinkable and unintelligible." Marso "Marriage

and Bourgeois Respectability," 147; see also Willse and Spade "Freedom in a Regulatory State?"

74. Mattis et al. "Intersectional Identities and the Politics of Altruistic Care in Low-Income Urban Community." *Sex Roles* 59 (2008): 418–14, 421. See also Ospina, Sonia and Celina Su. "Weaving Color Lines: Race, Ethnicity, and the Work of Leadership in Social Change Organizations." *Leadership* 5 (2009): 131–70; Su, Celina. "We Call Ourselves by Many Names: Storytelling and Inter-Minority Coalition-Building." *Community Development Journal* 45 (2009); Greenwood, "Intersectional Political Consciousness."

75. Hoban Kirby, E. and K. Kawashima-Ginsberg (2009) "The Youth Vote in 2008," CIRCLE (Center for Information and Research on Civic Learning and Engagement) Fact Sheet.

76. Bositis, David (2008). "Blacks and the 2008 Election: A Preliminary Analysis." http://www.jointcenter.org/publications_recent_publications/political_participation/blacks_and_the_2008_elections_a_preliminary_analysis. Accessed June 16, 2010.

77. Perhaps just as importantly, a recent experimental study of black attitudes toward black gay and bisexual men found that black women expressed more liberal attitudes about black male sexual activity with other men (Spence, "Episodic Frames, HIV/AIDS, and African American Public Opinion," 261).

78. Taylor and Keeter "Millennials," 19; the report suggests both generational and race-based differences; among Millennials the authors find an eight-percentage point difference between whites and nonwhites on the question of whether "Having a successful marriage is one of the most important things in life" to Millennials.

79. This kind of conversation opens a door to reveal the wider skepticism about interracial marriage among the most likely African American voters, black women, that is left unseen by the traditional frame of the interracial marriage survey question. Most questions ask how the respondent would feel about a family member marrying outside their race. In terms of their own lives, respondents aren't looking to marry a family member, so the traditional survey question is moot. Interracial marriage as an institution is more controversial among black women because since *Loving* it has often been perceived as a threat to their own prospects for marriage, given the discrepancy between their prevalence of out-marriage and black men's. While the gap in outmarriage for black men and black women is well documented empirically, the conclusion that interracial marriage is a legitimate threat is less an empirically documented phenomena than a cultural conceit repeated often in black public spheres.

80. Taylor, Paul, et al (2010). "Marrying Out: One-in-Seven New U.S. Marriages Is Interracial or Interethnic." Pew Research Center: http://pewresearch.org/pubs/1616/american-marriage-interracial-interethnic. Accessed June 16, 2010, 9.

81. The figures for black men have tripled between 1980 and 2010, leading to greater ambivalence.

82. Ibid.

83. Cantave, Cassandra and Roderick Harrison. "Marriage and African Americans Fact Sheet" Joint Center for Political and Economic Studies, http://www.jointcenter.org/DB/factsheet/marital.htm. 2001; accessed June 16, 2010.

84. When that person is white the acceptance rate is 81 percent, Asian 75 percent, Latino/a 73 percent.

85. Richardson, Bailey and Kandasharma, "Is Gay Marriage Racist?" 92–93.

86. The Los Angeles African American Women's Political Institute began in 2004. It is a ten-week intensive and comprehensive training program to prepare women for corporate advancement, to run for elective office, manage political campaigns, seek government appointments, understand public policy decision-making, and sharpen their leadership skills.

87. The group of black women also had far more positive responses to the teenage sons of the black gay male couple, one of whom told the story of having his dads essentially rescue him from some of the bad influences in his life—another statement that resonates in many African American middle- and working-class communities.

88. Pastor, Manuel and Rhonda Ortiz. *Making Change: How Social Movements Work and How to Support Them.* Program for Environmental and Regional Equity: University of Southern California, 2009, 11.

89. The following excerpt implies an availability of agency that is more con-strained than Young's interpretation of Sartre might lead us to believe: "Thus the concept of seriality provides a useful way of thinking about the relationship of race, class, gender and other collective structures to the individual person. If these are forms of seriality, then they do not necessarily define the identity of individuals and do not necessarily name attributes they share with others. They are material structures aris-ing from people's historically congealed, institutionalized actions and expectations that position and limit individuals in determinate ways in which they must deal...A person can choose to make none of her serial memberships important for her sense of identity. Or she can find that her family, neighborhood, and church network makes the serial facts of race, for example, important for her identity and development of a group solidarity. Or she can develop a sense of herself and membership in group affiliations that makes different serial structures important to her in different respects, or salient in different kinds of circumstances." Young, *Intersecting Voices*, 31.

90. "In the past month the black media has started to reframe black LGBT people as people who have families, rather than as 'threats' to the black family." Jefferson, Aisha I. "Partners in Parenting." *Essence* 41.2 (2010): 80; Chiles, Nick. "Daddy's Home." *Essence* 41.2 (2010): 154–60.

91. This of course is not a commentary on such authors, who are indeed breathtaking in their brilliance. But many authors cited here have

actively commented on the issues at hand and further, tend to be far younger than the established interlocutors, connecting with the attention to Millennials and their politics.

92. Though author Michael Joseph Gross mentioned his black gay friends in one sentence of the article, there was no further analysis or attention to their analyses—only the presentation of black allies like Representative Barbara Lee (D-CA) and former San Francisco mayor Willie Brown. Gross 2008/2009 http://www.advocate.com/News/Daily_News/2008/11/16/Gay_is_the_New_Black. Accessed June 18, 2010.

93. Farrow 2007, "Is Gay Marriage Anti-Black?" http://www.nathaniel-turner.com/isgaymarriageantiblack.htm. Accessed May 2010.

94. Martin, quoted in Mathis, "Is the LGBT Rights Movement Fighting for Equal Rights or White Privilege Rights?" http://renwl.org/is-the-lgbt-movement-fighting-for-equal-rights-or-white-privilege-rights-part-1/3809/comment-page-1/ Accessed March 30, 2010.

95. Lee, Eric P. *Proposition 8: The California Divide*, 77–78; see also Moore "Black and Gay in L.A., 192, 194.

96. Ferguson, Roderick. *Aberrations in Black: Toward a Queer of Color Critique.* Minneapolis: University of Minnesota Press, 2004, 45.

97. Yoshino, Kenji. *Covering: The Hidden Assault on Our Civil Rights.* New York: Random House, 2006.

98. Fogg-Davis, H. G. "Theorizing Black Lesbians within Black Feminism: A Case of Same-Race Street Harassment." *Politics and Gender* 2 (2006): 57–76.

99. The cultural demands of covering facilitate the perpetuation of the closet, although scholars like Mignon Moore are starting to document generational effects—class-privileged, gender-conforming black men and women in their twenties and thirties feel more comfortable "being out" in the black community than their similarly situated older counterparts. Moore, "Black and Gay in L.A.," 194–95). Indeed, one black male LGBT activist could draw upon the black cultural phobia of "down low" to explain that marriage equality for all members of the black community must be implemented to move the race forward. This activist, however, is more the exception than the rule. Ibid., 188–89.

While actual empirical evidence of "down low" men harming the black community is not yet available, black cultural narratives about down-low men persist and can be manipulated in issue frames about HIV/AIDS to produce different evaluations of the rights to be afforded black gay and bisexual men. Spence, "Episodic Frames, HIV/AIDS, and African American Public Opinion," 263, 266.

100. Meyer, "Gay Power Circa 1970."

101. Meyer, "Gay Power Circa 1970," 447.

102. Essex Hemphill, cited in Willse and Spade, "Freedom in a Regulatory State?" see also Farrow, "Is Gay Marriage Anti-Black"; Collins, Patricia Hill. *Black Sexual Politics: African Americans, Gender and the New*

Racism. New York: Routledge, 2004; hooks, bell. *Art on My Mind: Visual Politics.* New York: The New Press, 1995.

103. Lee, Eric P. *Proposition 8: The California Divide,* 73–74.

104. Lee, Eric P. *Proposition 8: The California Divide*; Granderson, "Gay Is not the New Black."

105. Granderson, LZ (2009). "Gay Is Not the New Black" http://www.cnn.com/2009/POLITICS/07/16/granderson.obama.gays/index.html. Accessed June 16, 2010.

106. Willse and Spade illustrate the problem with this set of organizations who attempt to speak for all but in actually represent a narrow part of the community: "A significant force of change has been the creation of funded organizations led primarily by white lesbians and gay men with economic and educational privilege that claim to represent a broad-based movement for LGBT rights. However, the agendas of those organizations have come to focus on the rights or people with occupational, educational, gender, and race privilege and to marginalize or ignore the struggles of transgender people, queer and trans people of color, and queer and trans poor people." Willse and Spade, "Freedom in a Regulatory State?" 317. While Strolovitch's work suggests this representational problem is not unique to the LGBT community, it is no less pressing a problem.

107. Richardson, Bailey and Kandasharma, "Is Gay Marriage Racist?" 88.

108. Ibid, 91.

109. Farrow, "Is Gay Marriage Anti-Black?" 2007.

110. Moore, "Black and Gay in L.A."

111. Ibid, 192.

112. Richardson, Bailey and Kandasharma, "Is Gay Marriage Racist?" 88.

113. It is also an invitation to think in more complex terms about the role of the state and multiple and overlapping patterns of relationship to it.

114. Greenwood, Ronni Michelle and Aidan Christian. "What Happens When We Unpack the Invisible Knapsack? Intersectional Political Consciousness and Inter-group Appraisals." *Sex Roles* 59 (2008): 404–17; Blackwell, Pastor and Kwoh, *Searching for the Uncommon Ground: New Dimensions on Race in America*; Pastor, Benner, and Matsuoka, *This Could Be the Start of Something Big.*

115. Andrea Smith quoted in Cole, "Coalitions as a Model for Intersectionality," 446.

116. Ibid., 448.

117. Greenwood and Christian "What Happens When We Unpack the Invisible Knapsack?" 405.

118. Cole "Coalitions as a Model for Intersectionality," 448.

119. See Pastor, Benner, and Matsuoka, *This Could Be the Start of Something Big.*

5

Viva Exploradora Dora: Intersectionality's Contributions to Public Policy

"!Hola! !Soy Dora! Let's Explore!"[1]

On August 14, 2010, the show *Dora the Explorer* celebrated the tenth anniversary of its premiere on Nickelodeon. Over the past decade Dora, a seven-year-old Latina character, has taken millions of preschoolers and their parents on interactive journeys in problem solving while teaching them simple phrases in Spanish along the way. In interviews about the tenth anniversary series creators and show runners Chris Gifford and Valerie Walsh Valdes reinforced the notion that Dora was a character who "turned fairy tales on their head," and traditional notions of gender along with them. Yet for most commentaries on Dora, it is her Latina ethnicity and her bilingual communication skills that generate the most interest. We now know from previous chapters the peril of this kind of attempted construction of ethnicity and gender as mutually exclusive.

Scholarly research on *Dora the Explorer* is scant, but the show, which initially planned to feature a male rabbit as the central character, employs cultural consultants to use both linguistic and cultural elements that are pan-Latino rather than reflective of a specific nationality. Indeed, the two young female voice-over actors who have portrayed Dora have been of Peruvian (Kathleen Herles) and Cuban (Caitlin Sanchez) backgrounds, a small surprise to the multitudes in the United States who assume Dora is Mexican American or Puerto Rican.

Dora's cross-generational symbolic value extends beyond popular culture and into commentary about political issues of the day. Drawing upon Dora's status as a nearly ubiquitous global commodity and the vast assumption of her Mexican identity, several Photoshop artists recently participated in an online contest calling for treatments of Dora following the unlicensed usage of Dora's face for a political cartoon in support of the Arizona legislature's passage of SB 1070, a draconian effort to step into the void created by the federal government's failure to comprehensively overhaul U.S. immigration policy over the past twenty-five years.[2] In the most infamous image, Dora the Explorer's mugshot features a bruised and bloodied Dora with a slate that reads:

Dora The Explorer

ILLEGAL BORDER CROSSING

RESISTING ARREST

666 666 66

In response to the contest call for submissions, the website FreakingNews.com, which sponsors such contests, posted thirty-four high-resolution entries, thirteen of which depicted Dora as someone who was in the United States illegally. Images included an armed white girl around Dora's age standing next to a "Wanted Dead or Alive: Dora the Explorer" poster and Dora's ever-present backpack, filled with the $1 million in reward money; an older Dora being attacked with a missile by Arizona Senator John McCain; Dora as a drug smuggler; Dora's head mounted over a fireplace as taxidermy; Dora as Elian Gonzalez;[3] Dora as part of a criminal gang, the Arizona 8, which includes her cousin Diego and a host of earlier cartoon characters, including Speedy Gonzalez and Frito Bandito; Dora's forged U.S. passport; Dora robbing the sturdy white couple depicted in the painting "American Gothic"; Dora as a day laborer at Home Depot; Dora as an MI-13 gang member;[4] and an Elmer Fudd-inspired hunting ad: "Dora Season," with "Illegal Immigration" written underneath. Two more entries attempted to mix metaphors, as Dora became the primary character in a Monopoly game of federal immigration policy, and another gave Dora an altered birth certificate from Hawaii, a clear reference to the lingering minority of Americans who refuse to believe that President Obama is a citizen. All of these images could in several respects be interpreted as efforts to tear Dora away from the apolitical, pan-Latino identity her creators have tried to preserve and to brand her not only as a specific nationality (Mexican) but as an undocumented immigrant as well.

These images, however, were not without challenge. Even among submissions to the contest itself, five arguably sympathetic portraits of Dora emerged: an older Dora with her green card; Dora the avenger, planting a hand grenade at the podium of Arizona Governor Jan Brewer; Dora entering the neighboring state of Utah, which through its Utah Compact has established a more humane approach to the failures of federal immigration policy; "The Passion of Dora"—Dora martyred on a cross; and Dora being denied entry to her cartoon home. These more "sympathetic" representations, while heartening, are limited in that rather than shift the preexisting terms of the debate surrounding immigration, they merely respond to them.

Of course, as Nickelodeon spokesman Dan Martinsen noted in reference to the controversy, "Dora" is just a cartoon character—albeit one that is broadcast in one hundred countries and thirty languages around the world. Dora doesn't have the special resonance with Millennials that Big Bird, Bert, Ernie, and Grover from *Sesame Street* do with Generation X, since all but a few had grown past the age of Dora's target audience (three to eight years old) by the time of her debut. So why start this chapter with Dora?

Dora's symbolic value and the recent controversy over usage of her image illustrate the twenty-first century tension that arises in the context of immigration. This chapter aims to use the Dora example to illustrate the complicated dynamics of the immigration debate in the United States. While many scholars consider tensions over immigration policy to be a routine part of American political development, contemporary demographers and sociologists have identified new challenges facing us in the twenty-first century.[5] As these scholars lay out the challenges, they unwittingly identify elements of the problem that suit it perfectly for intersectional analysis—particularly the interaction between generational dynamics, racial dynamics, and issues of national security. Chapter 3 explored the value of an intersectional approach to solidarity at the individual level, and chapter 4 explored its value at the group level. Chapter 5 will examine the ability of intersectionality to identify challenges to deep political solidarity at the policy level.

Dora's Diversity Narrative

One part of Dora's story is her ubiquity in popular culture. Historian and series consultant Carlos Cortes believes that Dora arrived at a specific moment when the world was ready for her.[6] Brown Johnson, the Nickelodeon executive who developed *Dora the Explorer* for the network, agreed that Dora's message is contemporaneous with twenty-first-century social dynamics: "It was important for us that Dora represented the idea that being multicultural is supercool."[7]

But what is this "supercool multiculturalism" Johnson refers to? Johnson, who has spent over twenty years in children's programming, uses the term "multiculturalism" as if it means the same thing to all people. The series creators' choice to embrace a pan-Latino identity for Dora is interpreted as a double-edged sword by some scholars. While some argue it adds to a more accurate portrayal of our twenty-first-century society,[8] the emphasis on pan-Latino identity erases much of the nuance and Diversity Within Latino/a culture that emerges from throughout the Latino/a diaspora.[9]

Turning to Dora as evidence of a multicultural narrative that is historically situated—one influenced by Time Dynamics—is important because Dora's brand of multiculturalism is reflected in prior studies of recent second-generation immigrants. The multiculturalism many immigrant families contended with during the post-1965 wave of immigration was profoundly affected by prior social movements focused on the empowerment of U.S. born people of color.[10] Perhaps ironically, the children of these more recent immigrants are in many ways uniquely suited to leverage their memberships in the traditional U.S. racial groups: public policy "designed to redress longstanding American racial [inequalities] turn out to work better for immigrants and their children than they do for the native minorities for whom they were designed."[11] By now we know the all-too-tempting Oppression Olympics interpretation of this finding (the production of Leapfrog Paranoia among U.S. born minorities), but what are those who wish to *end* the Oppression Olympics to make of this policy outcome?

In collecting a wealth of survey and ethnographical data about second-generation immigrants in New York City, authors Philip Kasinitz, John Mollenkopf, and Mary Waters found a "new kind of multiculturalism emerging that encourages hybridity and fluid exchanges across group identity boundaries and even public spaces."[12] In particular they and their collaborators found that despite a full-throated endorsement of a multiculturalism or cosmopolitanism that included high levels of social interaction and acceptance (or, as we know it, *tolerance*), the second-generation New Yorkers they followed were civically and politically *disengaged*.[13]

Both the *Dora* series creators' definition of multiculturalism—embracing those who are different from you—and the second-generation definition, which adds the embrace of hybridity, are notable for their *lack* of political engagement. Part of why the multiculturalism of Dora and the largely Generation X members of second-generation families followed by Kasinitz, Mollenkopf, and Waters is so apolitical

d greater public spending and an older, whiter group oriented
d less public spending.[32] Certainly Frey's analysis is consistent
more dire predictions of a despair-filled future, full of intergen-
nal and cross-cultural Leapfrog Paranoia, Movement Backlash,
ompassion Deficit Disorder.

t three years earlier demographer Dowell Myers argued for a
illed vision of the future. Myers contends that the battles over
ration that occurred in 1990s California present important les-
or how the rest of the country can acknowledge and come to
with the interdependence between both sides of the cultural
tion gap if the country overcomes its dependence on outdated
uctions of immigrant threat.[33] Myers believes that having ac-
information can save us. Each demographer has conducted
y analyses of the same demographic trends, but proposes two
t futures for your consideration. As empirical analysts, Myers,
nd their counterparts are merely the messengers regarding
ernatives. It is the intersectionality theorist's job to suggest
Millennials and Baby Boomers can do to avoid an Oppression
ics outcome in this domain.

mass media can play a key role in sending signals to gov-
t officials about items for the public agenda.[34] Most media
s cite a common complaint from critics of SB 1070: the law
ally sanction racial profiling[35] of those who "look" like immi-
Unfortunately most social science studies of public policy ig-
is kind of question: how do we interrogate the process by
who looks like immigrants" gets constructed? Although social
s have traditionally focused on the "WHAT"—government
ts, money, tax incentives—is at stake in policy debates, the
onstruction of target populations literature allows us to ex-
"WHO" is at stake and how that "WHO" is socially con-
over time. Authors Ann Schneider and Helen Ingram argue
people who are the intended targets of a public policy (e.g.,
ants) are socially constructed historically, as well as through
pes and media images at a particular point in time. Such so-
structions then influence policy design.

ter 4 suggested a path to finding new or counterintuitive
the struggle for marriage equality. In this section I want to
ously the implications of the photoshopped *Dora the Explorer*
or debates about immigration policy. Specifically, I want to
media representations of immigrant threat. Here I want to
another key contribution of intersectionality theory at the
vel: it can identify obstacles to solidarity among likely allies.

is its association with the twentieth-century discourse of tolerance and pluralism, which chapters 3 and 4 demonstrated was necessary but *insufficient* to produce the deep political solidarity so critical to avoiding mistakes of the past. Another prior nationwide cross-racial and cross-generational analysis of immigrant political participation similarly called Robert Dahl's twentieth-century pluralist theory of immigrant political incorporation into question when it comes to twenty-first-century immigrants. Dahl's pluralist theory suggests that immigrants represented an irresistible pool of potential votes for political parties and candidates in the early twentieth century. However, according to Karthick Ramakrishnan, the mere presence of caches of immigrant voters in the 1990s and 2000s was not sufficient to incorporate them as voters into the electorate—by either enterprising political challengers or incumbents focused on constituent service and representation. In fact, statewide laws like California's Proposition 187 in 1994 and Arizona's SB 1070 actually suggest that not only are immigrant voters not worth courting at the ballot box, they are troubling targets for exploitation in campaigns to win over other well-established voters, including those native-born citizens who are members of traditionally marginalized groups, like African Americans.

"Ahistorical, uncritical rhetoric of diversity"[14] may feel good, or even "supercool," but it stunts our growth as members of a society facing unprecedented challenges. This chapter demonstrates intersectionality's ability to address some of the problems facing pluralist theory by identifying challenges to solidarity and new approaches to public policy analysis.

Information-processing models of public policy making propose two sources of ambiguity of meaning in terms of signals and symbols: the substantive meaning of a signal like Dora (or the alterations of Dora) and the degree to which we can be sure of the interpretation itself.[15] The representation of Dora, given her widespread recognition and global reach, is an illustration of how powerful mass media phenomena can become,[16] representing Latinos to those who do not have contact with the people or cultures that fall under the umbrella term "Latino."[17] As a Latino cultural representative, Dora contradicts the messages Latinas often receive: "obedience to the church, submission to men, and limited participation in public discourse."[18] In so doing Dora is simultaneously communicating multiple messages—potentially empowering messages to young Latinos/as about behavioral norms—but also communicating messages to viewers unfamiliar with Latinas that then require viewers to fill in the blanks themselves, which may or may not be accurate.[19] These gaps leave wide-open opportunities for Leapfrog Paranoia, Willful Blindness, Defiant Ignorance, Movement Backlash, and Compassion Deficit Disorder to enter into such interpretations.

If Dora is so innocuous—an example of "innocent, asexual worldly knowledge"—then why were so many violent images targeting Dora produced in the controversy surrounding Arizona's SB 1070? Because "Dora's resourcefulness creates a positive image of Latino/a children and bilingualism"[20] *and* at the same time an anxiety about the implications of these new images for society. As one parent noted on Nickelodeon's Dora website:

> Dora use [*sic*] to be an ok show. Now I do not let my children watch it. There is way too much Spanish speaking in it. I do teach my kids to be willing to accept others as they are, but I feel that if the Spanish speaking descent are going to come here and live then they need to be taught and learn to speak our language. We should not have to learn Spanish. It's bad that even our cartoon programs have gone so far as to teach our children Spanish as much as it has. I feel that if you live here you need to speak our language. If not then leave. It should be a parent's choice to teach our children other languages, not a cartoon network.[21]

This parent's embrace of apolitical tolerance clearly does not extend very far politically. These concerns aren't just limited to television; Ramakrishnan notes that we have mixed feelings with regard to welcoming immigrants more generally.[22] Politically, such anxieties over changing norms of citizenship and belonging can be interpreted in two distinct ways—as a predictor of either a hope-filled or despair-filled future.[23] The direction of interpretation hinges directly on perception of threat, which has long been a key to immigration policy debate and discourse. It is this sense of threat to which we now turn.

THE NARRATIVE OF IMMIGRANT THREAT

While the United States has long embraced the slogan, "a nation of immigrants," the incorporation of immigrants has ebbed and flowed in terms of sheer numbers and citizen acceptance of the foreign-born since our nation's founding. Both the tug-of-war over Dora's meaning and the debate surrounding SB 1070 clearly suggest that "WHO" is at stake in policy debates matters as much as the costs and benefits of

the policy, commonly defined as "WHAT" Dora as a threat comes from the online subn selves. But the notion of immigrant threat has Contemporary perceptions of threat have be demographic trends and a signal event—Se have both received wide media coverage.[24]

Ramakrishnan analyzed the media co threat in the 1990s across three U.S. states as high, medium, or low.[25] In his sample coverage frequently focused upon the pred who began to identify a number of highly p occur among the U.S. population in the tw

- Latinos would surpass African America group in 2001.[27]
- First- and second-generation immigran for 25 percent of the national electorate
- By 2025, over half of all families with tural.[29]

What's unique about the twenty-first-cen produced by these demographic eventual tional and racial dynamics that current William Frey has identified what he call gap," which is the product of two twen trends: the aging of Baby Boomers, who in a United States that is a white majorit Millennials (and, increasingly, their child most racially diverse U.S. generation but centage of the foreign born.[30] For Frey thus highlights the potential for signifi state level between two generations wh more importantly, their political needs a each other. The implications of his analy of new racial and ethnic competition fo planted..."[31]

In the lingua franca of this book, Fre eration gap as a phenomenon ripe for ex Olympics. According to Frey, SB 1070 loom in the future; he identifies six Nevada, Texas, Florida, and New Mex predicted tension between a younger, ra

towar
towar
with
erati
and C

Ju
hope-
immi
sons
terms
gener
const
curat
unitar
distin
Frey,
the al
what
Olym
Th
ernme
analys
will le
grants
nore t
which
scienti
contra
social
amine
structe
that th
immig
stereot
cial con
Cha
allies i
take se
images
conside
illustra
policy l

Public identity operationalizes the logic of the social constructions of target populations argument into an empirically viable concept.[36] That is, public identity allows the identification, measurement, and testing of how immigrants are socially constructed.

Defining Public Identity

Quite logically, the meaning of socially constructed identities in a larger context is key to determining their influence in the political arena.[37] Schneider and Ingram assert that the social construction of target populations is an empirical phenomenon.[38] Unfortunately, previous scholarship on the social construction of target populations tended to identify target populations associated with a specific policy in a unitary fashion immune to the realities of Categorical Multiplicity and Categorical Intersections, much less more recent dimensions of intersectionality.[39] In short, public identity captures the influence of social constructions of target populations[40] in public policy making and is amenable to paradigm intersectionality analysis.

Public identities[41] consist of intersectional stereotypes (e.g., a stereotype about young Arab-American men) and moral judgments of multiple group identities (the combination of race, class, gender, sexual orientation, and national status) ascribed to groups targeted by a specific policy domain. Drawing upon chronically accessible perceptions, public identities are distinct from simple stereotypes because they are developed and shaped for political goals; specifically, they serve as ideological justifications for public policy and are disseminated strategically as such.

Public identities are grounded in history (Time Dynamics) because they provide a cognitive framework for political entrepreneurs to leverage chronically accessible stereotypes and moral judgments; they also emerge or decline over time. For example, in coining the welfare queen public identity, President Ronald Reagan leveraged chronically accessible intersectional stereotypes and moral judgments about single poor African American mothers that were presumed to apply to all people who were welfare recipients. Similarly shifting constructions of the "threat" that immigrants are assumed to pose to the United States are tied to the multiple identities of the immigrants, the transnational socioeconomic climate, and the specific stereotypes and moral judgments attributed to certain immigrants, which are then used to justify policy changes that cover *all* immigrants. In addition to accounting for Categorical Multiplicity, Categorical Intersection and Time Dynamics, public identity's political nature also highlights the Individual-Institutional Relationships dimension of the concept because it reveals how institutions and elites classify and frame individuals in ways that are available to the mainstream media and then disseminated to the general public. Incorporation of Individual-Institutional Relationships is especially important for the studies of policy implementation and evaluation of later immigrant generations[42] The case study I examine here takes data from the national print media using newspapers from around the country as a major resource.[43]

The role of moral judgment at the societal level is likewise a critical component of public identity as an empirical measure of the social construction of target populations. Social psychologists have found that in processes where judgments are made in common among individuals—rather than individuals judging alone or in isolation—the explanation of a particular outcome, the "why it happened," plays a significant role in the evaluation process and the kind of judgment that emerges. In these cases of social judgment, public identities serve as an information shortcut to determine the worthiness of the person's claim. Instead of evaluating the policy content of the message (the WHAT) public identities encourage individuals to focus on the WHO and to attribute negligence ("she should have known better"), responsibility ("she was coerced by powerful forces"), or blame ("the consequences were intentional and thus there is no excuse") based on the person's public identity as manipulated or presented by elites and disseminated through the mass media.[44] Myers, for example, notes that increased media attention to immigrant population growth interacted with California citizens' fears of negative consequences based on the social construction of immigrant threat.[45] In particular, outdated knowledge of crime rates and fear of crime long associated with specific race-gender stereotypes create a gap between Millennials and their Baby Boomer counterparts similar to the gap created by Dora for non-Latino viewers—a gap into which the Oppression Olympics can enter in the absence of counterframes.

Analyzing the narrative of immigrant threat using the concept of public identity provides a way to identify the key obstacles to solidarity facing those who would prefer to avoid the future of entrenched generational battles over policies governing allocations of public resources that Frey outlines for us. As in chapter 4, the first step is to comprehend the scope of the situation. In 2001, Millennials were as young as one and as old as twenty-one. Although most were unable to vote at the time, nevertheless 9/11 has been posited as a watershed moment in their political lives. How does their younger, more tolerant branding live up to the hype when it comes to issues of immigration, race, and border security? We again turn to the Collaborative Multi-racial Political Survey (CMPS) for further information.

MILLENNIALS, IMMIGRATION AND BORDER SECURITY POLICY

While Millennials are more tolerant on some social issues like interracial dating or gay rights than their older counterparts, the differences in public opinion didn't seem to produce significantly wide differences on policy attitudes when it came to same-sex marriage. How will Millennials fare on issues of border security? Will the searing impact of 9/11 make Millennials more like their Generation X counterparts, or will the experience of greater racial diversity make it "supercool" to pursue deep political solidarity with immigrants seeking humane and comprehensive reform? This section examines Millennials' attitudes toward immigration and border security using coded language to capture the intersection with racial profiling.

Chapters 3 and 4 illustrated the perils of depending on tolerance as grounds for major political change in this country at the individual (chapter 3) and group (chapter 4) levels. Chapter 4 demonstrated the regarding the limits of exploiting Millennials' tolerance of same-sex marriage. In the immigration policy domain, previous studies also challenge the notion that Millennials are "post-racial" by birthright when it comes to immigration policy attitudes. The distinctions among immigrants in 2002 in a snapshot survey, or even a year of media of coverage, may not be long lasting.

The Pew Center has found wide differences in tolerance of immigrants across generations. Millennials have split from Generation X between 2007 and 2009 in their perceptions of immigrants as threats; in 2007 both generations had the least number of respondents agree that "the growing number of newcomers from other countries threaten traditional American customs and values"—40 percent. That number unfortunately increased among members of Generation X while declining among Millennials, providing evidence of increased political tolerance of immigrants—an important baseline consistent with the discourse of tolerance and pluralism perpetuated by *Dora the Explorer*.[46] Again, however, Millennials' higher levels of tolerance did not translate into outright support of humane immigration reform. In the same survey 59 percent of Millennials also agreed that the United States should restrict and control immigrants more than it does now. This 59 percent is lowest among the generational cohorts, but nevertheless it is a solid majority.

To further analyze Millennial attitudes on immigration, we turn again to the 2008 CMPS. The CMPS, which by design sought to obtain a sample of respondents that was proportionately diverse based on a single category, race/ethnicity, ended up reflecting the intergenerational reality described by demographer Frey. The racial diversity of the Millennial sample is indeed distinct from the older sample. For example, white respondents represent 27 percent of the older sample, but only 14.2 percent of the Millennial sample, suggesting the possible existence of Frey's "cultural generation gap." In this section we will ask ourselves if Millennials are organically oriented toward policies that reflect deep political solidarity with immigrant rights groups seeking humane, comprehensive immigration reform. Should policy advocates blindly count on Millennials' support, based on increased racial diversity or their comparatively higher levels of tolerance?

The CMPS asked a split-sample question regarding border security, randomly dividing the entire set of 4,563 respondents into four equal sets of respondents (regardless of age or race), each receiving a different prompt that can cue certain aspects of the public identity of the "Bull's Eye." The four prompts shift either the border location (Canada or Mexico) or the cause for enhanced border security (illegal immigration or terrorism).[47]

Although we cannot conclusively link surveys conducted independently years apart (CMPS and Pew), it is in fact possible that the signal event of 9/11 does still have an impact on Millennials. One striking similarity between Millennials and their older counterparts is their support of increased border security to fight terrorism. As many as 57.5 percent of Millennials believe it is either "extremely" or "very" important to enhance border security to fight terrorism, while 60.2 percent of older voters agree. Interestingly, Millennials are focused on the Canadian border, while older respondents are focused on the Mexican border.

On the other hand, the two groups who were asked about enhanced border security to combat illegal immigration responded quite differently depending on their age. No matter the location, large majorities of older voters considered increased border security to keep illegal immigrants out "extremely" or "very" important (66.6 percent on the Canadian border, 64.8 percent on the Mexican border). Millennials, by contrast, were much more sanguine: only 40.3 percent of Millennial respondents thought enhanced enforcement on the

Canadian border "extremely" or "very" important, and even fewer, 38.4 percent, rated it that way for the Mexican border.

A one-sample chi-square analysis confirmed that Millennials do in fact respond differently to this question beyond what we might expect by chance on this topic. However, as with the questions on same-sex marriage in chapter 4 and using the same scale of 0 to 1, where 0 is no practical effect and 1 is the largest possible practical effect, the effect sizes were small for all four conditions: illegal immigration/Canada (.114);[48] illegal immigration/Mexico (.114);[49] terrorism/Canada (.172);[50] and terrorism/Mexico (.224).[51] The lack of a large statistical difference is even more striking when we remember the greater racial diversity among the Millennial sample noted earlier. As we saw in chapter 4 regarding marriage equality, to blindly count on the demographic differences among Millennials for significant political change remains a suspect political strategy.

The results of the CMPS provide some evidence that the threat of terrorism continues to linger among Millennials regarding border security, posing a potential obstacle for deep political solidarity on humane immigration reform. Millennials' enhanced tolerance does not automatically translate into deep political solidarity. Thus as with same-sex marriage, organizing and efforts to build deep political solidarity are key elements required beyond passive changes to the electorate. Given the charge of "racial profiling" leveled against SB 1070 and the "racialization" of Dora as Mexican in the Photoshop contest, I next focus on an analysis of racial profiling to examine the social construction of immigrant threat. Intersectional analysis of a past signal event—9/11—can point out particular challenges that must be overcome to build solidarity among likely allies—those who share the threat of racial profiling.

In addition to media constructions, signal events can lead to drastic changes in public policy at the behest of voters, political elites, or both. Certainly the most salient signal event for American Millennials has been September 11, 2001. Using a research design that incorporates Time Dynamics to address the sudden, unexpected nature of signal events like 9/11, I analyze media coverage of groups and individuals affected by racial profiling in the six-month period before and after September 11. The basis for the conclusions reported here stem from a content analysis of 400 randomly selected newspaper articles from around the United States—234 articles prior to September 11 and 166 afterward (a decline of 29 percent).[52] Again, my focus in this case study is on the social construction of profiling

targets, rather than any national study of who is actually racially profiled in numerous situations.[53] Keeping with the language of threat
and target populations, I term the public identity of those profiled
the "Bull's Eye."

Considering Categorical Multiplicity and Categorical Intersection
is an important value added by the intersectional concept of public
identity to the social construction of target populations approach.
Although the topic of racial profiling nominally privileges one category—race—over other categories of difference, public identity as
an intersectional concept obligates us for the purposes of this case
study[54] to deeply consider categories like gender, class, and national
status. The qualitative analysis of racial profiling targets indicates
that they are overwhelmingly male[55] but that they are of varying
national status. This evidence of the "Bull's Eye" public identity in
media coverage is echoed by earlier findings of second-generation
decline and persistent disadvantage among Dominican, African
American, and Puerto Rican men in New York City.[56] In this sense,
applying an intersectional analysis to a complex topic of immigration
and racial profiling reveals how intersectionality theory, no matter
its feminist roots, can articulate and reveal policy challenges facing
males in a way that brings people together rather than foster a "battle
of the sexes," or as Myers and Frey might fear, a "battle of the generations." This additional attention to multiple categories points out
a possible common ground upon which building deep political solidarity can start.

Some of the results of the study are to be expected. The intersection of racial profiling and immigration was low in the months
leading up to September 11, as African American citizens were
referenced as the targets of racial profiling in 102 of 234 articles
(nearly 44 percent of the sample). Following September 11, articles
containing references to the racial profiling of people who were perceived to be Arab American skyrocketed to 45 percent of the post-
September 11 dataset, after appearing in *zero* articles in the earlier
period.

As was the case in the previous chapters, attention to Categorical
Multiplicity, Categorical Intersections, and Time Dynamics is
not sufficient. Incorporating Diversity Within and Individual-
Institutional Relationships into the analysis reveals two particular
challenges to solidarity that, while not insurmountable, clearly illustrate the complexity of the relationship between immigration and
racial profiling issues. The "Bull's Eye" target of racial profiling is

associated with a specific set of profiling experiences in systematic ways, as we see next.

The Complexity of Solidarity for Mobilization

Surely groups do not stand pat when faced with a threat like Arizona's SB 1070 in 2010 or California's Proposition 187 in 1994. Unitary analyses like that of Myers, which quantitatively analyze groups based on a single dimension (e.g., "immigrants" *or* "Boomers") risk missing out on mobilization conducted by groups that may in fact bridge both categories—naturalized citizens, whose long-term residence in the United States is both an age-related dimension and an immigrant experience. Political scientists tend to agree that a perceived legitimate threat can spark increased naturalized citizen voters to turn out on election day,[57] but they disagree about how long the increase might last over time.[58] Part of perceiving threat is based on exposure to media coverage of the threat as well as experiences associated with that threat. The media dataset is thus well equipped to investigate not simply the social construction of the threat, but any discussion of possible policy responses or mobilization as well.

Table 5.1 places the presumed racial identity of the profiling policy target and the profiling experience in conversation with each other. From this table we can see that different perceived racial and ethnic backgrounds are associated with different types of profiling

Table 5.1 Public Identity of the Bull's Eye: Race of Subject and Profiling Experience*

	Airport Search	Airline Discrimination	Police Search	Traffic Stop	Police Detention
African Americans	48	5	330	1,005	150
Arab Americans**	381	890	0	0	992
Asian Americans	11	11	1	20	34
Latino/a Americans	0	0	78	153	0
Native Americans	0	0	0	20	0
White / Caucasian	24	0	0	4	0

*All numbers are in text units (lines of text in the original document). The total number of units coded for all races/ethnicities: 7,938. The total number of units coded for all profiling experiences: 5,497. Profiling experiences could be coded as not referring to any specific racial or ethnic group, or multiple codings, so numbers in the table are not additive.

**The Arab American category includes a number of subjects who are perceived to be of Middle Eastern descent based on their appearance, surname, or religious attire, but do not actually consider themselves Arab American (e.g., Sikhs and Somalis). While other categories are constructed solely based on the reported race or ethnicity, the level of misperceptions was especially egregious in the Arab American category.

experiences. People perceived to be African American and Latino have vastly different profiling experiences from those perceived to be Arab American. Both Latinos and African Americans, the focus of most articles prior to September 11 as targets of racial profiling, are portrayed as experiencing state and local police searches and traffic stops in the highest numbers. On the other hand, Asian Americans have a more evenly distributed set of racial profiling experiences, despite the overwhelming focus on a single incident: Dr. Wen Ho Lee's suspicious arrest and detention.

In contrast, people perceived to be Arab American experienced racial profiling at airports and in airplanes, in addition to police detention. The police detention category contains much of the controversy surrounding Attorney General John Ashcroft's decision to request "informational interviews" from over 5,000 men, mostly of Middle Eastern descent and aged eighteen to thirty-three, following the declaration of the "War on Terror." No comparable experience occurred with any other racial or ethnic group in the time period examined.

This systematic difference in profiling experience presents valuable information for activists and policy practitioners seeking to build deep political solidarity for comprehensive change, because this systematic Diversity Within the public identity of the Bull's Eye is replicated not simply in the profiling experience aspects of Individual-Institutional Relationships, but also in the arena of feasible policy responses, as indicated in Table 5.2.

How do groups mobilize in response to tangible threats? For African American and Latino targets, seeking federal legal intervention has been a long-standing strategy to combat their struggles with state and local law enforcement agencies. This method addressed racial profiling allegations of African Americans over the past fifteen years with the Cincinnati and Columbus (Ohio) police departments as well as the New Jersey state troopers. For Latinos, federal legal remedies (as a solution) were similarly a strong option, particularly with regard to the renegade Rampart division of the Los Angeles Police Department (L.A.P.D.). Indeed, this strategy is currently being implemented to fight Arizona's SB 1070, as the Obama administration successfully (as of the time of this writing) joined with the Mexican American Legal Defense and Education Fund (MALDEF) and its allies to file separate litigation to stay implementation of the parts of the immigration law expected to produce the most egregious forms of racial profiling. That said, the current implementation policies of the administration's Department of Homeland Security has led to higher numbers of detentions and deportations through its division of Immigration Control

Table 5.2 "Bull's Eye" Racial Identity and Proposed Policy Response*

	New Federal Law	New State or Local Law	Improved Enforcement of Existing Laws	Commission a Study	Legal Remedies	Pro-Profiling	Incident Not Racial Profiling
African Americans	44	259	27	141	913	73	65
Asian Americans	0	13	0	0	59	0	0
Latinos	3	52	0	18	178	0	51
Native Americans	0	0	0	0	0	0	0
Whites /Caucasians	0	0	0	7	0	10	0
Arab Americans**	9	62	3	0	45	137	75

*Again all text units here are combined across the one-year period. Figures from a specific period are noted in the text only where applicable.

**The Arab American category includes most significantly a number of subjects who were perceived to be of Middle Eastern descent (e.g., Sikhs, Somalis) based on their appearance, surname, or religious attire. While other categories are constructed solely based on the reported race or ethnicity, the level of misperception was especially egregious in the Arab American category.

and Enforcement (ICE) than any other president to date. Thus the idea of a complicated Individual-Institutional Relationship between Latinos/as and other groups caught within the ICE dragnet again signify caution about any assumptions of faith in a federal response without considering it in relationship to state and local levels.

In terms of deep political solidarity from an intersectional perspective, addressing Diversity Within must also include attention to the Individual-Institutional Relationships for Asian Americans and Arab Americans in this policy domain as well. Media coverage of Asian and Arab American racial profiling targets has focused on how the federal government is an *adversary*, not an ally, in contrast to the coverage of African Americans and Latinos/as. For example, among coverage of Asian American racial profiling, media coverage of legal remedies focused on the defense and exoneration of Dr. Wen Ho Lee, imprisoned and investigated by the FBI. Similarly, filing suit *against* the Justice Department was a focus of Arab American resistance in the legal strategies category.

Based on these findings, we can recognize that debates among groups regarding mobilization and policy responses may not simply be grounded in history or conventional practices but along lines far more substantive. Recognition of this reality emerged from an intersectional analysis of media coverage, but intersectional analysis of policy initiatives themselves and their enforcement can also produce similarly nuanced results,[59] a point to which I'll return in the final section of this chapter.

In addition to the complexity of consolidating support for policy strategies among likely allies, the second challenge identified by this analysis is similar to that illustrated by Dora the Explorer at the start of this chapter. How do we account for the different interpretations of a signal event—in this case, the tragedy of September 11?

Both the pre- and post-September 11 article samples included different interpretations of the profiling experienced by a variety of groups. The national media dataset included 73 and 137 lines of text *in favor of* profiling associated with African Americans and Arab Americans, respectively. In a vein perhaps most similar to the "Dora" debate, the experiences journalists categorized as racial profiling were labeled "not racial profiling" in numerous instances. When African Americans were the target, 65 lines of text debated whether the actions described were actually instances of racial profiling. Closely associated with the pro-profiling stance were the efforts of local and federal law enforcement to distinguish the actions of their agents from racial profiling. This effort occurred most frequently in connection with accusations from African Americans (65 lines of text), Latinos (51 lines of text), and Arab Americans (75 lines of text). Some government officials quite seriously sought to draw a distinction between racial profiling and effective police work. Again, however, attention to Time Dynamics is also key at the same time.

One sobering finding within the African American cell is that the majority of lines of text that discussed pro-profiling as a solution occurred following September 11 (66 of 73 lines of text, or 90 percent). These 66 lines focused on African Americans who were pro-profiling of Arab Americans, based on reports of survey research by the Kaiser Family Foundation and op-ed articles by prominent African American commentators like Stanley Crouch and African American law enforcement professionals. The hypocritical nature of such African American attitudes was the frequent topic—blacks, as prior victims of racial profiling, were now favoring the racial profiling of another group. This criticism resembles the accusations leveled at African American voters surrounding Prop 8 discussed in chapter 4. This finding was challenged, however, by survey research that suggested African Americans are much less willing to trade civil liberties for security than are whites and Latinos.[60] How might we think about these differing results?

Aside from actual error in either survey (an unlikely but possible explanation), the intersectional analysis provides two interesting avenues of interpretation. First, given the different types of profiling experiences, it is possible that the profiling experiences of African Americans and Arab Americans are so distinct as to not have a strong chronically accessible linkage in survey respondents' minds. In a manner analogous to chapter 4's discussion of civil rights, African Americans may not understand airport experiences and traffic stops as part of an umbrella concept of racial profiling. Unlike chapter 4, however, this is an open empirical question not resolved by prior analyses and therefore can't be confirmed.

The second possible explanation concerns the role of citizenship status as a complicating factor connected to the moral judgment aspect of the Bull's Eye public identity. In examining the relationships between civil liberties and immigration status, research in 2002 by the Kaiser Family Foundation found that respondents shifted their opinions when the subject's immigration status changed. When asked if "an Arab or Muslim who is not a U.S. citizen" should have the same rights as a U.S. citizen if arrested for stealing a car, 45 percent agreed and 46 percent disagreed—a difference of only 1 percent. However, when those 45 percent who initially favored equal rights were asked if they would continue to support giving equal rights for the suspect if the person was here illegally, 54 percent said no.[61] The attribution of social judgment in this instance is important, and relates to the prior definition of public identity as involving both intersectional stereotypes (e.g., men of African American, Arab American, Latino, or Asian American descent) and moral judgments (e.g., of prior legal or undocumented status). Regardless of which explanation is plausible, there is in this dataset empirical evidence of pro-profiling positions among African Americans that must be considered as an obstacle, however small or large, to solidarity on the topic. Although the 73 pro-profiling lines of text pale in comparison to the 1,384 lines of text indicating African Americans' overt action challenging racial profiling, it remains an obstacle that must be addressed.

An intersectional analysis of the media coverage six months before and after September 11 provided evidence that the public identity of the "Bull's Eye" is conditioned upon intersectional stereotypes and moral judgments of "WHO" is at stake, and that there is some overlap between "WHO" is at stake and the relevant policy responses considered or pursued. Moreover, these overlaps persisted even in a larger discussion about whether any remedy was even warranted. The substantive outcomes of this debate early in the twenty-first century are well documented: while there remains no federal law outlawing racial profiling, the PATRIOT Act, which created new crimes, penalties, and roles for government in direct response to the September 11 tragedy, was passed overwhelmingly by both houses of Congress and signed into law by President George W. Bush on October 26, 2001.

"There's a fine line between racial profiling and fine police work." With that comment African American comedian D. L. Hughley provided the punch line to a joke justifying the racial profiling of Arab Americans to a *Tonight Show with Jay Leno* television audience several months after September 11. Though we cannot claim that Millennials by their mere existence on earth to be harbingers of a postracial society, neither can we necessarily blame them. Studies of second-generation immigrants find little to no association between the minimalist multiculturalism they espouse as "supercool" and a political analysis that could reveal how much things desperately need to change. Absent intersectionality theory, their experience with multiculturalism remains stagnated at the *Dora the Explorer* level of diversity appreciation—exciting and appropriate for children aged three to eight, but a phase that even Nickelodeon has realized is fleeting.

It's time to go, as they say on Nickelodeon's educational website, "beyond the backpack."

MOVING FORWARD ON IMMIGRATION POLICY TOGETHER RATHER THAN SEPARATELY

The United States guarantees freedom of speech, and by no means are the doctored images of Dora a reason to restrict freedom of speech. But neither are these images completely innocuous. In a world of twenty-four-hour news cycles and the ability of images and videos to go "viral," blanketing the world within hours or days with a specific take on any given policy debate, they cannot be considered innocuous. As the persistent minority of Americans who deny President Barack Obama's citizenship indicates, such Internet rumors can be used both explicitly and surreptitiously to mislead citizens.

Immigration is a notoriously complex policy domain, with multiple overlapping constituencies and roots as deep as the founding of the United States itself. Using public identity as a paradigm intersectionality operationalization of the process of socially constructing target populations allowed us to identify key challenges to solidarity in a way that will ideally assist the next push for the DREAM Act, reform of ICE practices, and ultimately comprehensive immigration reform. Such an investigation is designed to facilitate effective pursuit of interdependence among social justice activists, fulfilling in part the prediction Canadian policy scholar Olena Hankivsky made in the introduction to this book: "to contribute an important...advancement in expanding policy discourse in relation to social justice."[62]

The empirical analysis conducted in this chapter, along with that of chapter 4, provide convincing evidence of the theoretical claim developed in chapter 3: increased political tolerance among Millennials in particular does not necessarily breed deep political solidarity, a bond of interdependence that is particularly important for individuals, groups, and policy practitioners in the area of social justice.

This chapter also introduced the intersectional concept of public identity as one instance of intersectionality's contribution to deepening analyses of public policy. In the case study of immigration and racial profiling, use of public identity embraced Categorical Multiplicity and Categorical Intersection by analyzing gender and national status dimensions at the same analytical level as race, revealing possible roadblocks to deep political solidarity and the benefits of intersectional analysis for men who find themselves in the crosshairs of the public identity of the Bull's Eye. The research design further incorporated other elements of paradigm intersectionality: Time Dynamics, Individual-Institutional Relationships, and Diversity Within.

Keeping our analysis in twentieth-century apolitical terms of "diversity" and "multiculturalism," as we saw from the Photoshop contest, does not prevent others from dragging one into the political debate through mobilizing a public identity of a target population. Pursuit of intersectional policy analysis through the use of public identity can reveal stereotypes and social judgments that must be called into question as we move through policy debates and highlight possible pitfalls for future solidarity. Yet intersectionality provides more than a single concept to the development of better public policy understandings of the connections between immigration and racial politics. How might intersectionality assist in the future to move like-minded policy activists "beyond the backpack"?

A paradigmatic intersectionality approach to public policy, instead of cueing the Oppression Olympics, replaces the simple model of structural subordinate relations inherent in analyses of policy domains like health disparities or health determinants with a causally complex dynamic matrix of social relations that produce groups and individuals that simultaneously experience both discrimination and privilege.[63] Another primary benefit of intersectional public policy has been to address the problem of unintended policy consequences.[64] Policy experts from the domains of public health and international human rights point us in important directions. Based on her expertise in international human rights, British scholar-activist Nira Yuval-Davis proposes a four-step process, which, when integrated with contributions from Canadian health policy scholars Olena Hankivsky and Renee Cormier and United States psychologists Elizabeth Cole and Lynn Weber, offers a number of practical questions to guide policy scholars in their ability to conduct intersectional analyses.

These scholars and practitioners generally assert that intersectional research begins at the stage of the research question, and is contingent upon deep political solidarity from the start.[65] Effectively evaluating public policy using the tenets of paradigm intersectionality involves crafting research questions collaboratively—that is, in concert with policy makers, grassroots activists, and community groups in a manner that fully attends to Diversity Within. While prior standards in qualitative, interpretive, and/or community-based research have emphasized collaboration between researchers and researched, intersectional policy analysis broadens the collaboration further in accordance with the tenets of paradigmatic intersectionality. Having token elite representation from marginalized groups (e.g., one gay white male or one straight Latino elected official) would not meet this standard of participation.[66]

Designing such a study also involves asking questions about power relations that are central to understanding the consequences of public policy—particularly those unintended consequences that emerge, like the benefit of prior policies to recent immigrants from policies designed to serve native-born minorities—in order to reform policies in ways that expand the pie rather than cut the same sliver ever thinner. To reveal such power relations, designing a study that both centers power relations within and between groups and properly determines an appropriate referent group for each group under study is key, instead of assuming that the referent group should always be the dominant societal group. Determining protocols for data collection collaboratively and setting a common criterion for consideration of power within and among the five dimensions of paradigm intersectionality—Categorical Multiplicity, Categorical Intersections, Time Dynamics, Diversity Within, and Individual-Institutional Relationships—are also important for the evaluation of public policy from an intersectional perspective. As well, unearthing disaggregated data pertaining to various social, legal, and identity categories[67] can better reveal the roles the social constructions of target populations play in public policy implementation.

One particular resource for this type of often original data collection is an expanded analysis of the "grey literature" in a policy domain. Hankivsky and Cormier define "grey literature" as "scientific and technical reports, patent documents, conference papers, internal reports, government documents, newsletters, fact sheets, theses and dissertations which have not been published in conventional channels such as journals or books and which may be more difficult to access."[68] Such searches, they argue, may not simply uncover relevant policy literature but also assist in producing an inclusive research collaboration: "through such a search community organizations conducting research on the same topic area might be identified and could be contacted for more details."[69]

Methodologically, intersectional evaluations of public policy involve contextual analysis of current policy outcomes to examine all of the possible determinants of such outcomes and intersectional review of policy initiatives and systems of implementation in terms of their efficacy to address the problems.[70] While mixed-method models provide the appropriate combination of the strengths of quantitative and qualitative research methods,[71] the final step of intersectional public policy research is critical to building the deep political solidarity that is the ultimate goal of this book.

In light of the collaboration demands at the start of the evaluation endeavor, it is probably unsurprising that having an effective knowledge translation plan is the final implementation aspect of intersectional approaches to public policy. Indeed, Hankivsky and Cormier argue that it is critical to intersectional policy work. They identify four key knowledge-translation questions that recognize both the reality of interdependence Myers seeks to communicate regarding immigrants and Baby Boomers and the justice standard of equity discussed in chapter 3:

1. Who are the key stakeholder groups and are they represented through all phases of the research and policy-making process?
2. Are research findings being communicated in a manner that is consistent with an intersectional perspective?
3. Are all the key stakeholders involved in all phases of the knowledge translation plan, ranging from knowledge creation to dissemination through to knowledge uptake and evaluation?
4. How will the knowledge translation plan be monitored and evaluated?[72]

As defined here, knowledge translation is much more than the standard "report back" so familiar to scholars and activists involved in community-based research. It extends to include questions of how knowledge is created and the transformation of knowledge not just into glossy brochures but into future action among all involved parties. In this sense the research represents a tacit commitment to working on making the changes necessary to rectify the situation. Both of our real-world scholar-activists in chapter 3, W. E. B. Du Bois and Hannah Arendt, recognized this aspect of their mission for their own groups; the trick for the twenty-first century is to expand deep political solidarity to include this form of action for multiple justice-seeking groups.

While these policy analysis standards are somewhat technical and nowhere mention Dora the Explorer, they assist in bringing together the widest possible coalition and considering the widest possible set of collaborative concerns for comprehensive policy evaluation, reform, and implementation. It would, of course, be politically naïve to think that a straightforward intersectional review would automatically produce a justice-oriented "groupthink" that could shift the world. Intersectional policy research designs can build the consensus to use policy to bring people together to overcome the cultural generation gap and other threats to our ability to function in a diverse, transnational context. But politics is politics, and tangible organizing must accompany any pen and paper intersectional analysis.

The next chapter concludes the book by returning us to our central question: in a new century, with a new generation, how can we bring new tools to the table to address the problems of the past? It intends to provide marching orders flexible enough to cross generations without minimizing the task at hand. Below are a set of opportunities to address the cultural generation gap identified by Frey and Myers.

How to talk to someone a lot older than you about the dangers of the cultural generation gap

- Together learn more about the work of the National Domestic Workers Alliance CARE campaign, which actively links the interests between the predominantly immigrant women who serve as care workers with the interests of the older generation that are being cared for: http://www.nationaldomesticworkeralliance.org/campaigns/20-caring-across-generations-national-campaign-for-the-care-act.

Examine how the relationship of interdependence already exists across the generations and can be built upon for broad social transformation that creates jobs, provides education and pathways to citizenship, and provides the opportunity for vast improvements in health care provision for seniors.

- Together watch the documentary, "Welcome to Shelbyville," which uses the election of Barack Obama to the presidency as a springboard for discussions about immigrant integration into the rural town of Shelbyville, Tennessee.

How to Talk to Someone a Lot Younger Than You About the Dangers of the Cultural Generation Gap

- Together learn more about the work of the National Domestic Workers Alliance CARE campaign, which actively links the interests between the predominantly immigrant women who serve as care workers with the interests of the older generation that are being cared for: http://www.nationaldomesticworkeralliance.org/campaigns/20-caring-across-generations-national-campaign-for-the-care-act.

Examine how the relationship of interdependence already exists across the generations and can be built upon for broad social transformation that creates jobs, provides education and pathways to citizenship, and provides the opportunity for vast improvements in health care provision for seniors.

- There are two websites that provide data, oral histories, and examinations of immigrant experiences from around the world. The Hypercities project is a research and educational project featuring nineteen cities around the world, including access to maps of tweets (trust your younger person to explain tweeting if you need it!) from Cairo during the recent ouster of President Hosni Mubarak: http://hypercities.com/.

Immigration Sites of Conscience is an international network of history museums of immigration across the United States and Europe. The network intends to start a new conversation about immigration around the world by providing opportunities for education and dialogue. http://www.sitesofconscience.org/resources/networks/immigration/en/

Notes

1. This is the welcome video offered on Dora's official NickJr. website: http://www.nickjr.com/dora-the-explorer. Last accessed September 3, 2010.
2. The last sweeping reform of immigration policy was the Immigration Reform and Control Act (IRCA) of 1986. Though many changes in policy have emerged since 1986, IRCA is traditionally referred to as the most recent comprehensive change.
3. Elian Gonzalez is, of course, a real-life little boy who was found floating in the waters between Cuba and Florida in a botched attempt by his

mother to reach the United States; when necessary, the federal government used force to return to the boy to his nearest biological relative, his estranged father, who remained a loyal citizen of Cuba.

4. Incidentally, this image was created by the same woman who created the mugshot image that gained such notoriety—Debbie Groben.

5. Myers, Dowell (2007). *Immigrants and Boomers: Forging a New Social Contract for the Future of America*. New York: Russell Sage Foundation; Frey, William H. (2010). "Will Arizona Be America's Future?" http://www.brookings.edu/opinions/2010/0428_arizona_frey.aspx Accessed July 26, 2010; Kasinitz, Philip, John Mollenkopf, and Mary C. Waters, editors. *Becoming New Yorkers: Ethnographies of the New Second Generation*. New York: Russell Sage Foundation, 2007; Kasinitz, Philip, John Mollenkopf, Mary C. Waters, and Jennifer Holdaway. *Inheriting the City: The Children of Immigrants Come of Age*. New York: Russell Sage Foundation, 2008.

6. Villarreal, Yvonne. "The Exploradora," *The Los Angeles Times*, August 10, 2010, D16.

7. Ibid., D17.

8. UCLA Chicano Studies Center Director Chon Noriega enthuses, "She really exemplifies the diversity of our [U.S.] culture, particularly among people under the age of 18, where one in four is Latino…" "Dora the Explorer's 10th Anniversary," NBC News, August 14, 2010.

9. USC sociology professor Jody Vallejo also notes: "At the same time it does allow people from those different origins to make her their own character, to take ownership. For non-Latinos who watch the show, it makes Latinos more relatable. It demonstrates that bilingualism is not that bad. But it makes it seem like Latinos come from a monolithic culture." Villarreal "The Exploradora," D17; see also Szabo, Liz. "Dora the Explorer Turns 10 as a Model for Pre-K Girls," USA TODAY, August 10, 2010.

10. Kasinitz, Mollenkopf, and Waters, *Becoming New Yorkers*.

11. Kasinitz, Mollenkopf, Waters, and Holdaway, *Inheriting the City*, 303.

12. Kasinitz, Mollenkopf, and Waters. *Becoming New Yorkers*, 16.

13. Foerster, Amy. "Isn't Anybody Here from Alabama? Solidarity and Struggle in a 'Mighty, Mighty Union." In Kasinitz, P., J. Mollenkopf, M. C. Waters, editors. *Becoming New Yorkers: Ethnographies of the New Second Generation*. New York: Russell Sage Foundation Press, 2004; Kasinitz, Mollenkopf, Waters, and Holdaway. *Inheriting the City*, 22 and 289.

14. Guidotti-Hernandez, Nicole. "Dora the Explorer, Constructing 'Latinidades," and the Politics of Global Citizenship." *Latino Studies* 5 (2007): 213.

15. Jones, B. and F. Baumgartner. *The Politics of Attention: How Government Prioritizes Problems*. Chicago: University of Chicago Press, 2003, 7.

16. Guidotti-Hernandez, "Dora the Explorer," 212.

17. Villarreal, "La Exploradora," D17.

18. Guidotti-Hernandez, "Dora the Explorer," 214.
19. Ibid, 216.
20. Ibid, 226.
21. Ibid, 211.
22. Ramakrishnan, S. Karthick. *Democracy in Immigrant America: Changing Demographics and Political Participation.* Stanford, CA: Stanford University Press, 2005, 30–31.
23. Myers, *Immigrants and Boomers*, 8.
24. Myers, *Immigrants and Boomers*; Ramakrishnan, *Democracy in Immigrant America.*
25. Ramakrishnan, *Democracy in Immigrant America*, 122.
26. Ramakrishnan found evidence of the ongoing development in real time: whites account for a smaller percentage of the second immigrant generation, and that generation will play a role in reshaping the composition of the United States, Ramakrishnan, *Democracy in Immigrant America*, 30–31.
27. Myers, *Immigrants and Boomers*, 36.
28. Ramakrishnan, *Democracy in Immigrant America*, 2.
29. NielsenWire. "The United States in 2020 in a Very Different Place".
30. Frey, "Will Arizona Be America's Future?"
31. Ibid.
32. According to data from the Current Population Survey, in 2000 eleven states had immigrant populations that exceeded 25 percent of the population. For California, New York, Hawaii, and Florida the percentage was 33 percent or more. (Ramakrishnan, *Democracy in Immigrant America*, 31).
33. Myers, Dowell. *Immigrants and Boomers*, 2007, 26.
34. Information-processing models of public policy best account for this causal influence on public policy (Jones, Bryan and Frank Baumgartner *The Politics of Attention: How Government Prioritizes Problems.* Chicago: University of Chicago Press, 2005).
35. Racial profiling, as defined in twenty-four or thiry-six documents within the media dataset, focuses on racial and ethnic minorities as persons profiled and law enforcement officials at the federal, state, and local levels as perpetrators of profiling. Several of these articles quote either federal proposed legislation or approved local and state statutes defining racial profiling. For example, the End Racial Profiling Act of 2001 defines racial profiling as "the practice of a law enforcement agent relying, to any degree, on race, ethnicity, or national origin in selecting which individuals to subject to routine investigatory activities," such as traffic or pedestrian stops and border inspections. Again this wording has not yet been passed into federal law. However, the Columbus, Ohio City Council did in fact define racial profiling in a unanimously passed amendment to its city code: "Racial profiling is defined as to 'stop, detain, investigate, search, seize or arrest' an individual based on that person's race or ethnicity." The city's antidiscrimination law has been on the books since 1994.

36. Hancock, Ange-Marie *The Public Identity of the Welfare Queen and the Politics of Disgust*. New York: University Press, 2004.

37. Huddy, Leonie. "From Social to Political Identity: A Critical Examination of Social Identity Theory." *Political Psychology* 22 (2001): 127–56; see also Brewer, Paul R. "Value Words and Lizard Brains: Do Citizens Deliberate About Appeals to Their Core Values?" *Political Psychology* 22 (2001): 45–64.

38. Schneider, Ann and Helen Ingram. "Social Construction of Target Populations: Implications for Politics and Policy." *American Political Science Review* 87 (1993): 335; see also Schneider and Ingram, "Social Construction: Response." *American Political Science Review* 89 (1995): 441–46.

39. Prior research, most notably in the area of AIDS policy making, has analyzed the social constructions of target populations in a unitary way—that is, based on a single aspect of their identity (e.g., sexual orientation, HIV acquisition process, or race/ethnicity). In this sense, earlier studies have failed to address Lieberman's critique of social constructions as being impermissibly vague regarding the well-established argument that citizens simultaneously possess many politically relevant identities (e.g., a gay male is not simply gay in a straight world; he is also male in a patriarchal culture).

40. While Schneider and Ingram deny that the focus is upon group identities, the examples in their original typology of advantaged-contender-dependent-deviant categories are largely grounded in prominent politically relevant group identities (e.g., minorities, communists, mothers) that have been studied by political psychologists. One key difference between the focus of this study and Schneider and Ingram's theory is the dependent variable. While their interest is in policy design, my attempt here is to test their assertion that social constructions matter in other areas of policy studies, namely the circumscribed universe of policy options (what they term "policy tools") considered feasible by legislators and ultimately the actual legislation passed into law.

41. Public identity is further amenable to intersectional analysis, to address the unitary categories within Schneider and Ingram's typology, which further testing has documented to be empirically unwieldy. Schroedel, Jean Reith and Daniel R. Jordan. "Senate Voting and Social Construction of Target Populations: A Study of AIDS Policy Making, 1987–1992." *Journal of Health Politics, Policy and Law* 23 (1998): 107–32.
Both issues are addressed with the usage of public identity, which codes on multiple dimensions as evidence of larger conceptual variables. This makes content analysis possible at the interval level using scales and indices, rather than dichotomous categorization. Yet the quantitative empirical utility of public identity does not obviate the need for rigorous qualitative analysis to determine the dimensions of public identity per policy domain and exploratory factor analysis to confirm the conceptual variables prior to proceeding with any methods of correlational or causal

analysis. Future research in these domains will hopefully shed light on how best to empirically measure what Schneider and Ingram argue is empirically measurable.

42. Prior studies have found evidence that educational institutions and other formal bureaucracies serve as "sorting mechanisms" with implications for policy implementation and evaluation. Kasinitz, Mollenkopf, and Waters, *Becoming New Yorkers*, 14.

43. This approach is well established in political behavior. In political science, see Sniderman, Paul, Diana Mutz, and Richard Brody. *Political Persuasion and Attitude Change*. Ann Arbor, MI: University of Michigan Press, 1996; and Kellstedt, Paul. "Media Framing and the Dynamics of Racial Policy Preferences." *American Journal of Political Science* 44 (2000): 239–55. In political psychology more specifically, see Huddy, "From Social to Political Identity," 144.

44. See Shaver, 1999.

45. Myers, *Immigrants and Boomers*, 26–28.

46. Taylor and Keeter, "Millennials," 79.

47. The following four questions were randomly split among the sample, meaning each person was asked one of these four options by chance:

    a) In order to keep **terrorists** out, how important do you think it is to increase surveillance of the U.S.-**Canada** border?

    b) In order to keep **terrorists** out, how important do you think it is to increase surveillance of the U.S.-**Mexico** border?

    c) In order to keep **illegal immigrants** out, how important do you think it is to increase surveillance of the U.S.–**Canada** border?

    d) In order to keep **illegal immigrants** out, how important do you think it is to increase surveillance of the U.S.–**Mexico** border?

    Each time respondents had the opportunity to respond: "Extremely important; Very important; Somewhat important; Not at all important; Don't know; Refused."

48. $\chi 2$ (3, N = 120) = 31.766, p <.005; Effect size r = .114

49. $\chi 2$ (3, N = 137) = 35.723, p < .005; Effect size r = .114

50. $\chi 2$ (3, N = 119) = 7.087, p < .010; Effect size r = .172

51. $\chi 2$ (3, N=128) = 12.912, p< .005; Effect size r = .224

52. In all, I analyzed 23,331 units of text (lines of text as delineated in the original) in the six months prior to September 11 and 18,486 lines of text post-9/11. The total number of units coded for all races/ethnicities: 7,938. The total number of units coded for all profiling experiences: 5,497.

53. Here I refer specifically to the several pieces of federal legislation that are not yet law: the End Racial Profiling Act of 2001 (H. 2074/S.989) and the Racial Profiling Prohibition Act of 2002. There are other pieces of legislation that deal in part with items associated with racial profiling (e.g., the PATRIOT Act), but both are primarily concerned with other domains of public policy than racial profiling.

54. As I noted in chapter 1, theorist Rita Dhamoon and others have convincingly demonstrated that there can be no a priori delineation of categories for an analysis—such a list must be derived based on the topic to be investigated.

55. The one cell that included a significant number of women was "Retail Store Harassment among Blacks," where African American women's experiences in stores were discussed in 83 of 163 (51 percent) lines of text about African American racial profiling targets. Women were not considered profiling targets in large numbers among any other racial group. While several articles about Arab Americans discussed women's fears, the fear was of hate crimes, not racial profiling.

56. Kasinitz, Mollenkopf, Waters, and Holdaway, *Inheriting the City*, 16.

57. Although this research was not available for media coverage during the time period examined, it is clear that there are possible responses, as Ramakrishnan notes here, that precede voter registration and turnout: "However, concerns over the 'war on terrorism' and the backlash against Arab Americans and South Asian Americans following the September 11 attacks may once again produce differences in the sense of threat among immigrants of different racial groups, religious affiliations, and national origins. Indeed, there have been reports of sharp increases in applications for naturalizations among immigrants of Middle Eastern descent following the repercussions of the present war on terrorism." Ramakrishnan, *Democracy in Immigrant America*, 143.

58. Ramakrishnan, *Democracy in Immigrant America*; Pantoja, Adrian, Ricardo Ramirez, and Gary Segura. "Citizens by Choice, Voters by Necessity: Patterns in Political Mobilization by Naturalized Latinos. *Political Research Quarterly* 54 (2001): 729–50; Ramakrishnan, S. Karthick, and Thomas Espenshade. "Immigrant Incorporation and Political Participation in the United States." *International Migration Review* 35 (2001): 870–909.

59. Yuval-Davis, Nira "Intersectionality and Feminist Politics." *European Journal of Women's Studies*, 13.3 (2006): 193–209.

60. Davis, D. W. and B. D. Silver. "Civil Liberties vs. Security: Public Opinion in the Context of the Terrorist Attacks in America." *American Journal of Political Science* 48.1 (2004): 28–46.

61. National Public Radio, Kaiser Family Foundation, and Kennedy School of Government. "Civil Liberties Update." 2002; accessed online August 15, 2010, 17.

62. Hankivsky, Olena. "Gender vs. Diversity Mainstreaming: A Preliminary Examination of the Role and Transformative Potential of Feminist Theory." *Canadian Journal of Political Science* 38 (2005): 977–1001.

63. Ibid.

64. Hankivsky, Olena, Renee Cormier, and Diego de Marich. *Intersectionality: Moving Women's Health Research and Policy Forward.* Vancouver: Women's Health Research Network, 2009, 3.

65. Hancock, Ange-Marie. "When Multiplication Doesn't Equal Quick Addition: Examining Intersectionality as a Research Paradigm." *Perspectives on Politics* 5 (2007): 63–79; Hankivsky, O., R. Cormier, and de Merich, *Intersectionality*; see also Yuval Davis, "Intersectionality and Feminist Politics," and McCall, Leslie (2005). "The Complexity of Intersectionality." *Signs: A Journal of Women and Culture in Society*,

66. Cole, "Coalitions as a Model for Intersectionality"; Hankivsky, Cormier, and de Merich, "Intersectionality."

67. Yuval Davis, "Intersectionality and Feminist Politics."

68. Hankivsky, Cormier, and de Merich, *Intersectionality*, 24.

69. Ibid.

70. Yuval Davis, "Intersectionality and Feminist Politics."

71. Hankivsky, Cormier, and de Merich, "Intersecitonality," 29; Hancock, "When Multiplication Doesn't Equal Quick Addition."

72. Hankivsky, Cormier, and de Merich, "Intersecitonality," 30–31.

Conclusion: A New Politics Manual for the Twenty-First Century

"Suddenly your heart chills. You turn yourself away toward the golden twinkle of the purple night and hesitate again. What's the use? Why not always yield—always take what's offered—always bow to force, whether of cannon or dislike? Then the great fear surges in your soul, the real fear... the fear lest right there and then you are losing your own soul; that you are losing your own soul and the soul of a people; that millions of unborn children... are being there and then despoiled by you because you are a coward and dare not fight!"[1]

W. E. B. Du Bois's challenge to us in this excerpt from *Darkwater* is to gather our courage and become active fomenters rather than passive supporters of social justice. After fifteen years of working with Millennials in a wide variety of capacities, I am convinced that they have the predispositions—from generally tolerant attitudes to often close-knit relationships with their family elders—that situate them well to make the change to work collaboratively toward the future. And yet the optimism of the 2008 election among Millennials and others counting on the presidency of Barack Obama to bring change to the country has been deeply chastened by the severity of Movement Backlash and Leapfrog Paranoia, as well as the daunting task of rebuilding the country following the Great Recession that lies ahead of us. In order to avoid feeling paralyzed by the need to end the Oppression Olympics, the major civic goal of this book has been to offer a path of deep commitment, which is accessible from the individual or group perspective. Quite simply I've argued that we can end the hegemony of the Oppression Olympics by analyzing politics with the paradigm intersectionality framework, which will light our way along the path to the deep political solidarity it will take to enable wide-scale social justice.

Solidarity Politics for Millennials did not spend a lot of time profiling activists or organizations involved in creating this societal transformation by design, although they undoubtedly exist and do tremendous work. Instead, this work sought to deeply engage with the commonalities among their projects from a different vantage point. Many times the dream of social justice is thought about as merely an end point or goal—where do we want to end up? How can we fulfill the common exhortation to "Be the change we want to see" without spending time thinking about the frameworks that are critical for the change we actually want to see? Instead of examining specific social justice objectives like ending racism, sexism, poverty, or homophobia, *Solidarity Politics for Millennials* sought to explore how to radically transform our path to achieving those objectives.

The empirical predictions of demographers and the contemporary controversies of the twenty-first century offer us the opportunity to rethink what we are doing and reconsider the implications and ongoing intersections between popular culture, politics, and social justice. While the introduction and early chapters highlighted the limitations of prior analyses of race, gender, sexuality, and class among movements of a certain age, chapters 4 and 5 have demonstrated that we will not automatically be saved by Millennials. Millennials are not born with vastly different political DNA than their parents or grandparents. These assertions are less criticisms of Millennials, because Millennials have not failed us yet; we have to provide sufficient inspiration and vision to encourage them to push beyond tolerance for something more. My goal has been to issue a clarion call for people across and within categories of difference who seek to pursue wide societal transformation to collectively think about what we are doing even as we pursue our shared goal.

Over the thirteen years that I've taught the concept of the "Oppression Olympics," innumerable Millennials have responded, "We need to get beyond the Oppression Olympics." Of course, their instincts are spot on. The real question, of course, has always been, "How?" In this book I have focused on how intersectionality theory can be translated for such a purpose. *Solidarity Politics for Millennials* has focused on consolidating and expanding what we know from the landmark insights of intersectionality theorists in a way that is useful for everyday politics—a five-dimension approach I term paradigm intersectionality. Attending to Categorical Multiplicity, Categorical Intersections, Diversity Within, Time Dynamics, and Individual-Institutional Relationships fosters a more inclusive engagement with our counterparts as we pursue wide societal transformation at the personal, intergroup, and policy levels. Essentially I've argued that paradigm intersectionality can contribute to the development of deep political solidarity, a key antecedent for wide-scale social change in the direction of social justice.

However, paradigm intersectionality *does not guarantee* a liberal or progressive outcome for every political battle in the future any more than Millennials are ATMs (Automatic Turn-key Messiahs, as I term them in chapter 4) of such outcomes by birthright. Moreover, it is clear that as intersectional approaches gain wider currency and have an impact on the currently challenging list of sociopolitical categories that drive social stratification, there is also no guarantee that other categories will not arise in their place. Sadly, this eventuality cannot be prevented by extant intersectionality of any sort.

What it can do, though, is better prepare us as individuals; as members of specific intersecting demographic groups and social justice organizations; and as policy advocates, architects, and practitioners to better handle the next set of categories. Through its attention to deep political solidarity, paradigm intersectionality can provide a "new politics manual" of sorts for folks already committed to the path, and a way for future generations to join the journey. Its inclusive and incisive approach seeks to reenergize people, groups, and policies to become active cocreators of an engaged democracy. We have to enter into the fray at some point, and it is my hope that this book assists us in doing so by strengthening the ties of interdependence and commitment to an equity standard of justice among us as like-minded individuals.

Although it draws upon the insights of intersectionality scholars and practitioners from around the world, one way to read this book is as an admittedly U.S.-driven and oriented work. As such may it provide limited purchase when it comes to the concrete policy issues discussed in this book—particularly for the few nations where same-sex marriage is already legal, or in political contexts where policies of dual nationality take the teeth out of pushes for draconian immigration policies. But a brief turn to the continent of Africa illustrates the limits of this kind of reading of the argument.

In 1994 the small African nation of Rwanda endured a level of ghoulishly efficient ethnic cleansing that had not been seen since the Holocaust. In the span of days more than one million Tutsis were slaughtered by organized bands of men of military age called the Interahamwe. The irony could not be greater. Peacekeeping forces under the aegis of the United Nations, the world's international institutional answer to the Holocaust during World War II, were incapable of protecting Tutsi lives.

In her efforts to comprehend that Nazi-driven paradigm shift in twentieth-century geopolitics, Hannah Arendt alerted us to the problem: "The end of a tradition does not necessarily mean that traditional concepts have lost their power over the minds of men. On the contrary, it seems that this power of well-worn notions and categories becomes more tyrannical as the tradition loses its living forces as the memory of it recedes."[2] While there are vast qualitative differences between Nazi Germany and Rwanda, it is the tyranny of traditions—cyclical as well as linear—that must concern us as we attempt to comprehend the past and reshape the future. In *When Victims Become Killers* Mahmood Mamdani[3] notes that despite their common language, genetic heritage, and kinship networks, a cyclical relationship to political power was grounded in a socially constructed binary between Hutus and Tutsis, who traded positions of having power and being powerless repeatedly. This cyclical relationship to power, marked by both unexpected and uneven shifts throughout eras of colonialism, revolution, and civil war, was mobilized by political elites in media transmissions hailing Hutu nationalism. Tutsi and Hutu identities were socially constructed over time as oppositional proxies for complex phenomena such as economic stratification and political power. Paradigm intersectionality and its applications can facilitate the foregrounding of these power relations at the individual, group, and policy level, outlining threats to deep political solidarity in advance of the next genocide.

In a similar vein, while one read of chapter 4 would focus on the public identity of the "Bull's Eye" as a purely American phenomenon, the fact remains that the mere tolerance has not protected us from genocide, war, hate crimes, or other structural forms of violence all over the world. As I complete the final preparations of this manuscript, the so-called "Arab Spring," the end of decades of authoritarian rule in Egypt and Tunisia and efforts to duplicate such a transfer of power to the people in Libya, the Sudan, and Syria continues to rage. The conventional wisdom again suggests Millennials are the saviors, given the numbers of youth involved in the protests.

"Welcome to Freedom," the rock formation in Cairo's Tahrir Square read. To those young people, this book will hopefully illuminate the limits of tolerance in a way that will empower them to avoid the pitfall of thinking mere tolerance will solve the challenges of deeply entrenched inequalities in their societies. Tolerance has not freed the disadvantaged in the United States and many European democracies. To them, I propose another across the cultural generation gap conversation, this time with another African who faced a similar dilemma. In *The Long Walk to Freedom* Nelson Mandela said, "For to be free is not merely to cast off one's chains, but to live in a way that respects and enhances the freedom of others. The true test of our devotion to freedom is just beginning."[4] In order to be free we cannot simply respect others' freedom—tolerance is necessary but insufficient. Instead we must also enact the other half of Mandela's formulation: to enhance others' freedom. That calls us to embark upon the path of deep political solidarity.

As I argued in previous chapters, attending to the tenets of paradigm intersectionality enables the cultivation of deep political solidarity at the personal level (chapter 3), facilitates deep political solidarity in intergroup contexts of deep political mistrust (chapter 4), and alerts us to possible threats to deep political solidarity at the policy level (chapter 5). The deep political solidarity discussed throughout the book, although focused on U.S. cases and contexts, seeks to provide a skeletal framework of practices that can be cultivated in societies around the world, with appropriate space and flexibility for adaptation to particular contexts, societal needs, and international concerns.

This book started out with a cross-racial conversation among a generation of women steeped in mid-twentieth-century approaches to politics. As a young(ish) interloper in the dialogue, I saw that it was nearly impossible to get off the Oppression Olympics train once it had left the station, despite my heartfelt belief that a train wreck between possible allies lay ahead. It is my sincere hope that this book fosters further dialogue across the cultural generation gap identified by Frey and Myers. In an effort to derail the dismal future predicted by Frey and to support the sunny outlook of Myers, I contend that cultivation of deep political solidarity is crucial. Hopefully, a shared reading of this book will allow such reflection.

It is, of course, in the older generations' interest that we correct our own lack of imagination in viewing race, gender, class, and sexual orientation that remains mired in the twentieth century and step into the new millennium armed with new ways of thinking about how to go beyond tolerance. After all, Millennials will be making decisions about our health care one day! In all seriousness, however, it is clear that Baby Boomers will live longer than any generation to date, and based on that fact alone, it behooves them to think deeply about the kind of world so many of them aspired to live in when they themselves were the youngest adult generation. Instead of simply exploiting Millennials for their technology or financial support of Medicare and Social Security, Boomers can play a role in restoring our faith in each other. But as with Millennials, this role is earned through common pursuit of interdependence and social justice, not one earned by birthright.

As my friend and colleague Robin D. G. Kelley wrote in his book *Freedom Dreams*, it is critically important to pause and envision a different future: "I'm not suggesting we wholly embrace their ideas or strategies as the foundation for new movements; on the contrary, my main point is that we do what earlier generations have done: dream."[5] Pausing to think about how to work together differently for common cause has been the mission of this book. *Solidarity Politics for Millennials* seeks to facilitate a common set of questions so that Boomers, X'ers, and Millennials alike can engage in the endeavor of social justice with humility and hope. Indeed, perhaps the experience can help to restore multiple generations', races', sexualities', classes', and genders' faith in each other to begin again—to pursue a shared freedom dream of social justice for this world and all of the people residing in it. In order to do so, of course, it is essential to be empowered with new frameworks that can inspire us to take on the challenging and daunting questions rather than feel defeated before we begin.

NOTES

1. Du Bois, W. E. B. *Darkwater.* Amherst, NY: Humanity Books, 1920/2003, 226.
2. Arendt, Hannah. *Between Past and Future.* New York: Penguin 1961/1993, 26.
3. Mamdani, Mahmood. *Colonialism, Nativism, and the Genocide in Rwanda.* Princeton, NJ: Princeton University Press, 2001.
4. Mandela, Nelson. *The Long Walk to Freedom: The Autobiography of Nelson Mandela.* Boston: Back Bay Books, 1995.
5. Kelley, Robin D. G. *Freedom Dreams: The Black Radical Imagination.* New York: Beacon Press, 2003, xii.

Bibliography

Anzaldua, Gloria and Cherrie Moraga. *This Bridge Called My Back: Writings by Radical Women of Color.* New York: Aunt Lute Books, 1987.

Arendt, Hannah. *Between Past and Future.* New York: Penguin 1961/1993.

Arendt, Hannah. *On Revolution.* New York: Penguin Books, 1963/1990.

Arendt, Hannah. *Men in Dark Times.* New York: Harcourt Brace, 1968/1993.

Banaszak, Lee Ann. "Women's Movements and Women in Movements: Influencing American Democracy from the Outside?" (2008). In: Wolbrecht, Christina, Karen Beckwith, and Lisa Baldez, Editors. *Political Women and American Democracy.* New York: Cambridge University Press. 2008, 79–95.

Barvosa, Edwina. *Wealth of Selves: Multiple Identities Mestiza Consciousness and the Subject of Politics.* College Station, TX: Texas A & M University Press, 2008.

Battlestar Galactica, "Miniseries," Original Air Date December 8, 2003.

Battlestar Galactica, "The Woman King," Air Date February 11, 2007.

Bell, Derrick. *Silent Covenants: Brown v. Board of Education and the Unfulfilled Hopes for Racial Reform.* New York: Oxford University Press, 2004.

Bell, James John. "An Army of One God: Monotheism vs. Paganism in the Galactica Mythos." In: Hatch, Richard, Editor. *So Say We All: An Unauthorized Collection of Thoughts and Opinions on Battlestar Galactica.* Dallas: BenBella Books, 2006.

Beltran, Cristina. "Patrolling Borders: Hybrids, Hierarchies and the Challenge of Mestizaje," *Political Research Quarterly,* 57 (2004): 595–607.

Berger, Michelle Tracey. *Workable Sisterhood: The Political Journey of Stigmatized Women with HIV/AIDS.* Princeton, NJ: Princeton University Press, 2004.

Beyond Same-Sex Marriage: A New Strategic Vision for All Our Families and Relationships. www.beyondmarriage.org, 2006; accessed June 2010.

Bhavnani, Kum-Kum, editor. *Feminism and Race (Oxford Readings in Feminism).* New York: Oxford University Press, 2001.

Bhavnani, Kum-Kum, John Foran, Priya Kurian, editors. *Feminist Futures: Re-Imagining Women, Culture, Development.* London: Zed Books, 2003.

Blackwell, Angela Glover, Stewart Kwoh, and Manuel Pastor. *Searching for the Uncommon Ground: New Dimensions on Race in America.* New York: WW Norton and Company, 2002.

Blahuta, Jason P. "The Politics of Crisis: Machiavelli in the Colonial Fleet." In: Eberl, Jason, Editor. *Battlestar Galactica and Philosophy*. Malden, MA: Blackwell Publishing, 2008.

Brah, Avtar and Ann Phoenix. "Ain't I a Woman? Revisiting Intersectionality." *International Journal of Women's Studies* 5 (2004): 75–86.

Bositis, David (2008). "Blacks and the 2008 Election: A Preliminary Analysis www.jointcenter.org/publications_recent_publications/political_participation/blacks_and_the_2008_elections_a_preliminary_analysis. Accessed June 16, 2010.

Brooks, David (2008). "The Class War Before Palin," *New York Times*, October 10. Accessed October 27, 2008.

Brown, Sonja Eddings (October 22, 2008). "Top African American Religious Leaders Join Apostle Frederick K. C. Price in endorsing YES on Proposition 8" www.protectmarriage.com/article/top-african-american-religious-leaders-join-apostle-frederick-k-c-price-in-endorsing-yes-on-prop-8. Accessed June 5, 2010.

Burack, Cynthia. *Healing Identities: Black Feminist Thought and the Politics of Groups*. Ithaca, NY: Cornell University Press, 2004.

Burgess, Susan. *The Founding Fathers, Pop Culture and Constitutional Law: Who's Your Daddy?* London: Ashgate, 2008.

Brewer, Paul R. "Value Words and Lizard Brains: Do Citizens Deliberate About Appeals to Their Core Values?" *Political Psychology* 22 (2001): 45–64.

Calhoun, Craig. *Critical Social Theory*. Cambridge, MA: Blackwell Publishers, 1995.

Carby, Hazel. "The Souls of Black Men." In: Gilman, Susan and Alys Eve Weinbaum, Editors. *Next to the Color Line: Gender, Sexuality and W. E. B. DuBois*. Minneapolis: University of Minnesota Press, 2007.

Cantave, Cassandra and Roderick Harrison (2001). "Marriage and African Americans Fact Sheet" Joint Center for Political and Economic Studies, www.jointcenter.org/DB/factsheet/marital.htm. Accessed June 16, 2010.

Chiles, Nick. "Daddy's Home." *Essence*, 41(June 2010): 154–60.

Cocco, Marie (May 15, 2008). "Misogyny I Won't Miss," *The Washington Post*, p. A15.

Cohen, Cathy J. "Punks, Bulldaggers and Welfare Queens: The Radical Potential of Queer Politics." *GLQ: A Journal of Gay and Lesbian Studies* 3 (1997) 437–65.

Cohen, Cathy J. *The Boundaries of Blackness: AIDS and the Breakdown of Black Politics*. Chicago: University of Chicago Press, 1999.

Cole, Elizabeth. "Coalitions as a Model for Intersectionality: From Practice to Theory" *Sex Roles* (2008) 59:443–53.

Cole, Elizabeth and Zakiya T. Luna. "Making Coalitions Work: Solidarity Across Difference within U.S. Feminism." *Feminist Studies* 36 (2010): 71–98.

Collins, Patricia Hill. *Black Feminist Thought: Knowledge, Empowerment and Consciousness*. New York: Routledge, 2000.

Collins, Patricia Hill. *Black Sexual Politics: African Americans, Gender and the New Racism*. New York: Routledge, 2004.

Cooke, Elizabeth F. "Let There Be Earth: The Pragmatic Virtue of Hope." In: Eberl, Jason, Editor. *Battlestar Galactica and Philosophy*. Malden, MA: Blackwell Publishing, 2008.

Crenshaw, Kimberle Williams. "Mapping the Margins: Intersectionality, Identity Politics, and Violence Against Women of Color." *Stanford Law Review* (1991).

Crenshaw, Kimberle Williams. "Demarginalizing the Intersection of Race and Sex: A Black Feminist Critique of Antidiscrimination Doctrine, Feminist Theory and Antiracist Politics." *University of Chicago Law Review* 139 (1989).

Crow, Graham. *Social Solidarities: Theories, Identities and Social Change*. Philadelphia: Open University Press, 2002.

Crowe, David (September 2005). "Katrina: God's Judgment on America." www.beliefnet.com; www.restoreamerica.com. Accessed October 28, 2008.

Davis, Darren and Brian Silver. "Civil Liberties vs. Security: Public Opinion in the Context of the Terrorist Attacks in America." *American Journal of Political Science* 48 (2004): 28–46.

Dawson, Michael. *Behind the Mule: Race and Class in American Politics*. Princeton, NJ: Princeton University Press, 1994.

Denizet-Lewis, Benoit. "Young Gay Rites." *New York Times Magazine*, April 28, 2010.

"The Devil Wears Prada," Screenplay by Peter Hedges, Revisions by: Howard Michael Gould, Paul Rudnick, Don Roos, and Aline Brosh McKenna (March 2005). *www.dailyscript.com/scripts/devil_wears_prada.pdf* Accessed June 11, 2008.

Dhamoon, Rita. *Identity/Difference Politics: How Difference Is Produced and Why It Matters*. Vancouver: University of British Columbia Press, 2009.

Dhamoon, Rita. "Considerations on Mainstreaming Intersectionality," *Political Research Quarterly*, Forthcoming 2011.

Diamond, Lisa M. and Molly Butterworth. "Questioning Gender and Sexual Identity: Dynamic Links Over Time." *Sex Roles* 59 (2008): 365–76.

Dottolo, A. L. and A. J. Stewart (2008). "Don't Ever Forget Now, You're a Black Man in America": Intersections of Race, Class and Gender in Encounters with the Police." *Sex Roles* 59:350–64.

DuBois, W. E. B. *The Autobiography of W. E. B. DuBois: A Soliloquy on Viewing My Life from the Last Decade of the First Century*. New York: International Publishers, 1968.

DuBois, W. E. B. *Black Reconstruction*. 1935.

DuBois, W. E. B. *Darkwater*. Amherst, NY: Humanity Books, 1920/2003.

DuBois, W. E. B. *Dusk of Dawn: Autobiography of a Race Concept*. Piscatawy, NJ: Transaction Publishers, 1968/2002.

DuBois, W. E. B. *The Philadelphia Negro*. New York: Cosimo Classics, 1899/2010.

DuBois, W.E.B. *The Souls of Black Folk*. In: Franklin, J.H., ed. *Three Negro Classics*. New York: Avon Books, 1972/1999.

Eberl, Jason, Editor. *Battlestar Galactica and Philosophy.* Malden, MA: Blackwell Publishing, 2008.

Egan, Patrick. "Findings from a Decade of Polling on Ballot Measures Regarding the Legal Status of Same-Sex Couples." Unpublished study, 2010.

Egan, Patrick and Ken Sherrill. "California's Proposition 8: What Happened, and What Does the Future Hold? " Unpublished study commissioned by the Haas Foundation, 2009.

El Sadaawi, Nawal. *The Hidden Face of Eve: Women in the Arab World.* London: Zed Books, 1977/2007.

Eyer, Katie R. "Have We Arrived Yet? LGBT Rights and the Limits of Formal Equality." *Law & Sexuality: A Review of Lesbian, Gay, Bisexual, and Transgender Legal Issues,* 19 (2010).

Faludi, Susan. *Backlash: The Undeclared War Against American Women.* New York: Anchor Books, 1991.

Farrow, Kenyon (2007). "Is Gay Marriage Anti-Black?" www.nathaniel-turner.com/isgaymarriageantiblack.htm. Accessed May 31, 2010.

Feldman, Ron. *The Jew as Pariah: A Collection of Essays and Letters Written from 1942–1966 by One of the Foremost Jewish Thinkers of Our Time.* New York: Grove Press, 1978.

Ferguson, Roderick. *Aberrations in Black: Toward a Queer of Color Critique.* Minneapolis: University of Minnesota Press, 2004.

Fetchenhauer, Detleft, Andreas Flache, Abraham P. Buunk, Siegwart Lindenberg. *Solidarity and Prosocial Behavior: An Integration of Sociological and Psychological Perspectives.* Groninged (Netherlands): Springer Science and Business Media, Inc. 2006.

Fields, Dorothy and Jerome Kern. "Pick Yourself Up" from the film *Swing Time.* Performed by Fred Astaire and Ginger Rogers, 1936.

Fiske, Susan T. and Shelley Taylor. *Social Cognition.* New York: McGraw Hill, 1991.

Foerster, Amy. "Isn't Anybody Here From Alabama? Solidarity and Struggle in a 'Mighty, Mighty Union." In: Kasinitz, Philip, John Mollenkopf and Mary Waters, Editors. *Becoming New Yorkers: Ethnographies of the New Second Generation.* New York: Russell Sage Foundation, 2004

Fogg-Davis, Hawley. "Theorizing Black Lesbianism within Black Feminism: A Critique of Same Race Street Harassment." *Politics and Gender* 2(2006): 57–76.

Forman, Tyrone and Amanda E. Lewis. "Racial Apathy and Hurricane Katrina." *DuBois Review* 3(2006): 175–202.

Foster, Kevin Michael (2003). "Panopticonics: The Control and Surveillance of Black Female Athletes in a Collegiate Athletic Program" *Anthropology and Education Quarterly* 34 (2003): 300–23.

Fraga, Luis, John Garcia, Rodney Hero, Michael Jones-Correa, Valerie Martinez-Ebers, and Gary Segura (2006). "Su Casa es Nuestra Casa: Latino Politics Research and the Development of American Political Science." *American Political Science Review* 100 (2006): 515–521.

Frankenburg, Ruth. *White Women, Race Matters: The Social Construction of Whiteness*. St. Paul, MN: University of Minnesota Press, 1994.

Frasure, Lorrie and Ange-Marie Hancock. "Black Politics after Obama: Preliminary Results from the Collaborative Multiracial Political Study." Unpublished manuscript, 2009.

Frey, William H. (2010). "Will Arizona be America's Future?" www.brookings.edu/opinions/2010/0428_arizona_frey.aspx. Accessed July 26, 2010.

Frymer, Paul, Dara Strolovitch and Dorian Warren. "New Orleans Is Not the Exception: Re-politicizing the Study of Racial Inequality" *DuBois Review* 3 (2006): 37–57.

Garcia-Bedolla, Lisa. "Intersections of Inequality: Understanding Marginalization and Privilege in the Post-Civil Rights Era" *Politics and Gender* 3 (2007): 232–48.

Giardina, Natasha. "The Face in the Mirror: Issues of Meat and Machine in Battlestar Galactica." 2006. In: Hatch, Richard, Editor. *So Say We All: An Unauthorized Collection of Thoughts and Opinions on Battlestar Galactica*. Dallas: BenBella Books, 2006.

Gilens, Martin. *Why Americans Hate Welfare: Race, Media and the Politics of Anti-poverty Policy*. Chicago: University of Chicago Press, 1999.

GLAAD (2010). "Talking About LGBT Equality with African Americans" New York: Gay and Lesbian Alliance Against Defamation and Movement Advancement Project.

Gilman, Susan and Alys Eve Weinbaum, editors. *Next to the Color Line: Gender, Sexuality and W. E. B. DuBois*. Minneapolis: University of Minnesota Press, 2007.

Goldberg, David Theo. "Devastating Disasters: Race in the Shadow(s) of New Orleans." *DuBois Review* 3(2006): 83–95.

Granderson, L. Z. (2009). "Gay Is Not the New Black" www.cnn.com/2009/POLITICS/07/16/granderson.obama.gays/index.html. Accessed June 16, 2010.

Grant, Judith. *Fundamental Feminism: Contesting the Core Concepts of Feminist Theory*. New York: Routledge, 1993.

Gratz v. Bollinger 539 U.S. 244 (2003).

Greene, Eric. "The Mirror Frakked: Reflections on Battlestar Galactica." In: Hatch, Richard, Editor. *So Say We All: An Unauthorized Collection of Thoughts and Opinions on Battlestar Galactica*. Dallas: BenBella Books, 2006.

Greenwood, Ronni Michelle. "Intersectional Political Consciousness: Appreciation for Intragroup Differences and Solidarity in Diverse Groups." *Psychology of Women Quarterly* 32 (2008): 36–47.

Greenwood, Ronni Michelle and Aidan Christian. "What Happens When We Unpack the Invisible Knapsack? Intersectional Political Consciousness and Inter-group Appraisals" *Sex Roles*, 59 (2008): 404–17.

Griffin, Farah J. "Black Feminists and Du Bois: Respectability, Protection, and Beyond." *Annals of the American Academy of Political and Social Sciences*. 568 (2000): 28–40.

Gross, Michael Joseph. Is Gay the New Black? www.advocate.com/News/ Daily_News/2008/11/16/Gay_is_the_New_Black_/2008. Accessed June 18, 2010.

Guidotti-Hernandez, Nicole. "Dora the Explorer, Constructing 'Latinidades,'" and the Politics of Global Citizenship." *Latino Studies* 5 (2007): 209–32.

Hancock, Ange-Marie. *The Politics of Disgust and the Public Identity of the "Welfare Queen."* New York: New York University Press, 2004.

Hancock, Ange-Marie. "When Multiplication Doesn't Equal Quick Addition: Examining Intersectionality as a Research Paradigm." *Perspectives on Politics* 5 (2007): 63–79.

Hankivsky, Olena. "Gender vs. Diversity Mainstreaming: A Preliminary Examination of the Role and Transformative Potential of Feminist Theory" *Canadian Journal of Political Science* 38 (2005): 977–1001.

Hankivsky, Olena, Renee Cormier, and Diego de Marich. *Intersectionality: Moving Women's Health Research and Policy Forward.* Vancouver: Women's Health Research Network, 2009.

Harris-Lacewell, Melissa. *Bibles, Barbershops and BET: Everyday Talk and Black Political Thought.* Princeton, NJ: Princeton University Press, 2004.

Hatch, Richard, editor. *So Say We All: An Unauthorized Collection of Thoughts and Opinions on Battlestar Galactica.* Dallas: BenBella Books, 2006.

Hawkesworth, Mary. *Beyond Oppression: Feminist Theory and Political Strategy.* New York: Continuum International Publishers Group, 1990.

Hawkesworth, Mary. "Confounding Gender," *SIGNS: Journal of Women and Culture in Society* 22(1997): 687–713.

Hawkesworth, Mary. "Congressional Enactments of Race-Gender." *American Political Science Review* 97 (2003): 529–50.

Hawkesworth, Mary. *Feminist Inquiry: From Political Conviction to Methodological Innovation.* New Brunswick, NJ: Rutgers University Press, 2006.

Hedges, Peter, Howard Michael Gould, Paul Rudnick, Don Roos, Aline Brosh McKenna.

Hendricks, Gay, and Kathlyn Hendricks. "Relationship Politics: Body Language of the McCain Marriage." *The Huffington Post.* Oct. 24, 2008. www.huffingtonpost.com/kathlyn-and-gay-hendricks/relationship-politics-bod_b_137042.html. Last accessed Oct. 24, 2008.

Hoban Kirby, E. and K. Kawashima-Ginsberg (2009) "The Youth Vote in 2008," CIRCLE (Center for Information and Research on Civic Learning and Engagement) Fact Sheet.

His Holiness the Dalai Lama. *Practicing Wisdom: The Perfection of Shantideva's Bodhisattva Way.* Boston: Wisdom Publications, 2005.

Hollibaugh, Amber. "Sex to Gender, Past to Present, Race to Class, Now to Future." *GLQ: A Journal of Gay and Lesbian Studies*, 10(2004): 261–65.

Honneth, Axel. *The Fragmented World of the Social: Essays in Social and Political Philosophy*. Albany: SUNY Press, 1995.

Hooks, bell. *Art on My Mind: Visual Politics*. New York: The New Press, 1995.

Hooks, bell. *Teaching to Transgress: Education as the Practice of Freedom*. New York: Routledge, 1994.

Hooks, bell. *Talking Back: Thinking Feminist, Thinking Black*. Boston: South End Press, 1989.

Huddy, Leonie. "From Social to Political Identity: A Critical Examination of Social Identity Theory." *Political Psychology* 22 (2001): 127–56.

Hurtado, Aida and Mrinalini Sinha. "More than Men: Latino Feminist Masculinities and Intersectionality" *Sex Roles* 59 (2008): 337–49.

In re Marriage Cases, 43 Cal. 4th 757 (2008).

Immordino-Yang, Mary Helen, Andrea McColl, Hanna Damasio, Antonio Damasio. "Neural Correlates of Admiration and Compassion" *Proceedings of the National Academy of Sciences* 106 (2009): 8021–26.

James, Joy. "Profeminism and Gender Elites: W. E. B. DuBois, Anna Julia Cooper and Ida B. Wells-Barnett." In: Gilman, Susan and Alys Eve Weinbaum, Editors. *Next to the Color Line: Gender, Sexuality and W. E. B. DuBois*. Minneapolis: University of Minnesota Press, 2007.

Jefferson, Aisha I. "Partners in Parenting" *Essence*, 41 (June 2010), 80.

Jones, Bryan and Frank Baumgartner. *The Politics of Attention: How Government Prioritizes Problems*. Chicago: University of Chicago Press, 2003.

Josephson, Jyl. "Romantic Weddings, Diverse Families." *Politics and Gender* 6(2010): 128–34.

Kasinitz, Philip, John Mollenkopf and Mary Waters, editors. *Becoming New Yorkers: Ethnographies of the New Second Generation*. New York: Russell Sage Foundation, 2004.

Kasinitz, Philip, John Mollenkopf, Mary Waters and Jennifer Holdaway. *Inheriting the City: The Children of Immigrants Come of Age*. New York: Russell Sage Foundation, 2008.

Kelley, Robin D. G. *Freedom Dreams: The Black Radical Imagination*. New York: Beacon Press, 2003.

Kellstedt, Paul. "Media Framing and the Dynamics of Racial Policy Preferences" *American Journal of Political Science* 44 (2000): 239–55.

Kirkpatrick, Jennet. "Introduction: Selling Out? Solidarity and Choice in the American Feminist Movement." *Perspectives on Politics* 8 (2010):241–45.

Koepsell, David. "Gaius Baltar and the Transhuman Temptation." In: Eberl, Jason, editor. *Battlestar Galactica and Philosophy*. Malden, MA: Blackwell Publishing, 2008.

Lax, Jeffrey and Jason Phillips. "Gay Rights in the States: Public Opinion and Policy Responsiveness" *American Political Science Review* 103 (2009): 367–86

Le Espiritu, Yen."Asian American Panethnicity: Contemporary National and Transnational Possibilities." In: Foner, Nancy and George Frederickson, editors. *Not Just Black and White: Historical and Contemporary Perspectives on Immigration, Race, and Ethnicity in the United States.* New York: Russell Sage Foundation, 2004, pp. 217–34.

Le Espiritu, Yen. *Asian American Women and Men: Labor, Laws, and Love.* Thousand Oaks, CA: Sage, 1997.

Lee, Eric P. *Proposition 8: The California Divide.* Los Angeles: Heat International Publishing, 2009.

Lenhardt, Robin. "Beyond Analogy: Perez v. Sharp, Antimiscegenation Law, and the Fight for Same-Sex Marriage" *California Law Review* 96(2008): 839.

Lewis, David Levering. *W. E. B. Du Bois, 1868–1919: Biography of a Race.* New York: Holt Books, 1994.

Lewis, David Levering. *W. E. B. Du Bois, 1919–1963: The Fight for Equality and the American Century.* New York: Holt Books, 2001.

Lieberman, Robert. "Social Construction (Continued)." *American Political Science Review* 89 (1995): 437–41.

Littlejohn, J. R. "A Sleeker Battlestar Galactica" www.usatoday.com, December 24, 2003. Accessed April 29, 2009.

Loftis, J. Robert. "What a Strange Little Man: Baltar the Tyrant." In: Eberl, Jason, editor. *Battlestar Galactica and Philosophy.* Malden, MA: Blackwell Publishing, 2008.

Loving v Virginia 388 US 1 (1967).

Mamdani, Mahmood. *Colonialism, Nativism, and the Genocide in Rwanda.* Princeton, NJ: Princeton University Press, 2001.

Mandela, Nelson. *The Long Walk to Freedom: The Autobiography of Nelson Mandela.* Boston: Back Bay Books, 1995.

Marable, Manning. *W. E. B. DuBois: Black Radical Democrat.* New York: Paradigm Publishing, 2005.

Marso, Lori J. "Marriage and Bourgeois Respectability" *Politics & Gender* 6 (2010): 145–53.

Martinez, Elizabeth. "Beyond Black/White: The Racisms of our Time." *Social Justice* 20 (1993): 22–34.

Martinez, Elizabeth. "Seeing More Than Black & White: Latinos, Racism, and the Cultural Divides." *Z Magazine,* 7(May 1994): 56–60.

Mason, Andrew. *Community, Solidarity and Belonging: Levels of Community and Their Normative Significance.* New York: Cambridge University Press.

Mattis, Jacqueline S., Nyasha A. Grayman, Sheri-Ann Cowie, Cynthia Winston, Carolyn Watson, Daisy Jackson. "Intersectional Identities and the Politics of Altruistic Care in Low-Income Urban Community." *Sex Roles* 59 (2008): 418–28.

Mathis, Derrick. "Is the LGBT Rights Movement Fighting for Equal Rights or White Privilege Rights?" http://renwl.org/news/lgbt-rights/is-the-lgbt-movement-fighting-for-equal-rights-or-white-privilege-rights-part-2. Accessed April 2010.

Matsuda, Mari. "Beside My Sister, Facing the Enemy: Legal Theory Out of Coalition." 43 *Stanford Law Review* (1991) 1183.

Maynard, Mary. "'Race,' Gender and the Concept of 'Difference' in Feminist Thought." In: Bhavnani, Kum-Kum, editor. *Feminism and Race (Oxford Readings in Feminism)*. New York: Oxford University Press, 2001.

McCall, Leslie. "The Complexity of Intersectionality." *SIGNS: Journal of Women and Culture in Society*. (2005): 1771–800.

Meyer, Richard (2006) "Gay Power Circa 1970: Visual Strategies for Sexual Revolution." *GLQ: A Journal of Gay and Lesbian Studies*. 12 (2006): 441–64.

Meyer, David and Steven Boutcher, "Signals and Spillover: *Brown v. Board of Education* and Other Social Movements" *Perspectives on Politics* 5(2007): 81–93.

Mills, Charles. *The Racial Contract*. Ithaca, NY: Cornell University Press, 1997.

Mink, Gwendolyn, editor. *Whose Welfare?* Ithaca, NY: Cornell University Press, 1999.

Monroe, Kristen Renwick. *The Heart of Altruism: Perceptions of a Common Humanity*. Princeton, NJ: Princeton University Press, 1996.

Moore, Mignon. "Black and Gay in L.A.: The Relationships Black Lesbians and Gay Men Have to Their Racial and Religious Communities." In: Hunt, Darnell and Ana-Christina Ramon, editors. *Black Los Angeles: American Dreams and Racial Realities*. New York: New York University Press, 2010.

Mosly, Tim and Shawn Carter. "Dirt Off Your Shoulder." Song lyrics, 2003. Performed by Jay-Z.

Myers, Dowell C. *Immigrants and Boomers: Forging a New Social Contract for America*. New York: Russell Sage Publications, 2008.

Naples, Nancy. *Community Activism and Feminist Politics: Organizing Across Race, Class and Gender*. New York: Routledge, 1998.

National Public Radio, Kaiser Family Foundation and Kennedy School of Government. "Civil Liberties Update." 2002. Accessed online August 15, 2010.

NBC News, "Dora the Explorer's 10th Anniversary." Airdate: August 14, 2010.

NBC Universal, May 20, 2008 "TODAY Show" Transcript.

Nielsen Wire. "The United States in 2020 in a Very Different Place," (July 2009). Accessed January 31, 2010.

"NOM Honors COGIC Presiding Bishop Charles E. Blake and Mother Willie Mae Rivers," June 2, 2010. www.nationformarriage.org/site/apps/nlnet/content2.aspx?c=omL2KeN0LzH&b=5075187&ct=8421183. Accessed June 5, 2010.

Ogundipe-Leslie, Molara. *Recreating Ourselves: African Women and Critical Transformations*. Trenton, NJ: African World Press, 1994.

Orbe, Mark P. Constructions of Reality on MTV's "The Real World": An Analysis of the Restrictive Coding of Black Masculinity." *Southern Communication Journal* 64(1998): 32–47.

Ospina, Sonia and Celina Su. "Weaving Color Lines: Race, Ethnicity, and the Work of Leadership in Social Change Organizations" *Leadership* 5(2009): 131–70.

Pantoja, Adrian, Ricardo Ramirez and Gary Segura. "Citizens by Choice, Voters by Necessity: Patterns in Political Mobilization by Naturalized Latinos. *Political Research Quarterly* 54 (2001): 729–50.

Pastor, Manuel, Chris Benner, and Martha Matsuoka. *This Could Be the Start of Something Big: Social Movements for Regional Equity Are Reshaping Metropolitan America.* Ithaca: Cornell University Press, 2009.

Pastor, Manuel and Rhonda Ortiz. *Making Change: How Social Movements Work and How to Support Them.* Program for Environmental and Regional Equity: University of Southern California, 2009.

Pateman, Carole. *The Sexual Contract.* Stanford, CA: Stanford University Press, 1988.

Phoenix, Ann and Pamela Pattynama. "Intersectionality." *European Journal of Women's Studies* 13 (2006): 187–92.

Potter, Tiffany and C. W. Marshall, editors. *Cylons in America: Critical Studies in Battlestar Galactica.* New York: Continuum International Publishing Group, 2008.

Ramakrishnan, S. Karthick and Thomas Espenshade. "Immigrant Incorporation and Political Participation in the United States." *International Migration Review* 35 (2001): 870–909.

Ramakrishnan, S. Karthick. *Democracy in Immigrant America: Changing Demographics and Political Participation.* Stanford, CA: Stanford University Press, 2005.

Ransby, Barbara. "The Deadly Discourse on Black Poverty and Its Impact on Black Women in New Orleans in the Wake of Hurricane Katrina" *DuBois Review* 3 (2006): 215–22.

Regents of the University of California v. Bakke, 438 U.S. 265 (1978).

Richardson, Mattie Udora, Marlon M. Bailey, and Priya Kandaswamy. "Is Gay Marriage Racist?" Transcript of a Conversation at the New College of California, 2004.

Rich, John and Gretchen Wilson. "Redneck Woman" Song Lyrics, 2004. Performed by Gretchen Wilson.

Roberson, Chris. "An Angel on His Shoulder." In: Hatch, Richard, editor. *So Say We All: An Unauthorized Collection of Thoughts and Opinions on Battlestar Galactica.* Dallas: BenBella Books, 2006.

Roberts, Adam. "Adama and Fascism" In: Hatch, Richard, editor. *So Say We All: An Unauthorized Collection of Thoughts and Opinions on Battlestar Galactica.* Dallas: BenBella Books, 2006.

Rudrauf, David, et al. "Rapid Interactions Between the Ventral Visual Stream and Emotion-Related Structures Rely on a Two-Pathway Architecture." *Journal of Neuroscience* 28 (2008): 2793–803.

Rusch, Kristine Kathryn. "Cheese Whiz and the Future: Battlestar Galactica and Me." In: Hatch, Richard, editor. *So Say We All: An Unauthorized Collection of Thoughts and Opinions on Battlestar Galactica.* Dallas: BenBella Books, 2006.

Schneider, Ann and Helen Ingram. "Social Construction of Target Populations: Implications for Politics and Policy." *American Political Science Review* 87 (1993): 334–47.

Schneider, Ann and Helen Ingram. "Social Construction: Response." *American Political Science Review* 89 (1995): 441–46.

Schreiber, Ronnee. *Righting Feminism: Conservative Women and American Politics.* New York: Oxford University Press, 2008.

Schroedel, Jean Reith and Daniel R. Jordan. "Senate Voting and Social Construction of Target Populations: A Study of AIDS Policy Making, 1987–1992." *Journal of Health Politics, Policy and Law* 23 (1998): 107–32.

Scott, Joan. "Gender: A Useful Category for Historical Analysis" *American Historical Review* 91 (1986) 1053–75.

Shapiro, Edward, MD. Talk Delivered at the "Living, Loving, and Voting Conference," Austen Riggs, October 17–19, 2008, Stockbridge, MA.

Sharp, Robert. "When Machines Get Souls: Nietzsche on the Cylon Uprising." In: Eberl, Jason, editor. *Battlestar Galactica and Philosophy.* Malden, MA: Blackwell Publishing, 2008.

Shields, Stephanie. "Gender: An Intersectionality Perspective." *Sex Roles* 59 (2008): 301–11.

Shingles, Richard D. "Black Consciousness and Political Participation: The Missing Link," *American Political Science Review,* 75 (1981), 76–91.

Solomon, Marc and Geoff Kors (2009). "Returning to the Ballot in 2010 vs. 2012" Press Release: www.eqca.org/site/pp.asp?c=kuLRJ9MRKrH&b=5190603 Accessed June 16, 2010.

Sniderman, Paul, Diana Mutz, Richard Brody. *Political Persuasion and Attitude Change.* Ann Arbor, MI: University of Michigan Press, 1996.

Spence, Lester K. "Episodic Frames, HIV/AIDS, and African American Public Opinion" *Political Research Quarterly* 53 (2010): 257–68.

Staples, Brent. "Barack Obama, John McCain, and the Language of Race" *New York Times,* September 22, 2008.

Steinem, Gloria. "Women Are Never Front-Runners," *New York Times,* January 8, 2008.

Stevens, Jacqueline. "The Politics of LGBTQ Scholarship." *GLQ: A Journal of Gay and Lesbian Studies,* 10(2004): 220–26.

Strolovitch, Dara. *Affirmative Advocacy: Race, Class and Gender in Interest Group Politics.* Chicago: University of Chicago Press, 2007.

Su, Celina. "We Call Ourselves by Many Names: Storytelling and Inter-Minority Coalition-Building" *Community Development Journal* 45(2009).

Sullivan, Andrew. "Goodbye to All That: Why Obama Matters." *Atlantic Monthly,* December 2007.

Szabo, Liz. "Dora the Explorer Turns 10 as a Model for Pre-K Girls." *USATODAY*, August 10, 2010. Accessed online August 15, 2010.

Tatum, Beverly. *Why Are All the Black Kids Sitting Together in the Cafeteria? And Other Conversations About Race.* New York: Basic Books 1997.

Taylor, Paul and Scott Keeter (2010). "Millennials: Confident, Connected and Open to Change" Pew Research Center Report.

Taylor, Paul, Jeffrey S Passel, Wendy Wang, Jocelyn Kiley, Gabriel Velasco, Daniel Dockterman. "Marrying Out: One-in-Seven New U.S. Marriages is Interracial or Interethnic" http://pewsocialtrends.org/assets/pdf/755-marrying-out.pdf (2010). Accessed June 2010.

Townsend, Tiffany. "Protecting Our Daughters: Intersection of Race, Class and Gender in African American Mothers' Socialization of Their Daughters' Heterosexuality." *Sex Roles* (2008) 59:429–42.

Villarreal, Yvonne. "The Exploradora." *Los Angeles Times,* August 10, 2010, D1.

Wachowski, Larry and Andy (1996). *The Matrix* Original screenplay.

Warner, Judith. "Compassion Deficit Disorder," *New York Times,* August 7, 2008; Accessed October 28, 2008.

Weber, Lynn and Deborah Parra-Medina. "Intersectionality and Women's Health: Charting A Path to Eliminating Health Disparities." In: Gender Perspectives on Health and Medicine: Key Themes. *Advances in Gender Research,* (2002) 7:181–230.

Weldon, S. Laurel. "Intersectionality." In: Goertz, Gary and Amy Mazur, editors. *Politics, Gender and Concepts: Theory and Methodology.* New York: Cambridge University Press, 2008.

Williams, Kimberly. *Mark One or More: Civil Rights in Multiracial America.* Ann Arbor, MI: University of Michigan Press, 2006.

Willse, Craig and Dean Spade. "Freedom in a Regulatory State? Lawrence, Marriage and Biopolitics." *Widener Law Review* 11(2005): 309–29.

Wilson, Angelia R. "Feminism and Same Sex Marriage: Who Cares?" *Politics and Gender* 6(2010): 134–45.

Winter, Nicholas J. G. *Dangerous Frames: How Ideas about Race and Gender Shape Public Opinion.* Chicago: University of Chicago Press, 2008.

Young, Iris Marion. *Intersecting Voices: Dilemmas of Gender, Political Philosophy and Policy.* Princeton: Princeton University Press, 1997.

Yoshino, Kenji. *Covering: The Hidden Assault on Our Civil Rights.* New York: Random House, 2006.

Yuval-Davis, Nira. "Intersectionality and Feminist Politics." *European Journal of Women's Studies* 13 (2006): 193–209.

Zatz, Noah. Beyond the Zero-Sum Game: Toward Title VII Protection for Intergroup Solidarity, 77 *Indiana Law Journal* 63 (2002).

Zerilli, Linda M. *Feminism and the Abyss of Freedom.* Chicago: University of Chicago Press, 2005.

Acknowledgments

Often political scientists are urged to remove the real-world politics from their political science research, a legacy of Cold War targeting of political activism by intellectuals and the reification of science that continues to influence our discipline. This book, however, endured a nine-year creative process precisely because real-world political events spoke to the United States' desperate need for an updated approach to social justice that goes beyond tolerance and mid-twentieth-century models of diversity and multiculturalism. As nine years pass, one accumulates a seemingly endless list of mitzvahs (good deeds) from an equally endless group of people and organizations.

Funding for this project has been generously provided by a number of resources, always in just the right way at just the right time. Research funds from the Institution for Social and Policy Studies (ISPS) at Yale University and support for a conference entitled "W. E. B. DuBois and the Scientific Study of Race," from the Yale Center for the Study of American Politics, were tremendously helpful in starting this project, permitting me research assistance, scholarly travel, and early opportunities to think about how precisely to frame the book. A 2006–2007 fellowship from the Center for the Comparative Study of Race and Ethnicity (CCSRE) at Stanford University provided me time, office space, and sabbatical support for the transformation of the book into one that addresses the contemporary pragmatic challenges of race, gender, class, and sexual orientation as intersecting processes and phenomena. At Stanford, Larry Bobo was prescient enough to push me on the challenge intersectionality can present to pluralism and gracious enough to wait until now for an answer. Hazel Markus, Al Camarillo, and Dorothy Steele provided a welcoming leadership collective for the center, and my fellow fellows—Michael Omi, Alison Isenberg, Moon-Kie Jung, and Mina Yoo—were a source of inspiration and information as I thought about refining the approach to paradigm intersectionality I first published in 2007.

This book began as a book of normative political theory in 2002, focusing on the lifeworks of Hannah Arendt and W. E. B. DuBois, while I was an assistant professor of political science and women's studies at Penn State University, where I had the good fortune to work with Holloway Sparks, Robyn Spencer, Frank Baumgartner, and Errol Henderson—perhaps the most unlikely intellectual cohort one could assemble, but friends who remained an important part of the emotional support for living with this project long after I left State College for Yale University.

At Yale University, I had the tremendous fortune to learn from ethnicity, race, and migration colleagues like Jonathan Holloway, Gerald Jaynes, Stephen Pitti, and Alicia Schmidt-Camacho. My colleagues in African American studies—most notably Elizabeth Alexander and Alondra Nelson—provided emotionally and intellectually inspiring examples of their own work and creative processes, combined with wonderful annual get-togethers to share good news, great tea, and always comforting fellowship. Political science colleagues Libby Wood and James Scott also provided important career advice and feedback on the work that helped me tremendously. My theory perspective broadened greatly by working with theorists as disparate as Ian Shapiro and Steven Smith, and the arrival of colleagues Karuna Mantena and Andrew March led to political theory workshop comments that helped me to identify the ethic of justice operating within deep political solidarity.

Despite the presence of a rivalry in football and other sports, my arrival at the University of Southern California (USC) did nothing to dampen the warm friendship shared with Mark Sawyer and the late Victor Wolfenstein of the University of California, Los Angeles (UCLA), each of whom provided repeated opportunities to present chapters from this work and offered supportive feedback each time. Political science colleagues at USC welcomed an applied political theorist with open arms. Janelle Wong, Jane Junn, Ricardo Ramirez, Jeb Barnes, Eliz Sanasarian, Christian Grose, Nick Weller, and Ann Crigler have all heard or read parts of this book and asked incisive questions that sharpened my thinking tremendously.

Chapter 1's analysis of the 2008 election was greatly enhanced by the peer-review comments provided by Nancy Burns for my piece "An Untraditional Intersectional Analysis of the 2008 Election," which appeared in *Politics and Gender*. Chapters 1–3 benefited greatly from the opportunity to direct USC's 2009–2010 New Directions in Feminist Research seminar, a program of the Center for Feminist Research, which included release time and a budget to invite smart people to both grapple with what I then called "intersectional solidarity" and work through the issues as they appear in their own work. In addition, the support of Dornsife College dean Howard Gillman and USC provost Beth Garrett has been singularly helpful in providing me with opportunities to present my ideas to lay audiences, providing me with a reality check on my own knowledge-translation plan.

My survey research expert colleagues across the United States who form the Collaborative Multi-Racial Political Survey (CMPS) collective—Matt Barreto, Lorrie Frasure, Sylvia Manzano, Karthick Ramakrishnan, Ricardo Ramirez, Gabe Sanchez, and Janelle Wong—tolerated the questions of an uninitiated applied political theorist, and revealed a wealth of possibilities in terms of research design and data to answer really tough questions about leaving the future of U.S. politics in Millennials' hands. Matt's overall leadership and Lorrie's work on the dataset itself made working with this dataset a user-friendly process that even a theorist could enjoy. Funds from the USC David and Dana Dornsife College of Liberal Arts and Sciences also supported data collection for this project.

Chapter 4 is dedicated to the memory of my brother-in-law, Paul R. Johnson, who died unexpectedly in 2011 and tragically before he could legally marry his partner of 19 years, Tim Hodges, in their home state of Arizona or their adopted home of California. It represents my first real foray into participant-observation research, and was significantly strengthened by my work as a board member of the Barbara Jordan/Bayard Rustin Coalition, a black lesbian/gay/bisexual/transgender (LGBT) organization led by board president Ron Buckmire, and my experience as a script supervisor and story producer on "The Wedding Matters" public service announcement production for the Courage Campaign. Chapter 4 also benefited greatly from my participation in the 2010 UCLA Critical Race Studies Symposium on Intersectionality, where I overcame my trepidation about meeting and presenting in front of Kimberle Williams Crenshaw herself, not to mention a slew of lawyers and law professors, whose sport it is to destroy arguments. Most importantly, presentations by the wealth of scholars facilitated my understanding of the equality as sameness argument before I could ever question its political utility.

Chapter 5 exists as a testimony of the possibility for an academic to actually possess a "dream" service appointment. My role as associate director of the Center for the Study of Immigrant Integration (CSII) at USC is truly a dream that helped me fully understand what it means to be an engaged scholar, not simply a public intellectual. The untiring work of core CSII staff Rhonda Ortiz, Juan de Lara, Vanessa Carter, Jackie Agnello, and Michelle Saucedo, and the CSII affiliated faculty, was only surpassed by their gracious acceptance of someone new to the area of immigrant integration and their deep political solidarity with California community organizations. Elements of chapter 5 and the conclusion were first presented through a talk at TEDxUSC, preparations for which alerted me to the connections that can be drawn between the introduction of this book, which begins with the 2008 United States election of its first African American president, and the 2011 activists in Egypt and Tunisia, who have toppled their authoritarian leaders.

My final USC thanks go to my colleagues and mentors, Michael Preston and Manuel Pastor. Both have provided incredible wisdom, a passionate commitment to social justice, and an ability to see *both* the forest *and* the trees simultaneously. As director of the CSII, Manuel continues to teach in every way that there is no contradiction between intellectual rigor, a great sense of humor, and social justice work. As vice-provost for strategic initiatives, Dr. Preston, as I have called him since graduate school, has supported me in all of the ways I did not know enough to ask for, even now as a tenured associate professor. I am grateful for both their time and ongoing support.

As I note in the conclusion, my teaching has been a large part of the inspiration for this book. Leading workshops for the Los Angeles African American Women's Political Institute (LAAAWPI), administered by Joy Atkinson, an indefatigable woman who lives daily the importance of cross-generational work, keeps me firmly committed to the grassroots. I must also thank my undergraduate students from the University of San Francisco and Yale in particular for repeating "We need to get beyond the Oppression Olympics" on their exams and papers for the ten years it took this professor to finally understand that it was up to her to think about how to do so. I further thank the USC undergraduates in my Political Participation and American Diversity course, who read PDFs of the chapters for class and helped me to clarify points where I lost the Millennial generation in the argument.

Academic book acknowledgments always seem to identify the personal commitments in the final section, interpreted by some as if they were, in the words of my eleventh-grade English teacher Mrs. Conklin, "a tacked-on ending." Though I follow this convention, my very ability to write this book is fundamentally dependent on the most personal of commitments—as a daughter and wife, sister and aunt, and of course, as a friend.

The very first day I set foot on Yale's campus as an assistant professor, I met James Vreeland and thought, this could be my new best friend. Our shared interests in Latin dance and culture then connected me with another dear friend—Rosalinda Garcia—who remains an important part of my heart. For them, as with long-time friends Pamela Balls-Organista, Cynthia Boaz, and Brian Vannice, the distance remains but the bonds remain strong.

My friends along the journey of thinking about and engaging in intersectional work and politics have been invaluable as together we think seriously about the contributions of intersectionality to political science in general and real-world politics in particular. Evelyn Simien (my coeditor for the *Political Research Quarterly* intersectionality mini-symposium), Rita Dhamoon, Edwina Barvosa, Heath Fogg-Davis, Cristina Beltran, and Anna Sampaio's work and friendship have helped me expand the intellectual history and merit of intersectionality by lifting up seminal contributions by lesbians, Latinas, and indigenous peoples—and true to intersectionality's spirit, contributions at times by authors and activists who were all three. John Bretting, Laurel Weldon, Andrea Simpson, and Olena Hankivsky's work and friendship continued to push me in the direction of the policy world. Susan Burgess provided an inspiring example of hard-fought intersectionality work in action and authored the book that gave me the courage to write a book that takes seriously a twenty-first-century world thoroughly and near-seamlessly imbricated with popular culture. New friend, coauthor, and colleague Karen Lincoln has provided laughter, lunch, gossip, and tears practically on cue depending on our joint need on any given day. I am called to a high standard of performance in this book in light of the contributions of these outstanding scholars. As has also been said in every set of research acknowledgments, all errors are of course my own.

I could not have written this book if I were not the child of Charles and Theresa Hancock, who met while integrating Louisiana State University at New Orleans and have shared their lifelong commitment to justice for African Americans in the most curious ways with their eldest daughter. They taught me the importance of a comprehensive education to social justice by enrolling me in kindergarten at the Albany, New York Jewish Community Center. They taught me the humanity of immigrants by enrolling me in the Albany Chinese Language School. They taught me the value of attending to multiple categories when they moved me to Columbia, Maryland, a planned community that emphasizes racial, religious, *and* economic integration. They eschewed the chance to ever use the phrase, "In my day, we ...," yet the stories they told of being black in the Jim Crow South left me with a profound respect for the importance they still place on racial solidarity, even as they have fully embraced the diversity within the black community *and* their nearly 50-year-old interracial friendships. I am lucky to actually have two parents who still tell me how much faith and confidence they have in me, as they do for all their daughters. It is for all of these reasons and many more held in the silence of my heart that this book is dedicated to them.

Finally, I am humbled to have a partner who has lived with this project throughout the length of our five-year relationship. My husband Stephen Hodges performed innumerable tasks related to this book, like transferring a 20-second clip of the film *The Fifth Element* from VHS to digital (only to see me discard it in favor of *The Matrix*), or forcing me to make the time every weekend to watch each episode of *Battlestar Galactica*, knowing only that I would enjoy it. He connected me with our friend Lori Chollar, a talented graphic artist who designed all the figures for the book, and read every chapter before it was sent to the publisher. During that five-year period, I have changed jobs, we have moved five times (including two cross-country moves), we have gotten married, sisters have gotten married and had babies, and brothers have lost long-time partners. Despite now knowing intimately that any move of this academic will involve his extensive use of a hand truck to load and unload a library of books, he continues to place my happiness and sanity at the top of his priority list—and understands that the solitude necessary for writing and creating is in the end a major part of it. For all of this and more, I feel eternally blessed and grateful.

INDEX